Organizing for Sustainability

Jan Jonker · Niels Faber

Organizing for Sustainability

A Guide to Developing New Business Models

palgrave
macmillan

Jan Jonker
Nijmegen School of Management
JAB MC BV
Doetinchem, Gelderland, The Netherlands

Niels Faber
Campus Fryslân
University of Groningen
Leeuwarden, Friesland, The Netherlands

ISBN 978-3-030-78156-9 ISBN 978-3-030-78157-6 (eBook)
https://doi.org/10.1007/978-3-030-78157-6

Translation from the Dutch language edition: *Duurzaam organiseren Template voor het ontwikkelen van nieuwe businessmodellen* by Jan Jonker, and Niels Faber, © Authors 2020. Published by Management Impact. All Rights Reserved.

Cover credit: Justus Bottenheft and Shirley Warlich and eStudioCalamar

This Palgrave Macmillan imprint is published by the registered company Springer Nature Switzerland AG
The registered company address is: Gewerbestrasse 11, 6330 Cham, Switzerland

Acknowledgements

Organizing for Sustainability is a sequel to the *Organising for the Circular Economy* workbook (2018) and has been made possible through sponsorship from the No-Waste Hackathon 2019 by a number of parties, namely: AVR (Rotterdam/Duiven), Cirkelwaarde (Apeldoorn), Midwaste (Delft), Radboud University (Nijmegen), Cyclus (Gouda/Moordrecht), and WEcycle (Zoetermeer). We are immensely grateful for their direct and indirect support in enabling this publication.

We would like to sincerely thank the co-authors, who gave their time, energy, and creativity free of charge. They are, in alphabetical order: Geanne van Arkel, Fons Claessen, Koen Dittrich, Moniek Kamm, Ivo Kothman, Naomi Montenegro Navarro, Erik van den Oord, Dorchanay Paykhar (first version only), Jos Reinhoudt, Dave van Schaijk, Mirella Soyer, and Egbert Willekes.

The following people have provided critical, constructive feedback on the original book concept and subsequently wrote a short review, which you can find at the beginning of the book. They are, in alphabetical order: Ron Boer, Maayke Aimée Damen, Ron Dijkstra, Hilde Engels, Frank Evers, Pieter Fritz, Timber Haaker, Isabelle Kock, Kim Poldner, Niels Smidt, and Edwin Tuin.

The final version of this book has also been realized through the active support of lecturers and students from, in alphabetical order: The Hague University of Applied Sciences (The Hague), Radboud University (Nijmegen), Rotterdam University of Applied Sciences (Rotterdam), and Saxion University of Applied Sciences (Deventer). Feedback on the template, which was deployed in these universities' courses, was received from over 300 participants from the above-listed universities where the template was deployed. Feedback from 20 companies who applied the template to their own organizations was also incorporated. We are very grateful to all of these individuals—unfortunately there are too many to name and thank individually—for giving their time freely and making valuable contributions.

We would like to thank the Boom/Management Impact publishing company, and in particular, Anneke van Dijk, Freek Talsma, Douwe van Randen, and Everdien ten Zijthof for the many years of pleasant cooperation (this is certainly not our first book, but it is our last) and also for having the courage to realize a publication that—in addition to a hard-copy version—is also available as a free e-book.

We are also very much indebted to Kien van Hövell tot Westerflier for allowing us to use the wonderful environment of her beautiful *Grootstal* estate in Nijmegen (see www.landgoedgrootstal.nl). This inspiring location has certainly helped create a beautiful book.

This publication would not have been possible without the financial support of The Hague University of Applied Sciences, Rotterdam University of Applied Sciences, Saxion University of Applied Sciences, and TMO Fashion Business School. We are very grateful to them. Through their support, this publication will be made available in Dutch and English as a free e-book.

This is also the last publication that will come about with the help of the Foundation *Our Common Future 2.0* (OCF 2.0, Doetinchem, NL). It is thanks to this foundation that over the last decade a wide range of whitepapers, workbooks, and books have been published in the field of sustainability, the WEconomy, the circular economy and, last but not least, business modelling. These publications have reached a large audience of tens of thousands of readers as a result of the relentless support and trust of the members of the OCF 2.0 Foundation board. We extend our sincere thanks to each of them, namely: Gerard Berendsen (chairman), Jan Jenniskens (secretary), Sjoerd Zeyl (treasurer), Dré Kampfraath, and Hans van Kranenburg.

Praise for *Organizing for Sustainability*

"Every few years, our current economic system falls apart because we have developed a monetary system based solely on capitalism. With this book and the Business Model Template, Jan Jonker and Niels Faber provide a step-by-step approach towards the necessary changes that our economic system requires to make the existing linear processes future-proof. Interesting, and very applicable in practice."

—Ron Boer, *Ecoron Relatiegeschenken*

"Over the past years, we have seen a growing trend in which the pursuit of multiple value creation in business is starting to occur—this constitutes a revolution relative to the status quo of mainstream business models. This book is for anyone who aims to challenge antiquated business models and design tomorrow's enterprises, in which social, ecological and financial value creation are essential. Good luck."

—Maayke Aimée Damen, *Founder Excess Materials Exchange*

"Our current economic system rests on the principles of private interests and profit maximization. More and more, we see that in many ways this is at the expense of our natural world thriving. This book shows how we can shape the transformation to a new economy. An economy in which cooperation and value creation are leading principles. The Business Model Template provides a useful tool for those who want to organize business according to these principles."

—Ron Dijkstra, *Founder LoyalGarden*

"This book is a compass in the adventure of entrepreneurship in a changing world. I feel that the BMT should stimulate people to the extreme: Think again, how can you make the world a better place? The rich countries are so rich because we have ransacked the earth, and gained our wealth on the back of others. We call this the externalities that are not included in the prices of the products. If we want to avoid these externalities, we should make our approach inclusive. This is true for the social domain and certainly also for the ecological domain. What becomes extinct will never come back. The BMT provides a basis for finding this much-needed inclusivity."

—Hilde Engels, *De Fruitmotor*

"Many companies that are considering, or reconsidering, their strategy still do so using traditional linear business models, in which pursuing higher profits are often at the expense of our earth. This book is an alternative for companies and students who want to be strategically innovative in a sustainable, circular manner so that they can create a healthy company in a healthy world."

—Frank Evers, *Senior Lecturer & Quality Control Coordinator, Windesheim University of Applied Sciences*

"Alongside hearing interesting speakers and thinkers in the Netherlands, such as Thomas Rau, Derk Loorbach and Jan Willem van de Groep, I got in touch with Jan Jonker during my studies at Erasmus University Rotterdam to discuss his theories. He has the unique gift of being able to lift you from the daily routine of *business as usual* and make it crystal clear why, how, and what things need to be changed as a society. He is an entrepreneur as well as a professional. This book has been written as a manual and guide for introducing transition into your organization. If you believe in *thinking, daring and doing* differently, to grow towards a resilient enterprise which, in terms of turnover, is structurally less dependent on the traditional economic factors and the current *business as usual*, this book will help you!!"

—Pieter Fritz, *Sustainability Developer, Xidoor (Berkvens, Svedex, Limburgia en Bod'or)*

"In our roles as citizens, consumers, students, employees, investors or decision-makers, we are facing the shared task of making our economy more sustainable. This requires radically different ways of production, consumption, and valuation, which must be sustainable, circular, and inclusive. This book gives both students and practitioners a hands-on approach to exploring new propositions and, in a collaborative effort, developing new business models."

—Timber Haaker, *Professor of Business Models at Saxion University of Applied Sciences*

"Over the past 25 years we at Interface have experienced how, by continuing to challenge your organization, you not only become future-proof, but successful as well. This book will help focus start-ups, existing organizations and new collaborations on how to address social and ecological issues in their business models."

—Ton van Keken, *COO Interface EAAA*

"An accessible book that takes the new generation of change-makers by the hand and supports them to develop new and innovative business models. This book is jam-packed with inspiring cases and concrete plans to help you get down to business straight away. Do not wait any longer: join the adventure to make your dream come true with the help of the BMT and have a genuinely positive impact on business and society."

—Kim Poldner, *Professor of Circular Business at The Hague University of Applied Sciences and Founder of the Circular Fashion Lab*

"With *Organizing for Sustainability*, the authors, led by Jan Jonker and Niels Faber, make the next step in the development of sustainable business models. This workbook is both in-depth and inspiring and provides practical tools for those who want to embark on sustainable propositions."

—Niels Smidt, *Specialist, Sustainability Strategy & Shared Value*

"*Organizing for Sustainability* and the BMT are the next steps towards sustainable organizations and ecosystems. The book offers a practical approach and contains plenty of examples from practice. The reader is challenged to get the organization to change as well in a world that is changing faster and faster. It is the very balance between sustainability, human dignity and profitability that is a precondition for successful business models in a world in which digitalization and (global) competition are becoming increasingly important. In this respect, the book also serves as a point of contact with other disciplines to bring about change."

—Edwin Tuin, *Change Expert*

"Over the past 25 years we at Interface have experienced how, by continuing to challenge your organization, you not only become future proof, but successful as well. This book will help focus start-ups, existing organization and new collaborations on how to address social and ecological issues in their business model."

—Jon van Nekam, CEO Interface EMEA

"An accessible book that takes the new generation of change makers by the hand ... [illegible]"

Disclaimer

Decisions that you make based on information in this publication are at your own responsibility and risk. We (editors-in-chief, co-authors, and publisher) have endeavoured to ensure that the information is correct, complete, and up-to-date at the time of going to press. Nevertheless, this publication may contain inaccuracies or sources that may no longer be available. When hyperlinks or references to third-party websites are used, this does not mean that we recommend products or services offered via these internet sites. The use of these hyperlinks is entirely at your own risk. We do not accept any responsibility or liability with regard to the content, use or availability of such internet sites. The veracity, correctness, reasonableness, reliability, and completeness of information on such internet sites have not been verified by us. It is not permitted to reproduce, forward, distribute, make public, or make available to third parties this publication for a fee, digitally or materially. We do not accept any liability for direct or indirect damage resulting from the use of this publication. You may print and/or download this publication for your own personal use, in accordance with the Creative Commons License for this work. Dutch copyright applies to this publication and the terms of use. The Dutch court has exclusive jurisdiction over any disputes that may arise in connection with this website.

About This Book

Over the last two decades the editors and co-authors of *Organizing for Sustainability* have written, individually, together, or with others, a large number of publications, working papers, research reports, and white papers about the topic that takes a central position here: What is a sustainable business model and how can such a model be achieved? In addition to formal, academic publications, texts have also been published on digital platforms such as SIGMA, Management Impact, Duurzaam Nieuws, TGTHR, Management Executive, and Nieuwe Business Modellen. When composing and editing this book, the authors made use of those previous texts and the ideas contained in them, both literally and freely. At some points, the text was *recycled* (so-called autoplagiarism), which could mean that some readers may come across texts they have seen before.

This manuscript also builds upon teaching materials that were developed for the *Sustainable Entrepreneurship (BKV 55)* course, which has been taught for the past decade at the Nijmegen School of Management of Radboud University (The Netherlands) commencing in 2011. The key objective of this programme is to teach participants about new business models as well as coaching them to develop their own (sustainable) business model. Over time, this process has been experimented with in multiple ways. The development of the Business Model Template (BMT) presented in *Organizing for Sustainability* stems from the need for a clear template that easily enables the development of sustainable business models. The BMT presented here has been tested extensively and with multiple iterations in various educational and organizational contexts between 2018 and 2019.

We are indebted to Ivo Kothman (Saxion University of Applied Sciences) for the constructive peer review of the very first version of the manuscript that became this book in 2018. Subsequently the book has gone through numerous edits. Although the greatest possible care was applied, there may still be some unintended errors. If this is the case, the reader is kindly requested to contact the editors (see contact details under *Feedback*). We are immensely grateful to all peer reviewers, co-authors, sponsors, companies, lecturers, and students who have made direct or indirect contributions to the development of this book.

Feedback

The BMT was created to enable people—both those starting new ventures and those within organizations—to work on their own sustainable business models. As far as we have come, there is always room for critical feedback, and therefore constructive feedback on the BMT is always welcome. Your constructive and concrete feedback can be sent to the editors by email at janjonker@me.com and n.r.faber@rug.nl.

COVID-19 Pandemic

Since early spring 2020 the world has been witnessing and trying to deal with COVID-19. The past year has been marked by great uncertainty, unrest and grief.

With unprecedented measures, governments around the globe have tried to curb the pandemic while providing care in various areas that was and still is urgently needed. Many people have shown unprecedented and courageous commitment which deserves more than just applause. We have also learned to appreciate indispensable professions that have turned out to be socially crucial. There have been diabolical dilemmas, which we have tried to address as they presented themselves. Despite all the pain, worry, and sadness in our society, we managed to transform, more or less overnight, from a *society as usual* to a society focused on society-wide disaster relief. We may be at a crossroads, unintentionally. The pandemic, painful as it may be, could be a blessing in disguise. Over the past few months, many have called for fundamental change. Let us not allow this moment, this momentum, to go unheeded. Let us focus on transition. We hope this book contributes to that challenge.

Contents

Student Testimonials on the Business Model Template

From profit maximization to value creation, the Business Model Template has helped us to develop a transparent business model to determine value creation in companies that take an interest in circularity. *Sygun van Arem, European Studies, The Hague University of Applied Sciences*

In the development of a circular business model for a company with a linear orientation, the BMT has added a great deal of structure, form and content to our idea. It also forced us to have a critical look at our thoughts. *Bilal Al Barkani, Business Economics, The Hague University of Applied Sciences*

Clear book with clear language. It really gives you a different view of companies. *Jelle Boers, Commercial Economics, Leiden University of Applied Sciences*

Working with the BMT has really been an eye-opener when it comes to sustainability. I can honestly say that this course has changed my perception of the world, which I had not anticipated when I signed up. *Ian Cornielje, Business Economics, Radboud University Nijmegen*

By going through the building blocks of the model, I gained an understanding of the sustainability aspects, which I would have missed without the model. *Naomi Hofland, Facility Management, The Hague University of Applied Sciences*

Finally, a template for drawing up a business model which makes my sustainable heart beat faster. *Lieke Hoogestijn, Environment & Society Studies, Radboud University Nijmegen*

Using the BMT has shown me that it is very simple to get a full picture of a company, even without an economics background. *Rowin Israël, Environmental studies, The Hague University of Applied Sciences*

The BMT has an outside-of-the-box mindset which helps us to make our ideas tangible without limiting our creativity. *Isabelle Kock, Nijmegen School of Management, Radboud University Nijmegen*

The BMT stimulates you to think differently and helps to make things clearer, starting with sustainability. *Ellen Kramers, Business Economics, The Hague University of Applied Sciences*

I was honoured to be one of the first to use the BMT. *Coen Neirinck, The Hague University of Applied Sciences*

The model is clear, user-friendly, well-structured and highly recommended. *Sander Post, HAN University of Applied Sciences*

Contrary to many traditional business models, the BMT allows for multiple value creation, long-term thinking and taking into account external factors. *Mitchell Sanwikarta, Business Economics, The Hague University of Applied Sciences*

After I finish my studies, I want to start a company with a circular business model. I will certainly be using this book. *Carlo Selbach, The Hague University of Applied Sciences*

With this approach, it is possible within a short time to put together a business model that has been developed for multiple value forms, including social and environmental ones, and forces you to think in a non-standard way. *Rik Seinhorst, International Business, Radboud University Nijmegen*

Even a freshman entrepreneur would be able to create a beautiful sustainable business model! *Wanyta van Son, Biology, Radboud University Nijmegen*

The BMT has enabled me to go from a *utopian* idea to a fully developed plan. *Maarten Smaling, Bachelor Geography, Politics and Society, Radboud University Nijmegen*

This book has contributed to giving me a better understanding of what I can contribute (now and in the future) to the circular economy. I thank the authors. *Shiwa Toewar, Entrepreneurship & Retail Management, The Hague University of Applied Sciences*

Readers' Guide

It makes no difference whether you want to start a company, collaborate with others to solve a problem, or make your company more sustainable: you always need a business model. A business model is a concept through which you can organize value creation. You always create value in collaboration with other parties, based on a certain strategy, and always within a particular context.

The choices you make inevitably lead to a specific type of business model. You organize a solution with a business model which has a certain impact, sometimes positive, but unfortunately also sometimes negative. In a business model, you think first and foremost about how to generate an economic return, the nature of the transactions involved, and the values that are created. In a nutshell, this is the central theme of this book, which comes together in the BMT.

This book consists of three parts, in which the three different stages and ten building blocks of the BMT are detailed. The three stages are (1) the Definition Stage, (2) the Design Stage, and (3) the Result Stage. Each of the stages is elaborated based on several building blocks. For the Definition Stage, these are (1) Motive and Context, (2) Dream, and (3) Proposition. For the Design Stage, these are (4) Business Model Archetypes, (5) Parties, (6) Strategy, (7) Core Activities, and (8) External Test. Finally, for the Result Stage, the building blocks are (9) Impact and (10) Value(s) Creation. The underlying theory for each building block is always outlined first. We then discuss its practical application with the help of various instruments. The elaboration is illustrated based on practical examples in the form of cases, quotes, tips, and checklists.

The book can be used in three ways (which are all discussed in more detail in Chapter 13):

1. **Entrepreneurial Approach:** This more basic approach is tailored to entrepreneurs and students who are working with the BMT for the first time. For this purpose, the three stages of the BMT are presented in landscape format. We recommend going through these three stages from top to bottom and from left to right which gives structure to the order of questions that must be answered to develop a business model. If, however, making a different way through the BMT makes more sense—if the parties with whom you want to collaborate are already known, for example, or if the choice of strategy is a given fact—then the BMT provides the freedom to do so.
2. **Intrapreneurial Approach:** The BMT can also be deployed by those who already have a business model with a proposition at its core, but who want to review it critically and make adjustments where desired. Here you might want to address the less sustainable aspects of the business model, increase its circularity, or investigate and reflect on the impact of the current way of organizing. The point of departure of this more in-depth approach focuses on improving what is already there, or incorporating new perspectives and novel ideas. For this purpose, we present an alternative view of the BMT, with the idea that you criss-cross through the different elements of the model.
3. **Network Approach:** Finally, you can also take a network approach to exploring your business model, whereby you map out your network, paying attention to the competencies that are present within it, and how this may contribute to the development of a new business proposition. This network approach focuses on the question of what is possible within the existing network. At the same time, it raises the question of where the network may need to be expanded. In essence, the network approach involves identifying the competencies and resources that are present in the network, and can be used for the development and implementation of a business model.

Whichever approach is used, the various choices made along the way in developing the BMT always impact each other. It is not a matter of precisely following all the building blocks one by one and filling them in, rather it is about exploring the different scenarios resulting from different choices at each step so that the choices are not *fixed*. Ultimately, a core value add of the BMT is enabling you to continuously check how new choices influence previous choices and adjust them until the business model as a whole is aligned.

But no matter how you work with the BMT, one thing we are 100% certain of is that when you reach the end of a design session, you will most likely have to reconsider and revisit one or more of the choices you made for the various building blocks.

Structure of the Chapters

The ten chapters in which we discuss the building blocks of the BMT are all of a similar structure but may vary in size (e.g. Chapters 3–12). After a short introduction, we offer some (concise) theory followed by tools and techniques (invariably referred to as *instruments*) followed by examples in the form of brief case study summaries. The case studies presented here predominantly come from cases done by students who have worked with the BMT, which have been edited to increase readability. Because we wished to keep the book as compact as possible, these cases do not always cover 100% of the ideas described in the chapter concerned. Each chapter is introduced with several quotes from companies, organizations, and institutions to illustrate the building block of the chapter. The quotes come from public sources (the internet, LinkedIn, company websites, etc.). Where possible, the source is given. We cannot guarantee the accuracy of the sources nor how up to date they are (see Disclaimer). Unfortunately, experience also shows that many digital sources cease to be operational after a relatively short time (*broken link*). The other chapters—Chapters 1 and 2, and 13–15—have no fixed structure. That is because of the freer nature of those chapters.

Working with Quotes[1]

The idea of collecting quotes to illustrate the BMT from professional practice was initially approached rather naively. Perhaps the most serious mistake here was to assume that there are sufficient organizations and institutions that, among other things, are working on translating sustainability and circularity into all levels of their business operations. After hours and hours of searching, and dozens or possibly hundreds of websites further, the inevitable conclusion is that this is simply not true. There are many laws, institutions,

[1]The quotes used in this publication were collected in November and December 2019 by (in alphabetical order) Niels van Almenkerk, Jan Jonker, Moniek Kamm, Ivo Kothman, Billy den Otter, Niels Peeters, and Egbert Willekes.

and customs in between dreams and reality. If it is only a matter of saying things correctly, there is little cause for concern. But there is still a very long way to go for many organizations as soon as what is said has to be concrete, visible, and measurable in practice. What stands out in this challenging and time-consuming process of collecting, arranging, and researching quotes and so on is that:

(a) Some quotes fit in more than one building block—often all building blocks. For the sake of clarity, quotes which could be applied in any of the building blocks have been avoided here as much as possible. In practice, some overlap between the building blocks will often be unavoidable.
(b) Many organizations/institutions, etc. produce beautiful, often somewhat heavy language, but it is by no means always clear what is meant precisely, let alone making the consequences of the generous promises clear from the outset.
(c) Filling the Motive and Context, Dream and Proposition building blocks with quotes is easiest—even though the distinction between Dream and the more concrete Proposition is not clear to everyone.
(d) The number of organizations that report that they have taken an external test to determine the viability or uniqueness of their product or service is minimal.
(e) Unsurprisingly, most organizations do not know how to report on their impact very well. It is interesting to see that there is a lot of well-meaning amateurism here.
(f) Even though it appears that the idea of multiple value creation (Building Block #10) is gaining some foothold, a tour of the organizations that are used here for quotes still leaves many unknowns regarding whether—and if so, how—it works out for them. That is not very surprising. After all, it is about the translation of impact into value(s) creation.
(g) The quotes used usually relate to the company as a whole. In the application, however, the building blocks can also be used for a business unit, individual product, idea, or similar.
(h) The quotes mainly focus on the creation of ecological and social value and much less on financial value. This does not mean that financial value is not important or comes second. For most companies and organizations, creating financial value is necessary for survival. The quotes mainly indicate how other forms of value can be created in addition to financial value.

Style and Tone

We have opted for a slightly informal style of writing, using *you* instead of a more impersonal style. By doing so we wish to address the reader more directly. We believe that this style fits this publication better.

Quick Scan

If you want to know whether the BMT could help you to create a business model to use for building a sustainable and circular future, fill out the *Quick Scan* in Appendix A.

The Business Model Template at a Glance

What Is a Template?

In a general sense, a template provides a structure with a specific application. You could think of a template for letters in Word, a drawing template, or the structure of a menu—starter, main course, and dessert. Similarly, the Business Model Template (BMT) provides a structure consisting of stages and building blocks, which helps to make several coherent choices that result in a design for a business model. This means that the user(s) themselves must work out the content clearly and logically and connect it consistently to develop a value proposition. There is, however, one big difference compared to conventional business model templates. For this BMT, the focus is to determine multiple values, and thus the financial margin is emphasized rather than profit being the dominant factor. The major challenge(s) facing users is to establish the negative and positive impacts as well as to arrive at a business model that creates more than one value. Ultimately, by organizing differently, we may contribute to solutions to the significant socio-economic and environmental challenges confronting us around the globe.

The Business Model Template consists of three stages and ten building blocks:

Key Points

Definition Stage

1. Motive and Context (Why): What is your problem, opportunity, or challenge, and what is its context?
2. Dream (What for): What goal are you dreaming of? Where are you going to make a difference?
3. Proposition (How): What will you do to solve the problem, seize the opportunity, or address the challenge?

Design Stage

4. Business Model Archetype (Logic): What type of business model will you use to create value?
5. Parties (Who): With whom will you do this?
6. Strategy (Route): Which route will you choose to realize your dream/goal?
7. Core Activities (Realization): What activities will you implement to realize this strategy?
8. External Test (Check): What do others think of your idea? Are you on the right track? Does it already exist? Is it allowed? Who can help you?

Result Stage

9. Impact (Indicators): What are the positive and negative consequences of your business model, now and in the future?
10. Value Creation (Transaction forms): How do you shape transactions and what do you exchange? What values are created as a result?

Being Ahead of the Crowd

In many cases, working with the BMT means coming up with a business model that is ahead of the curve. Current business practices hardly consider integrated costs, which refers to integrating externalities in costs, the impact of its business model (which is more than increasing turnover), or the creation of value other than financial ones. Working with the BMT is therefore exciting, if not challenging, because in our mind we sooner or later have a tendency to want to reduce everything to financial costs and revenues. With this BMT we want to show, in a number of practical steps, how this can be done differently. We show that this is directly linked to practice by illustrating each building block with quotes and examples from companies, organizations, and institutions. If you want to look at this in advance, we recommend that you read the last two building blocks in Chapters 11 (Impact) and 12 (Value Creation).

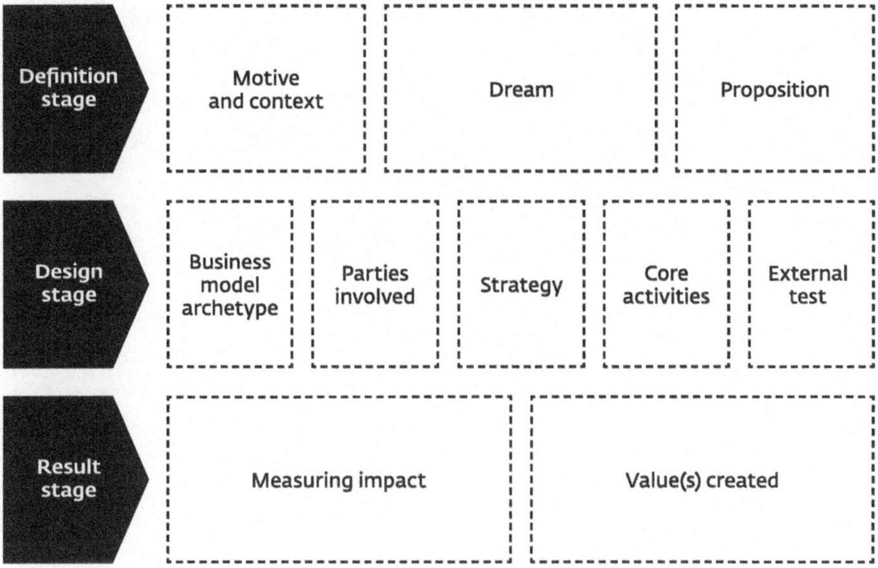

Business model template

About the Authors

Niels Faber is a Researcher at the University of Groningen (Campus Fryslan) and a Lecturer at Hanze University of Applied Sciences. His research focuses on the organizational aspects of sustainability and the circular economy. This translates into such themes as new forms of organization, in particular the circular economy, the ensuing transition and assessment of the progress made. He has produced numerous academic and professional publications and is co-editor with Jan Jonker of a series of online columns on the circular economy and the triple transition (climate challenge, energy transition, and circular economy).

Jan Jonker is Professor of Sustainable Entrepreneurship at Radboud University in Nijmegen. In recent years, he has also held the Pierre de Fermat chair at the Toulouse Business School in France and the Emile Francqui rotating chair at Vrije Universiteit Brussels. His work concentrates on three related themes: the emergence of the WEconomy, the development of new business models, and transaction systems with more than just money—*inclusive banking*. With the help of many people, he wrote, among other works, the bestsellers *Sustainable Thinking, Acting* (2010), *New Business Models* (2015), and *Organising for the Circular Economy* (2018). In recent years, his research has increasingly focused on the transition demanded by sustainability and circularity. For years he has been working with Niels Faber on columns, articles, and books on sustainability, the circular economy, and transition.

Abbreviations

B2B	Business to Business
BHAG	Big Hairy Audacious Goal
BMC	Business Model Canvas
BMT	Business Model Template
C2C	Citizen to Citizen
CBS	Central Bureau of Statistics
CMI	Clean Mobility Initiative
CO_2	Carbon Dioxide
COP21	UN Conference of the Parties No. 21 (2015)
CSR	Corporate Social Responsibility
DESTEP	Demographic, Economic, Social, Technological, Ecological and Political
DIY	Do It Yourself
EU CEAP	EU Circular Economy Action Plan
G2B	Government to Businesses
G2C	Government to Citizens
G2G	Government to Government
GDPR	General Data Protection Regulation
ICT	Information and Communication Technology
IoM	Internet of Materials
IoS	Internet of Services
IoT	Internet of Things
IPCC	Intergovernmental Panel on Climate Change
ISO	International Standards Organization
LCA	Life Cycle Analysis

LCO_2	Liquid Carbon Dioxide
LNG	Liquid Natural Gas
MOOC	Massive Open Online Course
NGO	Non-Governmental Organization
NWO	Dutch National Organization for Fundamental Research
P2P	Peer to Peer
PAAS	Product as a Service
PBL	Netherlands Environmental Assessment Agency
PDCA	Plan, Do, Check, Act/Adjust cycle
PEF	Polyethylene Furanoate
PEST	Political, Economic, Social and Technological
PET	Polyethylene Terephthalate
PPP	People, Planet, Profit
PSS	Product–Service System
REs	RE-Strategies
RVM	Reverse Vending Machine
SDG	Sustainable Development Goal
SMEs	Small and Medium-Sized Enterprises
SWOT	Strengths, Weaknesses, Opportunities and Threats
TNO	Dutch National Organization for Applied Research
UN	United Nations
USP	Unique Selling Point

List of Figures

List of Tables

1

Speaking of Transition

You must have noticed that politics, business, and society (is that us?) are confronted with increasingly pressing questions about economic and social transition. Things have to change—we are increasingly starting to agree on that, but how? What needs to change? We believe that it concerns three closely related and complex challenges.

1.1 The Triple Transition—Climate, Energy, and Circularity

Firstly, there is the climate challenge, which is encapsulated by the Paris Agreement of 2015 (a global agreement on the reduction of climate change negotiated at the 2015 United Nations Climate Change Conference—COP21), in which it was agreed to limit global warming to a maximum of 2 degrees above the pre-industrial era. For the first time in history, governments, NGOs, and businesses collaboratively agreed to address the climate challenge. This has led to national and international actions following from a shared understanding of the urgency of the problem. Both the severity of the consequences and the limited time available to address climate change dictate the agenda. To achieve the set goal to limit a global temperature rise, a reduction of greenhouse gas emissions of 45–50% is needed by 2030. By 2050, industrial activities will need to show net zero emissions. In the 2018 Intergovernmental Panel on Climate Change (IPCC, 2018) report on the speed of

J. Jonker and N. Faber, *Organizing for Sustainability*,
https://doi.org/10.1007/978-3-030-78157-6_1

global warming as a result of greenhouse gas emissions, the need for emission reduction is clearly proven.

The second challenge is directly in line with the climate challenge: the energy transition requires the switch from fossil energy sources (gas and oil) to sustainable energy sources (including solar and wind energy, hydrogen, and biogas). The Dutch national ambition is 16% renewable energy by 2023, on the way to entirely eradicating fossil fuels by 2050. In the European arena, the ambition is to become a CO_2-neutral continent by 2050. There are a lot of complicated issues involved, so it will certainly not be achieved without a struggle. But continuing with an economy that is addicted to fossil fuels is no longer a viable proposition going forward. Changes must be made no matter how difficult they might be technically, socially, and economically.

The third challenge is the pursuit of a circular economy: an economy of closed material loops, based on a policy initiated by the second Rutte administration (the cabinet of the Dutch government from 2012 to 2017), but actually driven by EU policy. The ambition is to achieve a substantially reduced use of virgin materials: 50% by 2030 and 100% by 2050. It is now widely recognized that the low-carbon agenda is fundamentally intertwined with a circular economy agenda—making scaling up the circular economy an imperative (De Wit et al., 2019; Material Economics, 2018). Whether that can be fully achieved remains to be seen. After all, we use a lot of materials such as meat, fuel, or heat. Moreover, a large percentage of (processed) raw materials is stored in buildings, roads, cars, and so on. All these items have different lifespans. The lifespan of a plastic bottle may be a few weeks, but a cycle tunnel or a block of flats will last for 30 if not 50 years—the materials used are effectively stored as stock. Circularizing as many raw materials, components, and products as possible therefore requires radically different ways of organizing.

These three challenges combined result in a call for radical and major changes in the configuration of our economies. The seriousness of this situation is clear from the protests of farmers, builders, and citizens (among others). Normally quiet squares across Europe—be it in Paris, Madrid, London, Berlin, The Hague—seem to have changed into *tournament fields* on which fierce confrontations take place, with banners and chanting slogans as the new weaponry. Although intentions to create change may be making themselves heard, some of this (verbal) campaigning aims at preserving and maintaining the existing order. Key figures such as the young Greta Thunberg and Malala are leading the movements respectively on fighting climate change or realizing emancipation and inclusivity. Although they are getting the message out, these counter voices have not as yet really challenged nor moved the economic and social status quo.

However, the three challenges outlined call for the reconsideration and redesign of systems. These new systems should be able to address not just one, but all three challenging questions simultaneously. And addressing these is by no means a silver bullet, because there are also other directly related issues, such as the pursuit of restoring biodiversity or promoting social inclusivity, as reflected in, among others, the *EU Green Deal*, the *Circular Economy Action Plan (CEAP)*, and the *Just Transition Mechanism*. The nature and scope of the issues are such that it is correct to speak of not one but of three challenges, and at the same time: a triple transition. After all, it concerns a climate challenge, an energy transition and a structural reduction of the use of resources. The aim to work on this systematically with definite goals in mind entails answering several (extra) questions.

> The transition to sustainability is […] our search for a new social contract: a *natural* social contract, with a radically different view on the relationship between man and his environment. This is a transition from ego-consciousness to eco-consciousness. Society is increasingly asking for a social order and environment that is ecologically sound, economically supported, and socially connected. *Patrick Huntjens, Social Innovations Lector in the Green Domain, InHolland University of Applied Sciences.*

These three Dutch challenges correspond with the EU policies on climate change, energy transition, and circular economy. These policies will hopefully provide the framework for a stable transition for the coming ten years. If we have the courage, and knowing that we have to, we will drastically change many of our systems and associated institutions. We have reached the end of the life cycle of the fossil fuel age. The decade 2020–2030 may, therefore, enter the history books as the period of the *Great Social Renovation* or the *Transition Decade*. The United Nations (the UN) speaks of the *Decade of Action*. In public debates, and sometimes also in political ones, the conservation and restoration of biodiversity is often referred to as a separate fourth dimension, as a transition of its own. The current international biodiversity treaty—the UN Convention on Biological Diversity (www.cbd.int)—agreed that the decline of biodiversity must be halved by 2020, that overfishing must be stopped, that agriculture and forestry must be sustainable, and that the amount of protected nature must have increased from 10 to 17% globally. Clearly this is urgent, and much must be done in this regard. One hundred and ninety countries are currently negotiating a new agreement. In this publication, we do not view this as a separate transition but as a central part of the climate change challenge. We hope that this choice will not offend anyone and certainly not harm nature, insects, birds, fish, chickens, and all other animals. At the very least this call for more biodiversity—and considering it an extra dimension or transition of its own—is often linked to a request for paying more attention to the social dimension of transitions. Sometimes it is even argued that this should also be viewed as a separate *transition.* Even though this is a very intriguing and challenging perspective, in this book we choose to see the social dimension as an integral interdependent part of the triple transition we highlight—Climate, Energy, and Circularity. We believe that this choice does not reduce the interests or importance of the biodiversity or social aspects of these transitions, but only expresses that these are both integral dimensions of these transitions.

Example

The Government of the Netherlands' National Climate Agreement and Climate Act

On 28 May 2019, the majority of the Dutch Senate approved a Climate Act (www.government.nl/topics/climate-change/climate-policy). For the first time, the climate objectives are now set in law. In addition, the law has a mechanism that ensures that the government also achieves its stated climate goals. The Climate Act sets three objectives: (1) a reduction of 49% (compared to 1990) of greenhouse gas emissions by 2030, (2) a 95% reduction (compared to 1990) of greenhouse gas emissions by 2050, and (3) 100% greenhouse gas neutral electricity by 2050. As part of the Climate Act, the Government of the Netherlands committed to presenting a National Climate Agreement setting out the measures that are needed to achieve the objectives of the Climate Act. In December 2019, the Netherlands presented a National Climate and Energy Plan to the European Commission, and from 2020 onwards, the fourth Thursday of October will be *Climate Day* in the Netherlands.

But the Netherlands is not an island. Transition frameworks are being developed continuously in Europe, and more specifically, in Brussels. For some people, the pace of progress at the EU level may not be fast enough, while others regard this as patronizing. The fact remains that we cannot move forward in (relatively small) Europe without common frameworks for the three transitions. Traditionally, programmes such as *Horizon 2020* and the *Mission Innovation* framework underpinning Horizon Europe are a step in the right direction. The current European Commission, which took office after the 2019 European elections, gives specific priority to these transitions as is evident from the *European Green Deal* published in 2019 and the new *Circular Economy Action Plan (CEAP 2.0) (2020).* See also the *European Climate Law* being proposed by the European Commission to write into law the goal set out in the European Green Deal—for Europe's economy and society to become climate-neutral by 2050: ec.europa.eu/clima/policies/eu-climate-action/law_en. Time will tell what the impact of these EU interventions will be.

Example

A sustainable Europe is one that opens up opportunities, innovates, creates jobs, and offers a competitive edge to its industries. The circular economy is key for developing Europe's future economic model. I will propose a New Circular Economy Action Plan focusing on sustainable resource use, especially in resource-intensive and high-impact sectors such as textiles and construction. To help drive the change we need, I will put forward my plan for a future-ready economy, our new industrial strategy. [...] We will be a world leader in the circular economy and clean technologies. We will work to decarbonize energy-intensive industries. Europe is an industrial economy, and for many parts of our Union the local manufacturer, plant or factory is the hub for our communities. This is why I believe that what is good for our planet must be good for our people, our regions, and our economy. Von der Leyen (2019, p. 7)

This is a sketch of the (large) national and European contexts within which citizens, companies, and governments must jointly find their way. These transitions will certainly not be without struggles. The fact remains that we live in organized societies and economies in which together we need to shape these transitions. In this book, we adopt the perspective that the crux of our economic activity consists of a series of transactions. Transactions are those actions in which two or more parties make an exchange, which is experienced as the creation of value. These may involve products, such as buying a loaf of bread at the local bakery, or services, such as having your hair cut and paying the hairdresser. When you see it this way, our daily economic and social actions consist of a continuous process of large and small transactions throughout each and every day.

Example

Brussels is going to invest hundreds of billions of euros to make Europe the first climate-neutral continent. Among other things, two billion trees must be planted and one million charging points for electric cars installed. The design plan for the Green Deal stands out for its comprehensive nature. Putting up some solar panels and windmills here and there is considered totally inadequate. With these ambitious plans, Europe must become the first climate-neutral continent in the world. (Peeperkorn, 2019)

1.2 A New Model for Organizing Multiple Value Creation

The deliberate designing and organizing of transactions and the value they create form the basis for the development of every business model. A central point of departure in this book is working on new forms of value creation. A business model shows how value creation is achieved and the resulting transactions. Transactions are those actions in which two or more parties make an exchange, which is experienced as the creation of value.

The Business Model Template (BMT) presented here is aligned with a long tradition of instruments or tools for modelling business or value propositions, and this is reflected in the attention this is given in various chapters (see Chapter 2—Business Modelling, Chapter 8—Strategy, and Chapter 12—Value(s) Creation). Such instruments help users to contemplate and create a business model. The BMT, however, distinguishes itself by providing a system to enable users to develop a sustainable business model based on multiple value creation. But ultimately what happens in the template is up to the users themselves. After all, a template by itself is an *empty* thing. It prescribes the form, consisting of stages and building blocks. The user(s) themselves must develop the content in a clear, logical, and coherent fashion, and connect it to a value proposition accordingly. The challenge is creating an infrastructure that enables users to come up with a concept that organizes multiple value creation in a step-by-step manner: this is the gap that the BMT seeks to address.

Humankind is depleting nature at an unprecedented speed when it comes to resources as well as ecosystems. Major transformations are needed to prevent this. If you are serious about the transformations that we are facing, you must also question economic growth at all costs (Kalse, 2019).

The concept of multiple value creation means working on more than one value simultaneously. Or to put it more precisely, it always involves creating more than just financial value. For some, this means promoting biodiversity, or keeping materials in productive use in the economy, or restorative entrepreneurship—which refers to entrepreneurial activities aimed at the restoration of ecological and social systems. And to make it even more complicated, it is not a matter of either/or but rather of and-and-and. So the aim of multiple value creation is to develop solutions which address enhancing biodiversity, stimulate social inclusivity and work on the idea of restorative entrepreneurship (see Fig. 5.1, Chapter 5.2). We will return to this in detail in Chapter 5—The Proposition.

Important

Three guiding principles
In light of the triple transition challenges and the different approaches in modelling the changing nature of value creation, three guiding principles play an important role: (1) being more sustainable (eco-efficiency), (2) designing and organizing closed loops with the aim of creating circularity, and (3) deliberately recreating the social fabric that underpins inclusivity. Together they provide the stepping stones for a new role of business models. Each of these principles is closely linked to the UN Sustainable Development Goals (SDGs) (see also Appendix D).

Being more sustainable means systematically reducing the use of resources and energy as well as reducing harmful side-effects such as pollution, destruction, and exhaustion. This applies to both the production of goods and their uses. This can be done by searching for new resources, using sustainably generated energy, recycling, and so on. This will increase the sustainability of existing processes and practices. Being more sustainable, however, does not question the underlying linear system; instead, the focus is on reducing and mitigating adverse effects. This debate has its origins in publications such as *Silent Spring* (Carson, 1962) or *The Limits to Growth* of the Club of Rome (Meadows et al., 1972). The arrival of the *Our Common Future* report by Gro Harlem Brundtland (WCED, 1987) gave a real boost to the debate. Since then, various institutions, such as the UN IPCC and the Resilience Institute in Sweden, have continuously and emphatically measured and visualized the degradation of our natural environment, while a wide range of platforms have advocated the urgency to take action. The urgency is now so high—as evidenced by melting polar caps, temperature rise, extreme drought, and resulting forest fires—that radical and collective action is urgently needed.

Circularity involves the organization of value retention of resources, semi-finished products, and products in loops, which requires a differently structured economic system. One of the key origins of the circular economy is generally attributed to Walter Stahel from Switzerland, who wrote a report for the EU in the late 1970s called *The potential for substituting manpower for energy* (Stahel & Reday, 1977) and referred to it as *The Performance Economy*. Circularity also has antecedents in the field of *Industrial Ecology* and is related to ideas like *Cradle to Cradle* (McDonough & Braungart, 2002), and the *Blue Economy* (Pauli, 2017). For a long time, these ideas were operating in isolation, until integrated and mainstreamed by the Ellen McArthur Foundation (see www.ellenmacarthurfoundation.org) who picked up the idea in 2013 and brought this philosophy to the attention of business, politics, and the general public in every possible way. The essential idea is that a circular economy replaces the traditional linear take-make-waste model.

> Even if consumers are generally willing to engage in a circular economy, actual engagement is rather low. Further efforts are needed to develop a comprehensive approach to foster sustainable lifestyles and consumption, keeping in mind the need for a fair and just transition. To guide consumers and public authorities towards sustainable choices, information requirements on products regarding reparability, durability, or availability of spare parts need to be made available. In addition, consumers' empowerment in a circular economy will benefit from an improved system to tackle green claims. Environmental Footprinting can be the methodology to substantiate these claims. *European Union Circular Economy Action Plan (New Circular Economy Action Plan, 2020* ec.europa.eu/environment/circular-economy/pdf/new_circular_economy_action_plan.pdf).

After all, circularity is not about more recycling, but rather it focuses on designing products for reuse, repair, and ultimately lifetime extension. This will result in new forms of high-quality reuse, conversion (converting waste into new basic products), and substitution (the replacement of, for example, mined resources with renewable resources). The twofold question is, however, to what extent we can (a) make the existing way of producing and consuming more sustainable (implying using fewer materials, and less energy and transport for example) and (b) which parts are suitable for circular organizing (for not everything is fit to be circularized). Many things are consumed (such as fuel, vegetables, or apple juice) and these do not come back in a form that is suitable for use in the same loop. Moreover, it is possible to organize loops that are not sustainable. After all, you can recycle paper several times, but every time you need more water, energy, and resources. Circularity therefore goes hand in hand with being sustainable, but what that means exactly and where the balance lies is not always clear. It is a matter of trial and error.

Definition

Towards a new definition of sustainable development
The pursuit of sustainable development is a process that follows the needs of people, society, and the environment in the present without compromising the ability of future generations to meet their own needs. That endeavour contains a continuous exploration to find a balance between the principles of being more sustainable, circular, and inclusive. Ultimately, this should lead to both a restorative and a regenerative society and economy.

Inclusivity has the social aspects of value creation as the central focus. Here, the point of departure is creating societies and economies in which people get equal access to social, public, and private goods and services. This includes offering jobs to people who cannot easily gain access to the labour market and giving equal rights to civic initiatives that currently apply to companies. When we look at a transition towards a sustainable and circular economy, all kinds of directly connected qualitative and quantitative social and labour market issues arise. Claims related to the potential of scaling up circularity to lead to a substantial increase in the number of jobs do not seem to be aligned with the required competence developments, knowledge agendas, and related training programmes required to implement circularity. Moreover, inclusivity explicitly concerns access to social and economic opportunities for people who are marginalized because they have no job or have insufficient financial means.

Finally, inclusivity also needs to apply to nature and ecosystems whereby nature and related ecosystems get a permanent place in decision-making processes. Biodiversity and everything related to it is crucial as a basis for a liveable planet and a healthy economy. Our business activities of the last century and a half have done considerable damage to nature and ecosystems. The pace at which biodiversity has been reduced in recent decades is so high that the question of what business is doing to restore it should be part of every corporate strategy and supported by every municipal and governmental plan.

While the urgency to take action is increasing, there remains a substantial gap regarding the scale of action required to address the triple transition outlined. Research by the Netherlands Environmental Assessment Agency (Planbureau voor de Leefomgeving, 2019) and Circularity Gap (De Wit et al., 2019), for example, shows that while we are generally quite good at recycling, we can barely connect this to higher order circular strategies, let alone social inclusivity. Many consider the forthcoming decade (2020–2030) to be crucial in shaping this transition. But the question remains as to how we go from the existing (dominant) linear economy to a different economy—one which is more sustainable, circular, and embeds inclusivity at its core? That is not possible by prioritizing one guiding principle or one transition above another, but by aiming at multiple transitions simultaneously. We refer to this as an integral approach. This sounds good, but it also makes things exponentially complicated, while uncovering the interdependence of the partial challenges in the pursuit of multiple transitions. We are facing an unprecedented challenge, which must materialize in the existing institutional and organizational fabric of our society that is still fundamentally geared towards economic activity which prioritizes short-term profit and the linear use of resources and materials. This existing order is a principal obstacle to the much-needed triple transition required across the globe.

> The climate and society are moving towards ever-greater extremes. Strong social contradictions that have arisen due to individual interests and beliefs being pushed to the extreme threaten the balance that we so desperately need. With the symbolic year 2020 ahead, solutions seem farther away than ever. *Peter van Vliet, editor-in-chief Sustainable News, Consulted on 15 December 2019.*

1.3 Measuring Performance

Many of our existing business models are developed from an organization-centric perspective, based on a strategic route focused solely on the growth of turnover, market share, and the level of profit or loss. Consequently, working on multiple value creation (the simultaneous realization of multiple forms of values that are of a social, ecological, and economic nature) and value retention is not in the DNA of these business models.

Traditionally, the performance of organizations is assessed on financial criteria, namely whether the organization has made a profit or a loss. This is starting to change since organizations increasingly need to take sustainability into account when assessing profit and loss. As a result, the interpretation of financial indicators will change. In the BMT, we adopt the set of non-financial performance indicators that were formulated and approved by the EU in 2019 with a focus on the *Significance of climate-related issues for the business model and the impact on strategy* (European Commission, 2019, p. 16). The performance indicators used include *Energy consumption* or *production from renewable and non-renewable sources, GHG emissions breakdown, energy efficiency targets,* and *renewable energy targets.* These indicators can also be (partly) linked to the SDGs. Together, these seem to be the guiding frameworks for the coming decade, creating the basis for a (practical) set of financial and non-financial indicators that provide insight into the integral performance of an organization. See the International Integrated Reporting Council (IIRC: www.integratedreporting.org) for an example of how these frameworks are used to report on these performances. For an overview of indicators entertained in the BMT, see Chapter 11.

Important

The BMT helps enterprising people and their partners to establish a successful and future-proof value proposition that contributes to solving social and ecological issues and results in multiple forms of value creation.

For business models that are intentionally designed to give form and content to the triple transition tasks discussed earlier in this chapter, their value creation must be measured within a system that does justice to multiple value creation. From this perspective, our current accounting system needs to change because it virtually excludes indicators other than financial ones. Moreover, depreciation methods are aimed at reducing the value of assets to zero, while a central objective of the circular economy is value creation based on value retention. Current accounting methods do not promote sustainability in any way, in the sense of sparingly using resources and maintaining value. Moreover, our institutional frameworks concerning taxes, accounting, and other regulations legitimize the externalization of ecological and social costs—and this must change.

It is here against this background that we introduce a business model template and associated system that is based on the pursuit of multiple forms of value creation. The BMT is based on two previously published publications. The first is the book *New Business Models; Working Together on Value Creation*, which was published in 2014 (Jonker, 2014). This publication has provided several principles and concepts that together constitute the foundation for the basic community-based business model. The second publication is the workbook *Organising for the Circular Economy, A workbook for developing Circular Business Models*, published in the spring of 2018 (Jonker et al., 2018), which underpins the foundation for the circularity-based business model presented here. The *Organising for the Circular Economy* workbook can be downloaded free of charge in Dutch and English via www.circulairebusinessmodellen.nl/product/werkboek-bmce. In the next section, we provide a brief overview of the BMT based on key questions, supplemented by several tips to enable the reader to get the most out of the BMT process.

1.4 The Business Model Template

The purpose here is to introduce you to the structure and style of this book and how the BMT is presented in the various chapters. The BMT system consists of three stages that are developed in ten building blocks. In Fig. 1.1,

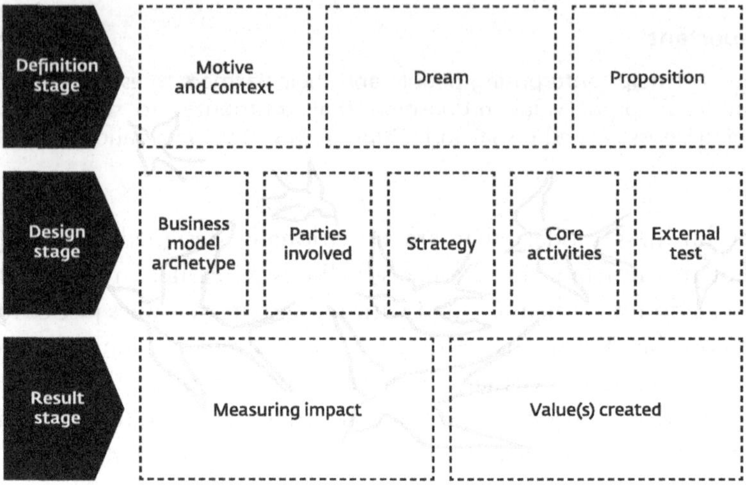

Fig. 1.1 Business Model Template

this is made evident in the building blocks being separated across three rows, with each row indicating a specific stage in the development process of a business model. The top row is the *Definition Stage*, the middle row is the *Design Stage*, and the bottom row is the *Result Stage* which together consist of ten building blocks. We will then walk through the template from top to bottom and from left to right.

Definition Stage: This stage consists of three building blocks: (1) Motive and Context, (2) Dream, and (3) Proposition. With these building blocks, you are trying to answer the following questions:

Questions

- What contribution will your business model make to sustainability challenges now and in the future?
- What do you think the *gap in the market*, or *the gap in society* is?
- What do you want to do and why?
- What is the problem, opportunity or challenge you want to address, and in what context?
- What is your internal drive and motivation?
- What dream goal do you want to achieve?
- Where are you going to make a real difference?
- Who are you going to do it for (who are your key stakeholders) and how will you sense-check whether they view the problem in the same way as you do?

The result of the Definition Stage is an overview of the context, the problem statement, the ultimate end situation/goal that you have in mind, and finally a high-level but clear-cut formulation of your proposal to achieve that ultimate end goal.

> **TIP**
>
> While you are still in the Definition Stage, it is advisable to take a good look around at existing initiatives. For example, go and search on the internet around the challenge you are exploring and see what suggestions you find. Allow existing initiatives to inspire you but try also to keep an open mind regarding what you could do differently.

Design Stage: After you have crystallized what you are going to do in the Definition Stage, the logical next step is to work out how you are going to go about it—you are going to design your business model (Design Stage). Four of the five steps in this stage help you shape the organization of your business model as concretely as possible, with the fifth step focusing on enabling you to test your model externally. The first four steps in this stage include the following building blocks: (4) Business Model Archetype, (5) Parties, (6) Strategy, and (7) Core Activities. The fifth step in the Design Stage encompasses all of the preceding building blocks and subjects them to Building Block #8—External Test.

With the building blocks in the Design Stage, you are trying to answer the following questions:

> **Questions**
>
> - How do you expect to achieve your dream/goal?
> - Which strategy do you choose to realize your dream/goal?
> - What activities will you undertake to realize this strategy?
> - What type of business model will you use to create value?
> - Who will you work with? With which stakeholders will you realize your value proposition?
> - Have you tested your business model idea with potential users/partners/suppliers (have you done an external test, for example)?
> - What do others think of your idea?
> - Are you on the right track?
> - Does your idea already exist in your context? What could you do better to make your offer unique?

If you have not found an answer to one or more of these questions, then seek advice from a new person and see who can help you find the answer. It may be necessary to go back to the Definition Stage, to make your context and value proposition more specific.

TIP

During the Design Stage, we recommend copying the basic BMT structure onto a large sheet of paper and working out the different building blocks in this stage with Post-its®, so that your choices can easily be changed or removed.

Result Stage: The third and final stage helps you to identify two essential building blocks of your business model: (9) the Impact that the business model has and (10) Value(s) Creation, in which it is made clear which values are being created.

Questions

- Which indicators will you choose?
- What are the positive and negative consequences of your business model, now and in the future?
- What value(s) are you creating and for whom?
- Which payment or transaction instruments will you be using?
- How do you shape transactions, and what do you exchange?

TIP

In the Result Stage, it is vital to be as concrete as possible. Do not be tempted to make big promises followed by a standard outcome—like the promise of a financially successful transaction model.

These last two building blocks provide insight beyond the conventional business model. In mainstream business modelling, often only the financial costs and benefits are considered. The impact that a business model has on its social, material, and ecological environment is not considered—regardless of it being an explicit question about the values that are being created. This is what differentiates the BMT from conventional business modelling: the BMT is one step ahead.

> We live in the aftermath of neo-liberalism which, with its *externalities*, has caused the biodiversity crisis and the ensuing climate crisis, and holds politics hostage worldwide. But an incredible thing is happening. Everywhere people are standing up to fight for the true values of our earth! Onwards to the coming decade of ecosystem restoration! *Sanne Copijn on LinkedIn* (Copijn, 2019)

In the next chapter, we will take a closer look at the history and background of business modelling. This is relevant because anyone who consults the literature in this field—even if only superficially—will find that the principles we address in the BMT are rarely, if ever, discussed, thus illustrating the gap which the BMT fills regarding the logic of multiple value creation.

References

Carson, R. (1962). *Silent Spring*. Houghton Mifflin.

Copijn, S. (2019). [LinkedIn post]. Retrieved on 4 November 2019 from: www.linkedin.com/posts/sonne-copijn-8abb20_vroege-vogels-sonne-copijn-strijdt-tegen-activity-6596719605442457600-YJEk/.

De Wit, M., Verstraeten-Jochemsen, J., Hoogzaad, J., & Kubbinga, B. (2019). *Circularity Gap Report 2019: Closing the circularity gap in a 9% world.* Retrieved on 24 September 2020 from:docs.wixstatic.com/ugd/ad6e59_ba1e4d16c64f44fa94fbd8708eae8e34.pdf.

Dutch Government. (2019). *The Government of the Netherlands National Climate Agreement and Climate Act 2019*. Retrieved on 19 February 2020 from: www.government.nl/documents/reports/2019/06/28/climate-agreement.

Ellen MacArthur Foundation. (2012). *Towards the circular economy Vol. 1: Economic and business rationale for an accelerated transition* (p. 98). Ellen Mac Arthur Foundation. https://www.ellenmacarthurfoundation.org/assets/downloads/publications/Ellen-MacArthur-Foundation-Towards-the-Circular-Economy-vol.1.pdf.

European Commission. (2013). *Europe in a changing world—Inclusive, innovative and reflective societies*. Retrieved on 24 September 2020 from: ec.europa.eu/programmes/horizon2020/en/h2020-section/europe-changing-world-inclusive-innovative-and-reflective-societies.

European Commission. (2019). *Report on climate-related disclosures*. Retrieved on 24 September 2020 from: ec.europa.eu/info/sites/info/files/business_economy_euro/banking_and_finance/documents/190110-sustainable-finance-teg-report-climate-related-disclosures_en.pdf.

IPCC. (2018). *Global warming of 1.5°C: An IPCC Special Report on the impacts of global warming of 1.5°C above pre-industrial levels and related global greenhouse gas emission pathways, in the context of strengthening the global response to the threat of climate change, sustainable development, and efforts to eradicate poverty*. Intergovernmental Panel on Climate Change. http://www.ipcc.ch/report/sr15/.

Jonker, J. (2014). *New business models; Working together towards value creation.* Academic Service.

Jonker, J., Stegeman, H., Faber, N., & Kothman, T. H. (2018). *Eén zwaluw belooft veel goeds – resultaten van het landelijke onderzoek 2016–2017 naar business modellen voor de circulaire economie.* Stichting OCF 2.0.

Kalse, E. (2019). Afzien van economische groei, kunnen we dat wel? *NRC Handelsblad*. Retrieved 10 May 2019 from: www.nrc.nl/nieuws/2019/05/10/afzien-van-groei-kan-een-economie-dat-a3959860.

Material Economics. (2018). *The circular economy: A powerful force for climate mitigation.* Material Economics. https://materialeconomics.com/material-economics-the-circular-economy.pdf?cms_fileid=340952bea9e68d9013461c92fbc23cae.

McDonough, W., & Braungart, M. (2002). *Cradle to cradle: Remaking the way we make things.* North Point Press.

Meadows, D. H., Meadows, D. L., Randers, J., & Behrens, W. W. (1972). *The Limits to Growth.* Universe Books.

Pauli, G. (2017). *The Blue Economy 3.0: The marriage of science, innovation and entrepreneurship creates a new business model that transforms society.* XLIBRIS.

Peeperkorn, M. (2019). Met deze ambitieuze plannen moet Europa het eerste klimaatneutrale continent ter wereld worden. *Volkskrant*. Retrieved 10 December 2019 from: www.volkskrant.nl/nieuws-achtergrond/met-deze-ambitieuze-plannen-moet-europa-het-eerste-klimaatneutrale-continent-ter-wereld-worden~bf2271ac/?referer=.

Planbureau voor de Leefomgeving. (2019). *Outline of the Circular Economy. The Hague:* PBL Retrieved from: circulareconomy.europa.eu/platform/sites/default/files/pbl-2019-outline-of-the-circular-economy-3633.pdf.

Stahel, W. R., & Reday, G. (1977). *The potential for substituting man-power for energy: Report to DG V for Social Affairs* (76/13; Programme of Research and Actions on the Development of the Labour Market). Commission for European Communities.

Von der Leyen, U. (2019). *A Union that strives for more: My agenda for Europe. Political Guidelines for the next European Commission 2019–2024.* Commission for European Communities. Retrieved on 24 September 2020 from: ec.europa.eu/commission/sites/beta-political/files/political-guidelines-next-commission_en.pdf.

WCED. (1987). *Our Common Future.* Oxford University Press.

2

Business Modelling

The triple transition that we are facing requires different models of entrepreneurship and organization combined with a different attitude towards value creation. The scale of the challenges facing society in the coming decade(s) necessitates business models that are based on collaboration and on value being co-created between parties in chains and networks.

Collaboration becomes mutually beneficial and is necessary for a business to thrive. Of course, organizing together is not something new in and of itself. The difference now is that parties need to look for ways they can differentiate themselves by creating new forms of value creation collaboratively, based on several shared principles and for longer durations.

Consequently, time becomes more critical in the process of value creation. Multiple customer engagements and transactions based on optimizing the value embedded in the same resources, materials, or (refurbished) products will become the norm, with partners creating value through the provision of additional services. This contrasts with the mainstream linear economic model, in which it is often only a single transaction that is important for value creation, and the producer's responsibility for the embedded resources in the product ends immediately after the transaction.

This concerted organization of value creation and retention demands both social and organizational innovation. The meaning of value creation is also extended from being purely monetary to including multiple values. Organizational models and business models become much more closely intertwined. When we start creating value with each other and among each other across the boundaries of an organization, the rules of the economic–organizational

J. Jonker and N. Faber, *Organizing for Sustainability*,
https://doi.org/10.1007/978-3-030-78157-6_2

game will change. It is no longer the *exclusive* responsibility of the organization to create value(s), but rather the network, society, and community. We move from organization-centred to network-centred or loop-centred value creation, retention, and capture, which leads to a fundamental revision of the logic of value creation.

Sustainability values are predominantly considered as externalities in the current dominant generation of linear business models. All kinds of social and ecological costs are therefore passed on to society or nature. This is because damage or risk, immediate or over time, both in the social and ecological domains, is, in principle, not included in the cost–benefit analysis. A transition from a linear economy to a more sustainable and circular economy therefore requires different business models. It is useful to look at the nature and logic of business models. Against this background, we propose three basic or archetypal business models: the platform, community, and circular economy models which are explained in Chapter 6—Business Model Archetypes.

2.1 A Short History of Business Modelling

Value creation is the core of a business model and is the shared task of the actors involved in the delivery of a business model. In essence, a business model is a description of how value creation between parties or partners—based on certain principles—is organized, at a particular moment, in a specific context, and given available resources. There is an unlimited number of combinations of factors that influence the design and functioning of a business model within a particular natural and institutional context, so it is inevitable that entrepreneurs and intrapreneurs make choices. Collectively, these choices reflect a certain logic.

As has already been said, the BMT is not the first template that has been created for business modelling, nor will it be the last. Therefore, before we dive into the BMT we will first briefly review existing templates.

The best known is the Business Model Canvas (BMC; Osterwalder et al., 2010), which has been widely adopted since its publication by both entrepreneurs and innovation training courses which describe, categorize, and develop business model innovations. There are many workshops and online tutorials on how to use the BMC which has become the go to framework for exploring business models. The BMC has been so widely used due to its straightforward depiction of the key building blocks of a mainstream business model. Its strengths include the fact that it can be used quickly without much prior knowledge, and because it enables the user to communicate business models efficiently with its clear visual representation. We used these strengths to shape and inform the design and usability of the BMT presented here.

However, despite the wide acceptance of the BMC, there has also been quite a bit of criticism (King, 2017; Koen, 2017; Murphy, 2014; Verrue, 2014). This criticism can be divided into three areas: criticism of the purpose of the model, criticism of the model itself, and criticism of the use of the model. Next, we summarize the main critiques of the BMC and compare it with the BMT.

1. The purpose of the BMC is to clarify how an organization creates value to make the core building blocks of a business model visible (Osterwalder et al., 2010). It is inherent in any framework or tool that seeks to simplify complexity that certain factors will fall outside the model, such as the implementation of the business model, the external environment, competitors, and preconditions. Therefore, the biggest advantage, its simplicity, is at the same time the biggest limitation of the model. In a sense, this critique can also be applied to the design of the BMT. However, with the BMT we pay more attention to the cause and context: an external test has been included, and you are invited to assess the impact of the model. The BMT aims to keep functionality as broad as possible without sacrificing simplicity.
2. The BMC model itself has been critiqued by various authors who draw attention to the building blocks' different levels of abstraction (some of which are more detailed than others) and contest the overlap between the different building blocks (Verrue, 2014). Additionally, the link between the categories is not always clear, and thus how the building blocks in the BMC influence each other is unclear. Moreover, the BMC is not suitable for not-for-profit organizations and other forms of social organization, largely due to the emphasis on financial returns (whereas, in principle, the value proposition could allow multiple value creation). There are also different levels of abstraction within the BMT. However, this is addressed by how these building blocks are grouped in the three stages of the model (Definition, Design, and Result Stages). In the BMT, creating multiple values as well as the impact of doing so is explicitly included in its DNA.
3. Regarding the use of the BMC, there is the argument that it results in insufficient attention being paid to strategy, long-term thinking, and time—a completed BMC model is a snapshot without the *time* component. In contrast, in the BMT, strategy and long-term thinking have been explicitly included in the form of the Dream (Building Block #2) and the

Strategy (Building Block #6) building blocks. The BMT also recognizes that the time component is important when considering and developing an accurate business model, and this becomes visible through the iterative process of business model innovation advocated for in the BMT method.

Additional criticisms of the BMC are that it is oriented towards existing companies rather than towards start-ups. In contrast, the BMT is specifically designed to apply to both new and existing companies. Another critique is that the BMC limits creativity by forcing the user to think in the described categories (boxes) and then fill them in. To a certain extent the BMT also has this limitation; however, we have formulated the building blocks so broadly, without compromising applicability, that they do not limit the creativity of the user. Lastly, the BMC does not offer any tools for comparing any value creation or costs other than monetized costs and revenues. In contrast, the BMT overcomes this by explicitly addressing the social and environmental impact of a business model in the Result Stage.

There are, of course, many more developments in the field of business models. Some of the adaptations to the BMC as well as alternative canvasses and models are discussed below:

- **The Lean Canvas Model:** Here the focus is explicitly on start-ups (Nidagundi & Novickis, 2017).
- **The Circular Business Model Canvas**: Here the focus is specifically on circular economy (Ellen MacArthur Foundation, 2016: www.circulardesignguide.com/post/circular-business-model-canvas).
- **The Triple Bottom Line Canvas**: Here both social and ecological values are included (Joyce & Paquin, 2016).
- **The Value Proposition Canvas**: Here competitor analysis is also considered (Pokorná et al., 2015).
- **The Business Model Innovation Canvas**: Here the BMC has been applied to Blitzscaling's business model with an emphasis on creativity and business innovation (Cuofano, 2018).
- **The Social Enterprise Canvas**: Here, as the name indicates, the focus is on social enterprises (Qastharin, 2015).
- **The Social Impact Canvas**: Here the focus is on the impact of a social enterprise in terms of creating both social and financial impact (traditional, economic growth) (TapToo, n.d.).
- **The Business Model Cube**: Here the network that a business model is situated in is given a central position (Lindgren & Rasmussen, 2013).

- **The e3-value approach**: Here the focus is on how value creation could be organized within a network (Gordijn et al., 2006).
- **The STOF model**: Here the focus is on developing the value proposition rather than the organization of value delivery and capture (Bouwman et al., 2008).

> Organizations need entrepreneurs who dare to challenge the complex quests of our world. We desperately need talents with a mindset to drive innovation and change with sustainable impact. *Free translation of Benjo van den Bogaard, consulted on LinkedIn on 1 December 2019.*

Why Conventional Business Model Toolkits Are No Longer Fit for Purpose

Thanks to the work of Osterwalder (2004) and others, over the last two decades, thinking in terms of business models has helped many organizations to make their value propositions explicit, to think about how they organize value delivery and capture, and ultimately helped businesses to reflect on whether their business model is optimized to deliver competitive advantage. But at the same time, conventional business modelling approaches have several weaknesses. The main point of criticism is that traditional business model frameworks focus almost exclusively on the perspective of one organization, with the emphasis on creating financial value. The consequence is that this method of approaching value creation and the associated business models reinforces binary profit-and-loss-account thinking. Indeed, some variants of mainstream business model toolkits now exist but they still remain a minority.

In reality, organizations are rarely, if at all, able to organize value creation, delivery, and capture on their own. Without exception, organizations work in a chain of suppliers, buyers, and partners. This applies to both the so-called operational activities (e.g. electricity, housing, mobility) and the core activities (see also Chapter 7—Parties and Chapter 9—Core Activities). However, the role of customers in a traditional business model often consists solely of generating revenue for the organization. Here a successful business model is one that makes explicit how an organization realizes its value proposition. In return, customers express their appreciation for the organization's proposition with a monetary transaction. This view on the value chain is rather limited and many authors (e.g. Teece, 2010; Vanhaverbeke & Cloodt, 2006; Zott & Amit, 2010) agree that the basis for value creation lies in what is usually called the *architecture of the organization* and the *network of parties*. Working together on value creation is a collective organizational task which occurs in value chains and/or networks. It follows that describing a business model for only one component of such a chain or network is of limited use.

Moreover, the type of value described in a conventional business model and associated toolkits is far from complete. Traditionally, the emphasis is on describing how financial value is created for the organization itself (explaining why the terms *business model* and *revenue model* are often confused). But just as you cannot run a business with only financial input, an enterprise can create more types of value than just financial. Starting up and maintaining an organization requires people, as well as raw materials, technology, tools, and knowledge. In the same way, an organization can also create social and ecological values. Here this is called *multiple value creation.*

Towards a Business Modelling Approach for a Sustainable Economy

The criticism of traditional business models and associated toolkits has resulted in all kinds of adjustments and extensions being proposed, but these lead to existing business or value propositions being *greened*. This approach fits in well with the ideas underlying conventional business modelling because it aims to develop products and services that are better, faster, more economical, and preferably also cheaper than those of the competitors. Here, greening becomes a matter of product innovation. The greening of a business model, in turn, leads to strategies that often go for *less* (less water, oil, energy, …) which we know as *eco-efficiency*.

Similarly, including non-financial values in the business model often only leads to incremental improvements, with the core focus on balancing financial costs and benefits remaining unchanged. Greening a traditional business model means working within the boundaries of one's (own) organization or existing value chain. The underlying paradigm of a linear economy is hardly, if at all, open to discussion, the business model remains intact, and the underlying organizational logic remains unchanged. At best, these cosmetic adjustments can lead to fragmented solutions: a tokenistic touch of sustainability is *added* to an existing mainstream model.

Example

Developing a business model for a community centre

A community centre in the town of Tenderlo in Belgium has a workshop for bike repairs and a restaurant using vegetables that are past their sell-by date. This project is seen as important in the context of fighting poverty but it is run by volunteers which limits its scalability and could threaten its long-term viability and continuity. Moreover, there is no *revenue* for the volunteers, making it hard to reward their time, nor are the people who collect the vegetables compensated for their modest travel costs. To make this initiative viable into the future they need a model that can create value for the volunteers either financially or in some other way. The originators of this project lack the knowledge and tools to make a business model for this case—can you take this example and explore what incentives and values could be created? For inspiration see also the case study on Cargonomia, a cooperative initiative in Budapest: www.climate-kic.org/insights/cargo-bikes-conviviality-and-conscious-food-creative-partnerships-and-the-circular-economy.

2.2 The Modelling Process

With the BMT, we try to resolve most of the criticisms of current business model toolkits. The greatest benefit of a template or a model lies in working with a common language which enables people within and between organizations to communicate unambiguously and work on organizing value creation. In this respect, the BMT is designed to help you to make clear choices that lead to a form of sustainable value creation. Traditionally the formulation of a business model sticks to a rather tight logic based on *three key business model elements or building blocks*: (1) making explicit the logic underpinning value creation, for example the value proposition, (2) clarifying the way the value proposition is organized, and (3) describing the earning capacity and costs from organizing the value proposition.

Key points

1. **Logic of value creation**: The first element describes the logic of value creation or the value proposition, answering the question *What value is created for whom?* The implicit outcome of this—certainly with conventional business models—is almost always the dominant pursuit of positive financial results. Although social and environmental values are increasingly important for organizations, these values in the business model rarely receive the attention they deserve.
2. **Organizational model**: The second element describes the way in which the value proposition is organized. Most often the point of departure is that this occurs within an organization in collaboration with other parties. But the organization-centred perspective is not the only perspective—this is also possible in loops and networks. Different building blocks such as customers, channels, costs, and activities must be connected logically, so that the aim,

the production, or the organization of a certain product or service can be carried out in such a way that financial profit is achieved.

3. **Revenue model**: The third element describes the earning capacity that the organization of the value proposition entails compared with the revenues that are realized. This leads to a revenue model: the logic of realizing monetary revenues and other benefits. When organizations describe this, a large number of fiscal, accounting, and auditing conventions and rules must be taken into account. This cost–benefit analysis is usually only organization-centred reflecting how the current institutional and fiscal structures work. All kinds of secondary social or ecological effects (both short- and long-term) are excluded from the cost–benefit comparison. In contrast, earning capacity in the BMT refers to creating multiple values, with revenue being one form of value creation.

In the BMT, we maintain these three elements from the conventional business model: value creation, organization, and earning capacity. But we define them differently, extending their meaning. This is possible because we have introduced three principles that help to make clear choices: being more sustainable, circular, and inclusive. Moreover, in the BMT, we add a fourth element to the traditional business model framework: *impact*, which refers to the impact the business model has on ecology and ecosystems, society, inclusivity, and the economy (Fig. 2.1).

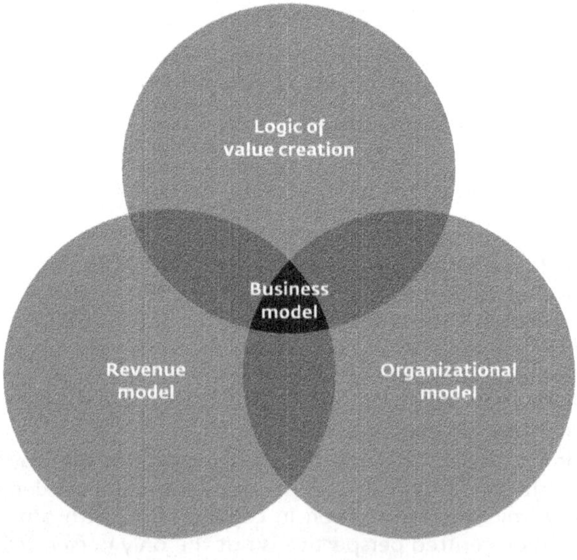

Fig. 2.1 Key elements of a conventional business model

2.3 Key Business Model Archetypes

In the BMT we make a distinction between three basic or archetypal business models. A brief description of each is outlined below—these will be discussed in more detail in Chapter 6—Business Model Archetypes.

Important

Platform model. The first business model archetype is a platform model which aims to make better and more efficient use of what we have through asset or performance management enabled by datafication and digitalization. At its essence this archetype is about better functional utilization—to sit on a chair more often, smarter and longer, for example; to use a car more efficiently; or to lease lighting. This is possible due to developments such as the Internet of Things (IoT), in which everyday devices are linked to the internet, so that usage can be registered and optimized. For instance, a *smart* refrigerator in a cafeteria can keep track of exactly what goes out per week, so that purchases are made more accurately, and waste is prevented. This datafication and digitalization of materials and objects leads to the development of new services delivered via digital platforms which we refer to as the Internet of Services (IoS). The platform business model archetype is also often labelled a *functional* or *sharing* economy. Once you start to look around there are plenty of examples: energy cooperatives are popping up like mushrooms, so-called *bread funds*[1] are showing unprecedented growth in the Netherlands, and now you don't need to buy your children's bikes but instead can access the different bikes as your children grow—see, for example thebikeclub.co.uk.

Community model. The second business model archetype refers to business models that are created around a community. Often a community is taken to refer solely to the *municipality* or the *society* that we live in, but this does not cover the full meaning from our perspective. In the BMT, the community business model archetype refers to the creation of multi-stakeholder thematic communities by citizens and/or public entities, together with companies related to health care, food, insurance, mobility, or energy, for example. Working together as a community—a group of people either physically or thematically connected—leads to what we have started calling *community-based business models.*

Circular model. The third business model archetype is based on the idea of designing raw materials, components, and products in such a way that they can be kept in circulation indefinitely (within the constraints of thermodynamics). The main aim of this model is to achieve value retention in and

[1]A bread fund provides a financial safety net when you become ill as a self-employed person. Self-employed entrepreneurs in a bread fund agree to support each other with donations in the event of a disability. The bread fund is an initiative of the Broodfondsmakers (source Taylor, 2017)—see www.broodfonds.nl/over_ons/de_broodfondsmakers.

through organizing loops which require circular business and organization models. [Open questions, which we will return to in Chapter 6—do business model archetypes relate to whether the circular economy is only driven by a raw material dimension? Or are there also social and ecological dimensions to circularity?]

Introducing the three business model archetypes at the heart of the BMT is essential here because they provide a clear and fundamental logic for developing sustainable business models. To sum up, the platform business model archetype is about better functional utilization, the community business model archetype is about forming thematic multi-stakeholder communities, and the *commons* and the circular business model archetype is about organizing value retention through closing material loops. And of course, it's important to remember that these archetypes are not strictly separable or mutually exclusive, but the clearer the logic you want to apply, the better the result.

2.4 Horizontal and Vertical Organization

Realizing the triple transition towards sustainable development—meaning a sustainable society and supportive economy—requires the generation of new business models. In fact, business models seem to play a crucial role in shaping these transitions (Bidmon & Knab, 2018). It is not enough to simply modify conventional business models, because then the underlying logic remains unchanged. Instead, a much more radical approach is needed, in which the core of value creation—anything that is of value or multiple values—is included in the *costs and benefits* in new, integral ways.

New business models that are future-proof are not organization-centred, but inter-organizational: dependent on a joint approach by different parties. It may be that one party takes the initiative or that several do, but in the end, there will always be a configuration of parties around a value proposition. New business models in this book refer to how those different parties (citizens, companies, and government) work together to organize a specific need or functionality. The focus is on configurations of parties that are composed in different ways from citizens, organizations, companies, or governments and that simultaneously pursue the creation of multiple value(s). The consequence is that value creation becomes collective, and the resulting value created is distributed and shared between parties.

Working on and with these new business models will result in different organizational relationships: more horizontal, in networks, and digitally facilitated. Suddenly we are simultaneously not only citizens, but also entrepreneurs and self-investors. You might call this DIY (do-it-yourself) entrepreneurship. Digitalization (for example the IoT) also strengthens the networks and interactions between parties enabling these new organizational relationships. We refer to this as the horizontal organization and see it emerging alongside the conventional vertical organization of the industrial model.

However, the horizontal method of organization cannot completely replace the vertical, industrial model. The hundreds of products and services we use every day are mainly the result of an industrial organization model that has been developed to perfection. One of the major challenges that we are facing today is to make this vertical model radically more sustainable while maintaining the power of industrial efficiency. New business models emerge at the very cutting edge of the horizontal and vertical organization described here.

2.5 Summary: Engaging with the Business Model Template

After this brief introduction to a number of the key elements of this book, it is time to advise on how to engage with the book and use the BMT. The BMT is an instrument that works best when you work on it iteratively with others. This makes it easier to make choices, to continue working out the next building block, and also to go back to review the implications of the choices made in previous building blocks. Every business model is created and evolves (by trial and error) through multiple iterations. At the crux of designing any business model, as well as when using the BMT, is the discussion and coordination of the choices made within each building block. The ultimate goal is to arrive at a well-defined set of decisions. Bearing the above in mind, it is of course feasible for individuals to use the BMT to test their business model ideas.

In Chapters 3–12 which follow, each of the ten individual building blocks is explained in greater detail (including the underlying theory) and illustrated with practical examples to support the business model innovation process. The ten building blocks are also grouped into three stages or phases described below and illustrated in an example of a completed BMT depicted in Fig. 2.2.

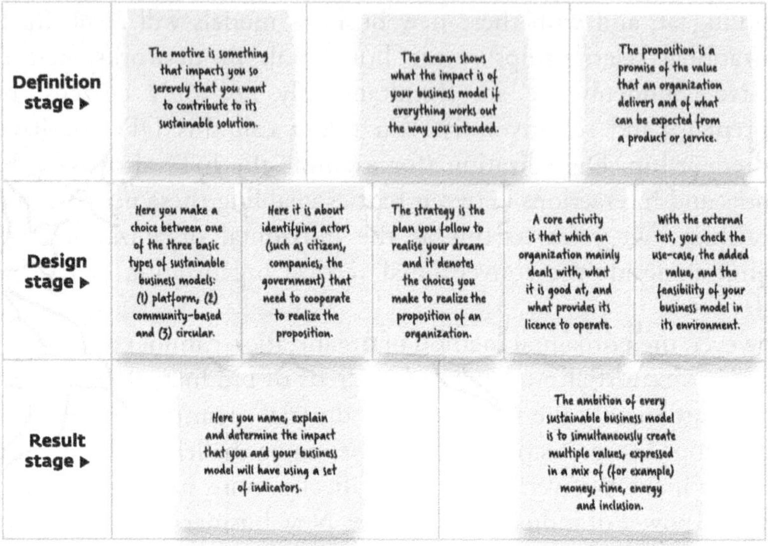

Fig. 2.2 Filled-in business model template

Key points

Definition Stage

Building Block #1: Motive and Context

Your motive is in response to something that has such an impact on you that you are driven to contribute to a sustainable solution to address it. The context concerns the actual social and economic situation in which your business-model-to-be has to function.

Building Block #2: Dream

The Dream indicates what will change as a result of your business model if you achieve everything you intend to.

Building Block #3: Proposition

A proposition is a promise that an organization or collaboration makes and that clarifies for the user what can be expected from the value of the resulting product or service or product–service system (PSS).

Design Stage

Building Block #4: Business Model Archetypes

Here you choose from the three basic types of business models: (1) platform, (2) community, and (3) circular, or a novel combination of the three.

Building Block #5: Parties

This is about identifying parties (such as citizens, companies, or government) that need to cooperate to realize the proposition.

Building Block #6: Strategy

A strategy is a plan that you use to make your dream come true and explains which choices are made to realize the value proposition.

Building Block #7: Core Activities

A core activity is what an organization or collaboration is primarily working on, what it is good at, and what gives it its right to exist.

Building Block #8: External Test

The external test is used to check the added value and the feasibility of the business model in the world around you.

Result Stage

Building Block #9: Impact

Here you describe, explain, and determine the impact that your business model will have, based on indicators.

Building Block #10: Value(s) Creation

The ambition of every sustainable business model is the simultaneous creation of multiple values, expressed in a mix of, but not limited to, money, time, energy, and inclusivity.

References

Bidmon, C. M., & Knab, S. F. (2018). The three roles of business models in societal transitions: New linkages between business model and transition research. *Journal of Cleaner Production, 178,* 903–916. https://doi.org/10.1016/j.jclepro.2017.12.198.

Bouwman, H., Faber, E., Haaker, T., Kijl, B., & De Reuver, M. (2008). Conceptualizing the STOF model. In H. Bouwman, H. De Vos, & T. Haaker (Eds.), *Mobile service innovation and business models* (pp. 31–70). Springer. https://doi.org/10.1007/978-3-540-79238-3_2.

Cuofano, G. (2018). *Blitzscaling Business Model Innovation Canvas in a Nutshell.* Retrieved on 13 June 2019 from: fourweekmba.com/blitzscaling-business-model-innovation-canvas/.

Ellen MacArthur Foundation. (2012). *Towards the circular economy Vol. 1: Economic and business rationale for an accelerated transition* (p. 98). Ellen Mac Arthur Foundation. www.ellenmacarthurfoundation.org/assets/downloads/publications/Ellen-MacArthur-Foundation-Towards-the-Circular-Economy-vol.1.pdf.

Gordijn, J., Yu, E., & van der Raadt, B. (2006). E-service design using i* and e/sup 3/ value modelling. *IEEE Software, 23*(3), 26–33. https://doi.org/10.1109/MS.2006.71.

Joyce, A., & Paquin, R. L. (2016). The triple layered business model canvas: A tool to design more sustainable business models. *Journal of Cleaner Production, 135,* 1474–1486. https://doi.org/10.1016/j.jclepro.2016.06.067.

King, R. (2017). *The business model canvas: A good tool with bad instructions?* Retrieved 13 June 2019 from: https://medium.com/%40RodKing/the-business-model-canvas-a-good-tool-with-bad-instructions-1829e4a66ac6.

Koen, P. (2017). *Front end innovation—Osterwalder's business model canvas doesn't work for start-ups.* Retrieved on 24 June 2019 from https://www.frontendinnovation.com/blog/08/14/2014/osterwalders-business-model-canvas-doesnt-work-for-start-ups.

Lindgren, P., & Rasmussen, O. H. (2013). *The business model cube.* Retrieved on 24 September 2020 from https://www.riverpublishers.com/journal/journal_articles/RP_Journal_2245.

Murphy, S. (2014). *Serious problems with business model canvas for startups.* Retrieved on 24 June 2019 from https://www.skmurphy.com/blog/2014/09/23/serious-problems-with-business-model-canvas-for-startups.

Nidagundi, P., & Novickis, L. (2017). Introducing lean canvas model adaptation in the scrum software testing. *Procedia Computer Science, 104,* 97–103. https://doi.org/10.1016/j.procs.2017.01.078.

Osterwalder, A. (2004). *The business model ontology: A proposition in a design science approach.* https://www.academia.edu/download/30373644/thebusiness-model-ontology.pdf.

Osterwalder, A., Pigneur, Y., & Clark, T. (2010). *Business model generation: a handbook for visionaries, game changers, and challengers.* Wiley.

Pokorná, J., Pilař, L., Balcarová, T., & Sergeeva, I. (2015). Value proposition canvas: Identification of pains, gains and customer jobs at farmers' markets. *AGRIS Online Papers in Economics and Informatics, 7*(4), 123–130.

Qastharin, A. R. (2015). *Business model canvas for social enterprise.* Proceedings of the 7th Indonesia International Conference on Innovation, Entrepreneurship, and Small Business (IICIES 2015) (pp. 116–125). Hak Cipta, Bandung, Indonesia.

TapToo. (n.d.). Social impact canvas van TapToo [Company Website]. Retrieved on 19 June 2020 from http://www.taptoo.nl/social-impact-canvas.

Taylor, M. (2017). *Report prepared by Bread Funds UK for the Independent Review of Employment Practices in the Modern Economy.* Bread Funds. Retrieved on 24 September 2020 from http://breadfunds.uk/wp-content/uploads/2017/05/BreadFunds-report-May2017-WEB.pdf.

Teece, D. J. (2010). Business models, business strategy and innovation. *Long Range Planning, 43*(2–3), 172–194. https://doi.org/10.1016/j.lrp.2009.07.003.

Vanhaverbeke, W., & Cloodt, M. (2006). Open innovation in value networks. In H. Chesbrough, W. Vanhaverbeke, & J. West (Eds.), *Open innovation: Researching a new paradigm* (pp. 258–281). Oxford University Press.

Verrue, J. (2014). *A critical investigation of the Osterwalder business model canvas: An in-depth case study.* Retrieved on 24 September 2020 from http://biblio.ugent.be/publication/5712151/file/5712152.pdf.

Zott, C., & Amit, R. (2010). Business model design: An activity system perspective. *Long Range Planning, 43*(2), 216–226. https://doi.org/10.1016/j.lrp.2009.07.00.

Part I

Definition Stage

A business model does not usually come out of the blue, but originates from an inspiration, an irritation, a great concern, an urgent need, or a passion. To direct these inspirations, irritations, concerns, and passions, in the *Definition Stage* of the BMT you will work out WHAT you are going to do. What keeps you awake at night? What contribution will your business model make to sustainable challenges now and in the future? What do you think the *gap in the market* is, or, even better, *the gap in society*? The first three building blocks of the BMT help you to structure and focus this thought process.

3

Motive and Context

If we don't clean up litter, it will be a long time before it disappears. The breakdown times for waste vary from several weeks to an eternity. Non-biological materials from conventional plastics to chewing gum do not decompose, but break apart into tiny particles that bioaccumulate in soil and water. *MilieuCentraal,* www.milieucentraal.nl

If we keep consuming the way we are now, by 2050 we'll need at least three planets to feed the entire world. A transition from animal to plant-based proteins is essential. *Dutch WeedBurger,* dutchweedburger.com

In 2050 there will be more plastic than fish in the sea. *Ellen MacArthur Foundation,* ellenmacarthurfoundation.org

A pair of jeans pollutes as much water as your body uses over ten years. *Damselfly London,* damselflylondon.com

All things considered, we have to go back to the circular thinking of the good old days, but with today's knowledge and insights. So, we are trying to design efficient production, at acceptable prices for the average consumer, and with attention to animal welfare, the environment, and the farmer. *Kipster,* www.kipster.nl

We see access to energy as a fundamental human right. To us, this is not an elusive goal, but an issue that requires immediate attention. It is a straight-up precondition for further development, because access to electricity means access to education, to communication, to income-generating opportunities, to self-belief, and to a better future. *WakaWaka,* waka-waka.com

J. Jonker and N. Faber, *Organizing for Sustainability,*
https://doi.org/10.1007/978-3-030-78157-6_3

3.1 Exploring the Challenge and Opportunity

When you start working on a new business model, the main question is: Why are you doing it? What problem, challenge, or opportunity have you identified within a specific (existing) context? You could think of the necessity of working in a CO_2-neutral way or the increasing demand for modular elements in construction or electronics in the context of the transition to the circular economy. Or your business model could focus on improving biodiversity, abolishing single-use plastics, or making bikes from recycled materials. If the immediate reason and motive driving you to develop your business model is not clear, then this needs to be the first thing to consider. Building Block #1—Motive and Context deals with this aspect and is about capturing as clearly as possible the nature and context of the problem, the challenge, or the opportunity posed.

Slowly but surely, sustainability will become central to every business model. It follows logically that there will still be business ideas that are initially conventional (for conventional, read purely market-oriented). If this is the case for you/your team, it is important to use this building block to look carefully for the social and ecological components and the context of your idea. Which themes are playing a role? Which ones affect you the most and which ones can you use to turn the market opportunity into a social and ecological opportunity? In this way, you can expand your conventional reasoning and motivation into one in which sustainability is central, because that is what we are aiming for with future-oriented sustainable entrepreneurship: it is an integral part of your business model rather than something you do *on the side*.

> What it is really about is developing a vision of what our food system will look like 30 years from now. Today's agriculture is based on ideas from 50 years ago: produce as much as possible at the lowest possible cost. We have gone overboard in that respect. Zanders (2020)

Everyone can identify reasonably quickly where the problems are in his or her environment, what bottlenecks exist, and where the shoe pinches. But one step further is to look for hidden opportunities. The idea of looking carefully at the context is essential here because this will steer the possibilities and choices that you have at a later stage of the development of the business model. There may also be real starting points within the context that you are looking at. Consider, for example, a municipality that wants to promote citizen participation, or a company that has a specific waste stream and has no current opportunities within its value chain to do anything with it.

In everyday reality, the context within which we are operating is complex, ranging from the immediate environment to, for example, the sector or industry in which you are seeking to operate. What at first glance might have seemed self-evident and clear-cut is not always so. Add to this context the societal and macro-related issues, such as labour market developments in the coming decade, possible sectoral resource scarcity, or government ambitions such as circular agriculture or a circular economy by 2050. At the same time, there are all sorts of institutional frameworks that impose constraints through legislation and regulations that you need to be aware of.

A motive to construct a new business model can also be very pragmatic, and this is certainly applicable to existing entrepreneurs. Consider, for example, a CO_2 performance ladder which directs companies and their value-chains to reduce their CO_2 footprint. Or the ambition of the EU to become a CO_2-neutral continent by 2050. Many entrepreneurs do not focus on the transition itself, but want to respond to expected changes, developments of this kind in their markets, affiliated customer behaviours and the relevant institutional setting (e.g. rules and regulations to guide the ambitions).

The Context of Everyday Normal

People's habits and routines also play an important role in everyday activities—whether business or private. Much of what we do is done on auto-pilot—*that's the way we always do it*—and has been done that way for years. We are often symbolically stuck because habits are very comfortable and implicitly reflect the status quo of arrangements and agreements.

The fact that all these unstructured developments are dynamically changing complicates matters even further. It would be nice to be able to take a snapshot of the status quo, find a solution for it, and then put it back, but, unfortunately, that is not possible. Everything and everyone is on the move all the time. What is *in* the spotlight today is *off* tomorrow (but not resolved, if that is what you think). Problems change in nature and scope while you are looking at them and in the process your interpretation of them changes. Perhaps the issue you started looking at is not as interesting as it seemed in the beginning. Looking at a context with respect to its complexity is of the essence: not simplifying things or sweeping them under the rug, and trying your best to discover what truly matters, as well as where you see the opportunities to do something. Getting clear about what motivates you to start working on a specific issue is, after all, the basis for further shaping the business model. Sustainable business models take shape within the socially and economically quasi-stable context sketched above.

Important

Purpose economy

If anything is characteristic of meaningful entrepreneurship, it is that purposeful entrepreneurs are mindful of the fact that the market is a fictional narrowing of reality. The market only exists in our minds. The real place of companies is not the market, but society and Mother Earth.

3.2 Tools for Visualizing the Motive and the Context

Even if you intuitively understand your motive and context, it is both prudent and can be advantageous to make a slightly more thorough analysis and to make both explicit. Using multiple different instruments to perform this analysis should help you to obtain a clearer and more nuanced view of the current situation. We recommend that you conduct more than one. After all, instruments are lenses which will reveal different aspects of the same issue. For this purpose, we propose several groups of instruments which could be a useful resource, with the caveat that we cannot vouch for the theoretical foundation or methodical quality of the instruments and advise that any instruments should be handled critically, since all tools have inherent blind spots.

(a) **A quick scan of facts**:The simplest method is to gather facts about the issue you want to address and organize them properly. For instance, you could start with a basic internet search and see what information comes up when you enter some fairly random keywords. For fun, also look at the rising or falling popularity of the issue via, for example, Google Citations. Make sure that you also use proper sources from reputable institutions. In the Netherlands, these include the Central Bureau of Statistics (CBS), the Netherlands Environmental Assessment Agency (PBL), or most government websites. In the UK, you can use the Office for National Statistics (ONS). In addition, the European Commission provides a large database of reputable publications on a wide range of topics. Supplement this with scientific publications and research reports from credible commercial institutions. We do not recommend relying on the popular media (digital or in print). Whatever you do, always use multiple sources so that you can compare and cross-check assumptions and figures. Make sure that you note the source references and above all ensure that you separate facts from opinions.

(b) **Macro-analyses like DESTEP and SWOT**: The DESTEP analysis, also called the PEST analysis, is an analytical framework to map the Demographic, Economic, Social, Technological, Ecological, and Political factors at the macro-environmental level. These are six perspectives (variables) that together produce a picture of the macro-economic environment of a company or organization. Combined, they give insight into the elements around a market that cannot be influenced directly. The aim is to gain insight into the short- and long-term impacts of these factors. There are dozens of (public) sources that help you to carry out a DESTEP analysis in a neat and methodological manner. The so-called SWOT analysis—SWOT stands for Strengths, Weaknesses, Opportunities, and Threats—is a complementary analysis to a DESTEP analysis. The SWOT is a tool that creates a structured representation of an organization's perspective of internal strengths and weaknesses relative to perceived information in the analysis. A crucial benefit of this analysis is the confrontation matrix, in which you develop insight into the relationship between your plan and the market or context. Again, a multitude of tools, instructional videos, and canvasses can be found online.

(c) **Life cycle analysis**: Life cycle analysis (LCA) shows the environmental impact during the various life stages of a product. This can also be applied to a chain, a loop, or an (entire) organization. An LCA is also referred to as a cradle-to-grave analysis because it covers the whole process from the extraction of the necessary raw materials, to production, transport, use, and waste processing. The LCA was first used in the 1980s. It is based on a *closed* process that provides insight into the use of energy and materials as well as pollutants and emissions into the environment in all stages of its life cycle. The process helps to identify where in the product's lifespan the impact is strongest and where opportunities exist for sustainable improvements. Thinking about LCAs has been methodically developed to a great extent. For example, the International Organization for Standardization (ISO) has developed a standard for LCA: the ISO 14040 series. The continued use of the LCA is evident from the UN's *Life Cycle Initiative* (see: www.lifecycleinitiative.org) and the European counterpart the *European Platform on Life Cycle Assessment* (see: eplca.jrc.ec.europa.eu/LCDN). Consultancy agencies or research institutes can do extensive LCAs, but possibilities exist to perform a simple LCA yourself to get an initial idea (do an internet search for *LCA tool*).

(d) **Trend analysis & scenarios:** The so-called trend analysis is a different ballgame. This involves extending specific trends into the future, for example, for a period of five or ten years. What the future will bring appeals to the imagination and is instrumental in determining the market. Of course, there is also such a thing as *trendology*, and there are quite a few professional forecasters, but those who look at the matter seriously end up with scenarios and scenario planning. Scenarios are useful instruments for developing and exploring different future possibilities. In short, a scenario is a chronological description of a particular event that has taken place or is yet to take place. Shell developed the scenario methodology in the 1980s. Their definition is 'Scenarios are not predictions of the future. They are stories about how the future might look and are underpinned by models that provide the backbone logic and rigor to these future possibilities' (Shell, 2017a). Their methodology is open to the public. Check out Shell's accompanying website (Shell, 2017b) for an impression.

(e) **Environmental analysis:**Anyone who looks into the multitude of instruments and methods for making an environmental analysis will soon no longer be able to see the forest for the trees. Below, in random order, is a brief (and incomplete) list in addition to DESTEP, SWOT, LCA, and Scenario Methodology:

- Blue Ocean strategy
- brainstorming techniques
- capabilities analysis
- competition analysis
- need finding
- stage-gate
- open-space
- five forces model
- value proposition canvas.

And this is just the tip of the iceberg. So, whatever you choose and whatever combination you make, keep a close eye on why you are doing this analysis, because the available tools are only tools.

3.3 Case Studies: Motive and Context

Below are three short case studies that each address the motives and context in which a business model can emerge.

Case study: CO_2

Greenhouse gases are a natural phenomenon in the atmosphere, but human actions, such as the large-scale burning of fossil fuels and forest clearing, have caused far more greenhouse gases to be released into the atmosphere than the planet can naturally adapt to. The increase in these greenhouse gases, especially the enormous increase in CO_2 from burning fossil fuels, is causing global warming. There is a clear correlation between the demonstrated temperature rise and the increased CO_2 concentration in the atmosphere. The earth's temperature is expected to rise by 1.4–5.8 degrees if the way products are made and utilized does not change. Such an increase in CO_2 will cause major problems. Think, for example, of rising sea levels, droughts, heatwaves, and ocean acidification. The high CO_2 concentration is not the only cause of climate change. Methane gas, emitted by sources such as cows, and various minerals in manure and the associated nitrogen, phosphates, and ammonia that leak into the groundwater are also causing an ever-increasing problem. Farmers cannot get rid of their manure and are left with a surplus. They are obliged to process this surplus, for example by burning it, having it processed into fertilizer, or treating it to make dried digestate (Woltjer & Smits, 2019). In recent years, more and more companies have begun to take measures to reduce CO_2 emissions or to remove CO_2 from the atmosphere and use it for other purposes, such as biofuel, growing plants, or insulation. The latter concept is also called *Carbon Capture and Utilization*. In this concept, CO_2 is regarded as a renewable resource for the replacement of or an alternative to virgin raw materials. Instead of storing carbon dioxide, using it to produce valuable chemicals, materials, and fuels might be a better long-term solution (Al-Mamoori et al., 2017). The question remains as to what applications are most suitable for CO_2. For example, it can be used for growing vegetables, soft fruits, flowers, and plants, especially in the summer and autumn, but also for producing fuel or as an additive in concrete.

Case study: Mixed plastics

How we are currently dealing with raw materials is not effective or sustainable economically, ecologically, and socially. The EU has recognized the need for *waste regarded as resources* in the 2020 Circular Economy Action Plan (CEAP 2.0). In a sense, most EU countries are doing fairly well with such materials as paper and glass. However, we do have a problem with the handling of plastics. Plastic is predominantly used only once (referred to as *single-use plastic*) and is regarded as waste rather than a raw material from which new products can be made. Addressing this issue requires identification of alternative substitutes for single-use applications: developing better systems for the collection and recovery of plastics and the utilization of fewer mixed plastics in packaging, as well as developing more products from recycled plastic. Despite the many improvements made so far, most municipal recycling systems are still far from circular. In the Netherlands, for example, around 26–30% of the sorted plastic ends up as residual waste (Jetten et al., 2011). A large part of this is mixed plastic and consists of a wide variety of plastics such as polypropylene, polybutene, polystyrene, and polyethylene terephthalate, the latter better known as PET. Moreover, this waste flow tends to be mixed with things like organic material, sand, metals, glass, and paper. Currently, it is still too difficult to filter out the mono-flows. Therefore, the residue is burned. We need to find an innovative way to save the still-usable substances in residual waste (Bergsma et al., 2011; Jetten et al., 2011).

Case study: Plastic caps

Every year more than 300 million tons of plastic products are produced worldwide. Many of these products have a short life cycle, and the vast majority are single use only. In 2018 some 86 tons of plastic found its way into the oceans (Plastic Soup Foundation, n.d.). WasteBoards (wasteboards.com) wants to change this and has developed a product that highlights both the problem (plastic that ends up as litter) and offers a beautiful solution (skateboards made from plastic caps). With a so-called *bakery*, they produce high-quality skateboards with a considerably smaller environmental impact than that of regular skateboards. The skateboards have been on the market for several years now. However, it is a fairly labour-intensive production process for a small niche market. Furthermore, the considerable amount of plastic in the oceans exceeds the demand for skateboards by far, motivating WasteBoards to explore and develop new products, addressing new markets. A key requirement for Wasteboards is that any new products they develop can be produced anywhere in the world on a relatively large scale: they should be products that many people want to have and can be made by melting plastic caps.

3.4 In Conclusion

These three cases illustrate that the motives and the context for getting started with a particular issue can be completely different. These examples also show that perhaps *everything and anything* can be the reason to start working on a business model. This is stimulating, on the one hand, but also a bit overwhelming on the other. For it suggests that we live in a world where new problems are constantly emerging, which may become increasingly difficult to solve due to their complexity.

References

Al-Mamoori, A., Krishnamurthy, A., Rownaghi, A. A., & Rezaei, F. (2017). Carbon capture and utilization update. *Energy Technology, 5,* 834–849. https://doi.org/10.1002/ente.201600747.

Bergsma, G., Bijleveld, M., Otten, M., & Krutwagen, B. (2011). *LCA: recycling of household plastic packaging waste* (Final report 11.2430.79). CE Delft. www.ce.nl/publicatie/lca:_recycling_of_household_plastic_packaging_waste_/1208.

Ellen MacArthur Foundation. (2012). *Towards the circular economy Vol. 1: Economic and business rationale for an accelerated transition* (p. 98). Ellen Mac Arthur Foundation. www.ellenmacarthurfoundation.org/assets/downloads/publications/Ellen-MacArthur-Foundation-Towards-the-Circular-Economy-vol.1.pdf.

Jetten, L., Merkx, B., Krebbekx, J., & Duivenvoorde, G. (2011). *Onderzoek kunststof afdankstromen in Nederland*. Berenschot Groep B.V. www.rvo.nl/sites/default/files/bijlagen/Onderzoek%20kunststof%20afdankstromen%20in%20Nederland%20-%20December%202011.pdf.

Plastic Soup Foundation. (n.d.). Retrieved on 20 February 2020 from: www.plasticsoupfoundation.org/plastic-probleem/feiten-en-cijfers/plasticcijfers.

Shell. (2017a). *Windows on the future: Modelling scenarios* [YouTube]. Retrieved on 24 September 2020 from: youtu.be/l4MDcGYif4k.

Shell. (2017b). *Shell scenarios*. Retrieved on 24 September 2020 from: www.shell.com/energy-and-innovation/the-energy-future/scenarios.html.

Woltjer, G., & Smits, M.-J. (2019). *De betekenis van mestverwerking in een circulaire economie* (No. 2019–029). Wageningen Economic Research. library.wur.nl/WebQuery/wurpubs/fulltext/475439.

Zanders, R. (2020). De 'groenste' kippenstal ter wereld: Beuningen is klaar voor een milieu-revolutie. *Volkskrant.* Retrieved on 20 February 2020 from: www.volkskrant.nl/nieuws-achtergrond/de-groenste-kippenstal-ter-wereld-beuningen-is-klaar-voor-een-milieurevolutie~b9f50166/.

4

The Dream

We want to accelerate the […] transition from a carbon-based economy to a sustainable economy, by reducing the demand for energy, investing massively in renewable energy sources, and by keeping the use of energy as low and efficient as possible. *Triodos Bank,* www.triodos.com.

Kromkommer, [a Dutch wordplay on the words *komkommer* (cucumber) and *krom* (wonky)], continues until the goal is achieved: *equal rights for all fruit and vegetables* and, therefore, less waste. *Kromkommer*, www.kromkommer.com/english.

We can all be involved in the transition and we can all benefit from the opportunities it offers. We will help our economy to be a global leader by moving first and moving fast. We are determined to succeed for the sake of this planet and its inhabitants—for Europe's natural heritage, for biodiversity, for our forests and for our seas. By showing the rest of the world how to be sustainable and competitive, we can convince other countries to move with us. *European Commission,* 2019, ec.europa.eu.

By investing in energy-saving, renewable energy, and reuse of our waste flows, we strive to generate as much sustainable energy worldwide in 2020 as we are using. *IKEA*, www.ikea.com.

We want to put more beautiful, sustainable products on the market, give new life to valuable material, reduce the heaps of discarded clothes, and inspire and unburden as many brands and consumers as possible. With a passion for our product and the process, and love for the planet, we want to make the world a little nicer and healthier. *Loop a Life,* www.loopalife.com.

Together we'll make chocolate 100% slave free. *Tony's Chocolonely*, www.tonyschocolonely.com.

J. Jonker and N. Faber, *Organizing for Sustainability*,
https://doi.org/10.1007/978-3-030-78157-6_4

To be able to close the Roof2Roof cycle, the cooperation of all parties in the Roof2Roof chain is required. Only then will it be possible to achieve the ultimate result: no waste! *Roof2Roof*, www.roof2roof.nl.

4.1 The Bright Spot on the Horizon

In addition to Motive & Context (Building Block #1), the Dream provides a second tool in this stage to help you build your business model. The Dream can also be seen as a Big, Hairy, Audacious Goal (BHAG) (Collins, 2021 on which you are going to work. In essence, it is simple. What is the goal of your Dream? How and why will your business model idea/value proposition really make a difference? The Dream building block demands thinking big. You have previously indicated which major social and/or ecological issues you want to solve. Now you will determine what the result of that solution could be, what the ideal final image would look like. What is the bright spot or opportunity you see on the horizon? In this process, it is vital to refrain from all kinds of *yes, buts*. Note and park all of the challenges you see and actively think outside your mental box. Beyond the problems, roadblocks, challenges, and opportunities you see, you are already dreaming about the future. The Dream can—and should—be broadly defined and based on seeking to address so-called *Wicked Problems* (Weber & Khademian, 2008). Your solution should seek to go beyond just tackling one issue: it is the very building block in the transition towards sustainable development in society. It offers a solution for either the climate challenge, the energy transition, or the realization of a circular economy. Or perhaps it seeks to address this triple transition simultaneously. That is your Dream.

Example

Tokou's Dream

My name is Tokou Hinbridias, and since 2017 my team has been working hard on solving the waste problem in Corfu. We want to achieve a waste-free island. Thanks to our activities, events, and social media, we have inspired thousands of people in Corfu to help out over the past two years. The first unofficial recycling centre was opened in Spartylas in May 2018. Another village, Arillas, aims to be the first truly clean village on the entire island. The problem is that there are not enough companies to collect and process waste. Besides, there is much corruption and little cooperation from the existing companies. We need help to ensure that the government does not cover up the problem of corruption. I want to keep working to make Corfu the cleanest, greenest island in Greece. *Tokou Hinbridias.*

About Dreaming

It is possible to get lost in thinking about dreams. Is dreaming purely a matter of well-informed creativity or are there theories about dreaming? For as long as humanity has existed, people have engaged in dreams. 'The Greek philosopher Aristotle believed that dreams were an omen of illness. Egyptians, Romans, and Jews saw them as messages of the gods. The Chinese thought they were messages from an entirely different world. This changed in the nineteenth century because a number of psychoanalysts (including Freud and Jung) had a completely different theory about dreams' (Khan, 2011). What exactly dreams are and the purpose they serve is still largely unknown, despite these centuries of reflection. However, dreaming is a crucial part of the development of a business model. We need dreams to imagine the future. To realize these dreams, you could make use of the scenarios that we described in the previous chapter. Another option is through *framing*.

About Rhetoric and Framing

Framing is originally a persuasion technique in communication science. The essence of this technique is to choose a combination of words and (primarily) images in such a way that it highlights a specific set of aspects or properties. An example is: 'Windmills are run on subsidies'. Framing can be done explicitly with the help of rows and *bullets*, or more implicitly, in the form of a quote or a (short) story. The latter is also called a *narrative*. Next we illustrate how framing is used in politics and what you can learn from it.

Framing Example #1

A Dutch member of parliament, El Fassed (Dutch Green Party), was concerned about the lack of policy on nature in the first Rutte administration[1] and the impact this was having on accelerating the decline in species of plants and animals. He framed his concern as follows:

> Biodiversity is not a luxury. It is a necessity and an important economic value. El Fassed (2010).

What is interesting when one reflects on this message is that he fell into a classic trap. By actually saying that biodiversity is not a luxury, he strengthened the link between the concepts of *biodiversity*, *environment*, and *luxury*. In most cases, denial of a frame leads to its practical confirmation. The later usage of the words *necessity* and *important economic value* are no longer registered by most people, regardless of the meaning that these additions may or will have. This is because people tend to first and foremost look for confirmation of an image they are already familiar with.

Framing Example #2

US President John F. Kennedy (1917–1963) and his race to the moon with Russia is probably one of the most infamous examples of framing. There follows an excerpt from his speech delivered at Rice University's Stadium in front of 40,000 people on 12 September 1962:

> We set sail on this new sea because there is new knowledge to be gained, and new rights to be won, and they must be won and used for the progress of all people. For space science, like nuclear science and all technology, has no conscience of its own. We choose to go to the moon! We choose to go to the moon in this decade and do the other things, not because they are easy, but because they are hard; because that goal will serve to organize and measure the best of our energies and skills, because that challenge is one that we are willing to accept, one we are unwilling to postpone, and one we intend to win, and the others, too.[2]

History is full of people who recognized the importance of framing to depict a valuable, inspiring future in order to influence and change the course of history. Just think of Rachel Carson (*Silent Spring*, 1962), Martin Luther King (*I have a Dream*, 1963, www.youtube.com/watch?v=vP4iY1TtS3s) and in the Dutch context, the admired and later despised Dutch Minister of Agriculture Sicco Mansholt (the architect of the *Never hungry again* policy of 1958).

If you want to read more about the extensive research that has been done in this field, we recommend that you take a look at *Metaphors we live by* (1980) by the authors George Lakoff and Mark Johnson. With their unsurpassed axiom, 'To win, one must frame the debate', we end this rhetorical excursion.

4.2 Using Framing to Bring Your Dream to Life

So framing is about the conscious and effective use of visual and language tools to inspire and convince others. Here we want to show you how to use

[1]The first Rutte cabinet, also called the Rutte–Verhagen cabinet, was the sitting cabinet of the Government of the Netherlands from 14 October 2010–5 November 2012.

[2]John F. Kennedy, *Moon Speech*, 1962. To read the full speech, visit er.jsc.nasa.gov/seh/ricetalk.htm.

framing to transform the initial seed of your dream into a convincing and inspiring image of a possible future.

But the real question is: How do I apply framing? Here we use the work of Sara Gagestein: *Don't think of a Pink Elephant* (2014). She offers five rules of thumb for effective framing, which we recommend, albeit in a slightly adjusted form:

Key points

1. **Values first, then words and images:** When you want to convince someone of something, the first step is to identify which values you share. These shared values are the basis for developing a frame. Which ideals and motives does the person you want to convince hold? Think of values such as freedom, justice, commitment, and of course, sustainability. The closer the values you select match the values of the other, for example your customer or stakeholders or partners, the stronger the emotional impact. Once you have discovered a number of values that are important both to you and to others, you can develop your frame based on those values by carefully searching for matching words and images and fine-tuning this process until a convincing story has emerged.
2. **Be clear, go for simplicity:** If you really want to have an impact on another person, it is important to make your story as clear and straightforward as possible. Steer clear of the fallacy that it is about mere simplification. Instead, opt for explicit language and avoid abbreviations and jargon. You will find that doing this in practice is quite difficult. Moreover, never assume that others know what you mean. Words like *sustainability*, *circular economy*, or *inclusivity* are seldom understood immediately, let alone interpreted in the same way by everyone. Always keep in mind that you cannot convince people of things they cannot imagine or relate to.
3. **Blacklist of keywords to avoid:** In addition to looking for suitable words and images, it is crucial to consider which words you should *not* use. These are words that run counter to the selected values or, consciously or unconsciously, evoke negative associations. Gagestein recommends creating a *blacklist* of words to avoid to ensure the wrong choice of words don't become barriers to your frame reaching others. We suggest that you make a frame of your idea with right and wrong words and then test your *ideal words* and your *blacklist* in a small group.
4. **Be consistent and keep repeating your message:** Research shows that frames are particularly effective when they are repeated and confirmed continuously. The more often the other person is confronted with your frame, the more your idea, your image, or your point of view is anchored in the other person's brain. Therefore, you are advised to keep repeating the frame consistently. Always do this with the same keywords and the same images: the more you vary, the less firmly a frame settles in the brain.
5. **Enjoy the framing game:** Many people consider framing to be a necessary evil. But let us be honest: framing can also just be a fun *game*. Thinking up frames, discovering shared values, and selecting appropriate words makes communication about your soon-to-be business model not

only more adequate and effective but also much more fun and exciting. And last but not least, with a little bit of framing knowledge, and by flexing this muscle, you will watch (political) debates and discussion programmes differently and will be able to identify when someone is actively trying to influence the debate using this technique.

Our take-home message here is that you can achieve a lot with the language resources available to you. Note: doing this right requires a little inspiration, but more importantly, hard work until you hit the right note. Simple, clear, appealing messages are often the result of hours of tinkering and trying, refining, putting aside, and trying again. So take your time and don't get upset when people knock your words or just don't understand them. Just pick yourself up and start again!

Tip

This may be the most important tip: do not sit at your screen, staring at your carefully crafted frames/key messages and visuals. Go and try them out on real people and use their feedback to develop them *and* keep doing this exercise until your framing lands with people and your key messages are so intuitive they become a part of you. When will you get to this point? It's hard to say but you will know when the time comes.

Example

Ray Anderson's Dream (Interface)

In the 1990s, for the transformation of his company, Ray Anderson was inspired by Paul Hawken's book, *The Ecology of Commerce* (1994/2010). Anderson not only wanted to be a successful entrepreneur but also wanted to make a restorative contribution to the environment and society. Have a look at his TedTalk on 18 May 2009, entitled *The Business Logic of Sustainability*, www.youtube.com/watch?v=iP9QF_lBOyA.

4.3 Case Studies: Dream

Case study: WashingGreen

WashingGreen's dream is to combat climate change. WashingGreen aims to play a decisive role in promoting laundry cleaning using CO_2, thus positively impacting global water shortages and reducing greenhouse gas emissions. In this way, WashingGreen contributes to a greener world and the transition to a circular economy. *WashingGreen*, www.washing-green.com.

Case study: Litter

Our ultimate dream is to achieve a circular economy. We would like to transform plastics value chains through closing loops, ensuring that the embedded value in products is maintained. We do so by bringing plastic litter back into the plastic chain. We also seek to create social values by encouraging a collective approach to combating litter. *Litter* (no website available at the time of publication).

Case study: GreeNet

At GreeNet we dream of contributing to the resolution of the litter problem and how it is separated. Our dream is that all of today's *waste* will be our future resources. Not only do we want to generate financial value, but we also want to make a positive contribution to society, from an ecological and social point of view. We want to realize our dream by correctly separating waste at public transport stations throughout the Netherlands. We hope to create one unified Dutch collection network based on a single collection system. *GreeNet* (no website available at the time of publication).

Case study: Polyethylene Furanoate (PEF) plastic

Our dream is to make the world a little more environment-friendly by turning corn waste and CO_2 into PEF plastic. With our PEF, we want to make large events such as football matches, concerts, and festivals more sustainable by creating a mono-stream of PEF. This way everyone can enjoy a snack and a drink during a football match or a performance by their favourite artists. This could be done by means of a deposit system for cups at the events. This makes the event more sustainable because less single-use material is being used.

Case study: CO_2Trade

The community-based platform CO_2Trade aims to make CO_2 a raw material for various production processes. Knowledge sharing brings new applications of CO_2 to the market, which leads to new enterprises. Due to sustainable applications of CO_2 as a raw material, less CO_2 is released into the air, which counteracts climate change in the long term. *CO_2Trade*

Case study: WasteBoards

Plastic pollution is a growing problem. All over the world, rivers, oceans, beaches, and cities are becoming more and more polluted with plastic. WasteBoards wants to turn the tide by involving as many people as possible, creating value from plastic waste while having fun doing it. We start small, but we dream big. Today we bake boards in our small factory in Amsterdam. But how cool would it be to create WasteBoard bakeries in cities around the world, like the favelas in Rio de Janeiro or the slums of Delhi? We dream of a world without littering, where when we wake up, our business is redundant. *WasteBoards*, www.wasteboards.com.

4.4 Curating Dreams

Putting all the steps together, you have now *dreamed up* something—something big—that you want to go for with words and images. For some more inspiration, think of dreams like 'No more famine in the world, starting with our neighbourhood', or 'In ten years we will have created the Wasteless Supermarket', or 'Wouldn't it be nice if people could not only pay with money but also pay with their time, their waste, or by sharing access to their car?' But between these dreams and their realization, there is the inflexible, tough, and often harsh everyday reality. Work hard, persist, and don't give up. Moving from dream to implementation requires formulating a clear and explicit value proposition.

References

Carson, R. (1962). *Silent Spring*. Houghton Mifflin.

Collins, J. (2021). BHAG. *Jim Collins*. https://www.jimcollins.com/concepts/bhag.html.

El Fassed, A. (2010). *Kamer buigt zich over geld voor natuur. Nu.nl*. Retrieved from www.nu.nl/politiek/2373725/kamer-buigt-zich-geld-natuur.html.

European Commission (2019). *Report on climate-related disclosures*. Retrieved on 24 September 2020. ec.europa.eu/info/sites/info/files/business_economy_euro/banking_and_finance/documents/190110-sustainable-finance-teg-report-climate-related-disclosures_en.pdf.

Gagestein, S. (2014). *Denk niet aan een roze olifant*. Haystack.

Hawken, P. (1994 & revised 2010). *The ecology of commerce: A declaration of sustainability* (rev. ed.). HarperBusiness.

Khan, S. (2011). *Philosophy and science of dreams: The interface between two seemingly antithetical approaches*. Bachelor, Pennsylvania State University. https://honors.libraries.psu.edu/files/final_submissions/906.

Lakoff, G., & Johnson, M. (1980). *Metaphors we live by*. University of Chicago Press.

Weber, E. P., & Khademian, A. M. (2008). Wicked problems, knowledge challenges, and collaborative capacity builders in network settings. *Public Administration Review*, 68(2), 334–349. doi.org/10.1111/j.1540-6210.2007.00866.x.

5

The Value Proposition

Borrow clothing when you want to, without being tied to anything. *Lena Library,* www.lena-library.com.

Sharednd is a platform with a strong feel-good factor, where home cooks invite strangers into their home for a dinner party. *Sharednd*, www.sharednd.com.

Snappcar is a platform on which you can rent out your own car to strangers or, of course, rent a car from a stranger. *Snappcar*, www.snappcar.nl/en/.

Using twenty-first century craftsmanship, we turn every type of raw material into fascinating products. *Triboo*, www.triboo.nl.

With Pure Baby Foods, we try to offer a tasty and healthy alternative to homemade baby food. *Pure Baby Foods*, www.purebabyfoods.nl.

Peerby GO is a website that lets you rent things directly from your neighbours—delivered and picked up again at the place and time of your choice. *Peerby*, www.peerby.nl.

Our ideal is to have meat enthusiasts experience our products and have them realise they don't have to miss out on anything if they take meat out of their diet for one or more days. *The Vegetarian Butcher*, www.thevegetarianbutcher.com.

We collaborate with the world's most iconic brands helping them unlock the hidden value in their waste, and reduce their impact on the world. Join us. *Pentatonic*, www.pentatonic.com.

We offer a better alternative to new and used products. And that—thanks to the refurbed carefree package—without any risk for our customers. Our goal is to make the refurbed idea known throughout Europe and thereby

J. Jonker and N. Faber, *Organizing for Sustainability*,
https://doi.org/10.1007/978-3-030-78157-6_5

contribute to a more sustainable world. *Refurbed*, www.refurbed.de/unternehmen.

We help you activate your circularity. We work with procurement professionals/suppliers/producers. Our mission is to empower your transition towards a restorative and regenerative circular economy. *CircularIQ*, www.circular-iq.com.

With our brand, retail, and operational partners, we are building a global ecosystem for the reuse movement that maintains the convenience and affordability that we have come to enjoy with a throwaway lifestyle. Loop is on a mission to *Eliminate the Idea of Waste®* in an approachable way that is accessible to all. *Loop Store*, www.loopstore.com/our-vision.

5.1 Developing the Perfect Proposal

A business model is underpinned by a value or business proposition. Such a proposition solves a problem, meets a current need, or appeals to new, often still undiscovered, needs. It consists of a smart and immediately recognizable combination of products and/or services that implicitly and explicitly meet the requirements of a customer or user. It communicates what you are going to do to solve the problem, seize the opportunity, or take up the challenge, and for whom you are going to do it. The trick is to state in your proposition, as precisely as possible, which values will be created and who will benefit from them. This proposition may identify a potential target group or indicate who the customers or stakeholders could be. The more precisely you indicate the nature of that value, the better you will be able to design an appropriate (organizational) logic at a later stage. It is important to also take impact and value creation into account when developing your proposition, factoring in social, ecological, and economic values (the so-called *Triple Bottom Line*, or *People, Planet, Profit* (PPP) by John Elkington, 1997).

TIP

It may help to use a matrix when you draft your proposition. On one axis list all stakeholders involved in your business model and on the other axis the various values that are created for them. Describe what that value looks like in practice for each stakeholder. Make it concrete, specific, targeted.

Example

Stakeholders and Value Creation: The City of Amsterdam

The City of Amsterdam strives for zero-emission mobility in the city. Apart from the technical challenges that this poses, this ambition is of value to multiple stakeholders. Think of the general practitioners who are confronted with a decrease in the number of respiratory diseases (health, social), think of cleaner playgrounds for children (quality of the living environment, social), or think of pollution reduction (pollution, ecological).

All in all, a business model is a description of how value creation is organized, at a specific moment in a particular context, for certain people or parties, and given the available resources. It is common to describe value creation from the perspective of one organization. However, a proposition can also be written from the perspective of a group of people (a *community*) who work together to create value, or with the help of an intermediary platform that facilitates it. Implicitly assuming one organization is as the very centre of what we organize all too easily blocks thinking differently about value creation. In other words, there is not one vision, or a *one size fits all* perspective. What is of value, how it comes about, and which principles and points of departure underlie it can be organized in many ways. Sometimes a proposition can be very innovative and call for a so-called *disruptive* approach. This does not stand in the way of a value proposition being built on already-existing propositions. This does not imply just adding some *green* features to the existing status quo of a business model and leaving the fundaments untouched. Without wanting to open up the fundamental debate on *deep sustainability*, we are really advocating a transformation of the logic of value creation. In addition, when addressing a wicked problem linked to sustainability, we think the disruptive approach will be more prevalent.

Moreover, the result cannot be measured in absolute, let alone objective, units. What is of value to one person may not be of any value at all to another. That is why it is not possible to translate everything around us into financial value (the so-called *monetizing* step). No matter which way you think about it, it is ultimately the user who determines whether the proposition creates value(s) that they are willing to pay for.

5.2 Speaking of Value Creation

So much has and continues to be written about value creation, that when representing it here it is challenging to do it sufficient justice. Instead, we

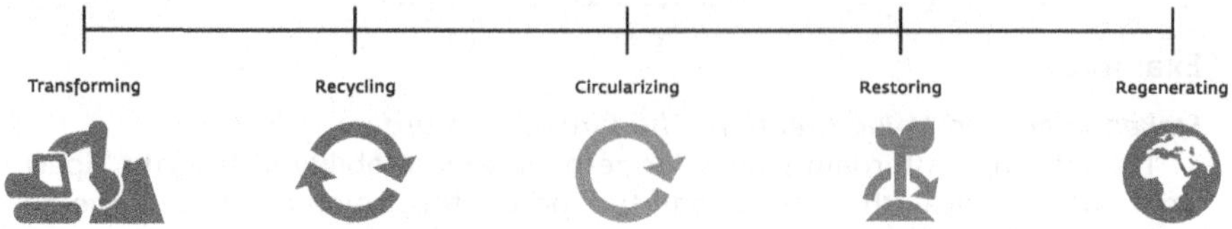

Fig. 5.1 Five positions of value creation

only summarize our framework of five positions of value creation, namely (1) value creation based on the *transformation* of commodities (meaning the extraction and conversion of raw materials), (2) value from the *recycling* of already-existing products, spare parts or commodities, (3) value creation by organizing value *retention* through loops, (4) value creation by *restoring*, and finally (5) value creation by organizing *regeneration* of natural habitat, social cohesion, etc (Fig. 5.1). These five positions can be linked to different economic schools of thought. Regardless of the nature of an economy, value creation is the shared task of economic actors.

Key Points

Value creation from transformation (Transforming) is most directly related to the linear economy. This form of creation involves the transformation of raw materials into products or services with the transactions being primarily expressed in money, leading to a *pure* monetary revenue model.

Value creation from recycling (Recycling) fits the linear economy because within that economy, sustainability is realized through design or redesign based on the eco-efficiency principles *reduce, reuse, recycle.* Retention of value from recycling focuses only on the very last link in the economic chain. The character of this linear economy remains unaffected.

Organizing value retention (Circularizing) is seen as being key to the circular economy. The core of this is the organization of various types of cycles in which value is created by better use of materials, extending the life of products and parts and making smarter use of products and raw materials. The search for possibilities for conversion (converting waste into raw materials) and substitution (replacing an unsustainable raw material with a sustainable one) plays an important role here. Unlike recycling, this does not concern the processing of materials into a low- or lower-grade product at the end of the chain (e.g. green glass into mixed glass), but the use of residual flows and bio-based flows as raw materials for high-quality applications (e.g. CO_2 into chemical building blocks).

Organizing value recovery (Regenerating and Restoring) refers to two different, and for many people still new, positions of value creation. Both forms concern the idea that companies contribute more to challenges in society and the habitat (ecological environment) than the mere pursuit of organizing sustainability in their own organization, the organization of (material) cycles, or the sustaining of value chains. In this view of value creation, organizations consciously work on one or more often long-term social and ecological goals simultaneously, way beyond the scope of their business proposition.

Important

Value Creation and Different Economies

Taking another step in thinking about value creation shows they can offer the basis for five different economies. We distinguish between (1) a clean-cut linear economy, (2) a linear economy with recycling, and (3) a circular economy based on value retention. These first three types of economy are familiar: we live in a confusing and unbalanced amalgamation of them. The fact that we should move towards a different breed of business model is a direct result of this knowledge. But this is not enough. We should go one step further and work towards (4) a recovering economy, or, finally (5) a regenerative economy. The latter refers to an economy that focuses on, for example, restoring biodiversity (and not exhausting it) or an economy that delivers more than it uses. We are far from having reached that point.

This tentative, and by no means perfect, typology of value creation shows that the debate about value creation needs to become much broader to allow for sustainability, circularity, and inclusivity. Nowadays, conversations about value creation are still too often implicit and mainly concern financial value creation. Many of the current organizational efforts are not focused on setting a new economic course—advocating multiple value creation in particular—but on reducing adverse effects of efforts tailored to the rules of the current economic game. If we want to progress in the transition towards an economy that fosters a sustainable society, a more intense debate is required. Moreover, considering multiple forms of value will demand a translation into rules and legislation in many different areas (the so-called institutional environment) and of course a new generation of business models that will ultimately be regenerative and restorative in nature. Just think outside the box about insects that convert food waste into edible proteins in short-cycles, or an organization that redevelops withered land into forest. We already know of sporadic and inspiring examples, though this is still far from mainstream.

5.3 Value Creation and Change

In the BMT, we assume that value creation has several facets that are equally important. We call this *multiple value creation*, which means that we always aim to simultaneously realize multiple forms of values that are social, ecological, and economic in nature. We believe that this is at the heart of what we usually call *sustainable development*. At its core, the Proposition building block answers the question of what you will do to solve the problem or to realize your dream and indicate for whom you create which value(s).

Therefore, the essence of the proposition is a proposal that describes what kind(s) of value is created by which product or service and for whom. The product or service is only a means to this end, with the value as experienced by users being central. There can be a variety of values at stake simultaneously (financial, social, ecological) and they can be shared or collective. A shared value is a value that I possess and is also shared by all members of a certain group. The reason it is shared is irrelevant: it just is. A collective value is a value that is shared among group members, because they are members of that group. Not sharing the value means that you are not part of the group.

The question is also about the extent of the proposed value creation. Are you seeking to future-proof your organization, or are you seeking to contribute to a broader social change? Essentially it comes down to a strategic choice between three possible approaches regarding the nature and depth of creating change: change through improvement, change through transformation, and change through transition[1]. These three modalities of change have their own scope, timeline, and impact.

TIP

Without wanting to make things extra complicated here we suggest you reflect on the nature of change and the impact you want to create with your business model. This not only *sounds* difficult but *is* difficult since you are trying to assess what the scope and related impact of your business model is, now and over time.

Example

Commonland

Commonland works with multidisciplinary teams building long-term partnerships dedicated to restoring ecosystems through a robust socio-economic model. Landscapes and water systems meet our basic needs—food, water,

[1]There is a vivid debate regarding the meaning of the terms *transformation* and *transition* and the relationship between these two notions—a useful summary article can be found here: www.sciencedirect.com/science/article/pii/S2210422417300801.

clean air, a stable climate, biodiversity, health, and safety—and contributes to our wellbeing. Yet at present, more than 25% of our natural areas worldwide are degraded through deforestation and over-exploitation. *Commonland* seeks to bring a holistic approach to landscape restoration by working with multidisciplinary teams to build long-term partnerships dedicated to restoring ecosystems through a robust socio-economic model. *Commonland* focuses on creating four values: inspiration, social capital, natural capital, and financial capital (*Commonland*, n.d.) (www.commonland.com).

Improvement means companies working on the basis of their existing business model and making it a bit more *sustainable*, for example, by using less water, energy or fuel. This is a practice that can be found in almost any organization working on sustaining what they do. Improvement has a deep-rooted history in the theory and practice of quality management, materialized in methods such as the Plan Do Check Act or PDCA cycle. Organizations in every step of the value chain can independently take these measures to make their processes more sustainable, by working more efficiently, reducing the use of raw materials, or reducing waste. Measures are often—but not always—taken by the organization at hand. The motto is therefore *We are going to do things better*, but operating within the earlier chosen logic of value creation.

> The society in which we live will go through unprecedented transformations in the next 15 years. Businesses must take a leading role in managing these changes. We are well beyond philanthropy and CSR [corporate social responsibility]. It's time to brutally confront the facts of our own business models and act to make them sustainable. *Peter Bakker, President and Director of the World Business Council for Sustainable Development (WBCSD), speech at Nyenrode University (Breukelen), 20 November 2018.* (Nyenrode, 2018)

Transformation means that a different, if not to say novel, logic of value creation is looked for. This means that next to an (already existing) economic revenue model, ecological and social values are deliberately also taken into account. This could take many forms and shapes, for example by collaborating with sheltered employment to give a second life to products that are returned after use. But it could also mean to use large-scale collection of *green* household waste from vegetables and fruits to be used for the improvement of biodiversity instead of being burned or left to rot. Transformation can start at the company level, but in order to have scale, it often implies changes in the value chain or in networks and loops. Here the motto is: *We are going to do things differently*, leading to a novel logic of value creation.

Transition means changing an entire functional system. Value chains, laws, and regulations, and the behaviour of companies, governments, and consumers will have to change simultaneously to enable a (complete) transition. This shows that a transition goes together with major social challenges in, for example, the fields of energy, mobility, transport, food, or health care. For example, with improvements only, it is still not possible for individual companies or the collaboration of a configuration of companies in the value chain to realize the intended transformation to reduce CO_2 emissions to a desired level. Or, to get rid of our economic and social *crude oil* addiction, more is needed than individuals installing solar panels. What is required is a new approach: a new system to generate energy. Motto: *We are going to do entirely new things.*

Important

Transition Offers Radically Different Opportunities for Insurers

Paradoxically, insurers pay as much money to compensate for the damage caused by heavy rainfall in cities, like Amsterdam, as it would cost to provide the city with green roofs. However, if the money is used for green roofs, insurers can no longer sell insurance. That said, the proposition that could be developed with the help of the BMT involves climate-proofing the city by installing green roofs. This proposition would not only solve the problem of water stress but would also contribute to cooling the city (preventing heat stress). Moreover, it would create space for biodiversity, improve air quality, and create a greener living environment. Various studies show that people feel better in a greener environment. The proposition in which these multiple values are realized demands working with different problem owners.

5.4 Some Reflections on the Scope of Value Creation

Unlike in all the other chapters of this book, we encounter a dilemma here. This entire book, and therefore the BMT, is essentially an elaborate *instrument* for organizing multiple value creation in a structured way. So, providing some sub-instruments here is quite paradoxical. In our view, organizing is neither more nor less than realizing the promised value(s) through an organization, and is almost always linked to a configuration of parties either in a value chain or in loops. Organizing, therefore, is making and realizing that promise at the same time. It is not without reason that we say *stick to your promise* or *deliver your promise*. But allow us to make a small theoretical side-step on the scope of value creation.

Organizations have five (internal and external) parties to whom they make a promise of value creation. We consciously use *parties* here and not *stakeholders*, because that could subconsciously lead to a narrower view of the idea of value creation. Those parties are the individual, the team, the organization, the customers, and society. The very fact that all these parties must derive value from what is being organized is crucial. The task of an organization is to create value for all these parties simultaneously. Combined, therefore, these parties can be seen as the Value Creation Circle (Fig. 5.2).

In addition to the Value Creation Circle focusing on the various parties at stake, the current business-oriented literature also distinguishes the nature of value creation, leading to five strategies (Fig. 5.3). The assumption is that each strategy offers a clear organizational perspective. We present them here as they are commonly set out but we invite you to reflect on their relationship with the three guiding principles of this book: sustainability, circularity, and inclusivity.

The first three strategies for value creation are Product Leadership, Operational Excellence, and Customer Intimacy (Treacy & Wiersema, 1999):

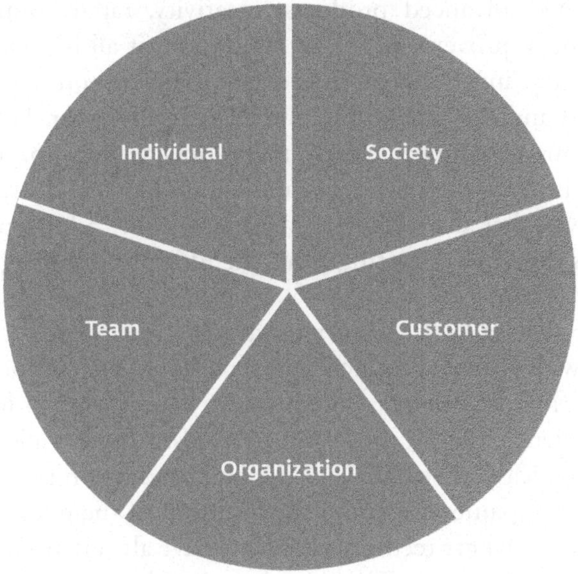

Fig. 5.2 Value Creation Circle

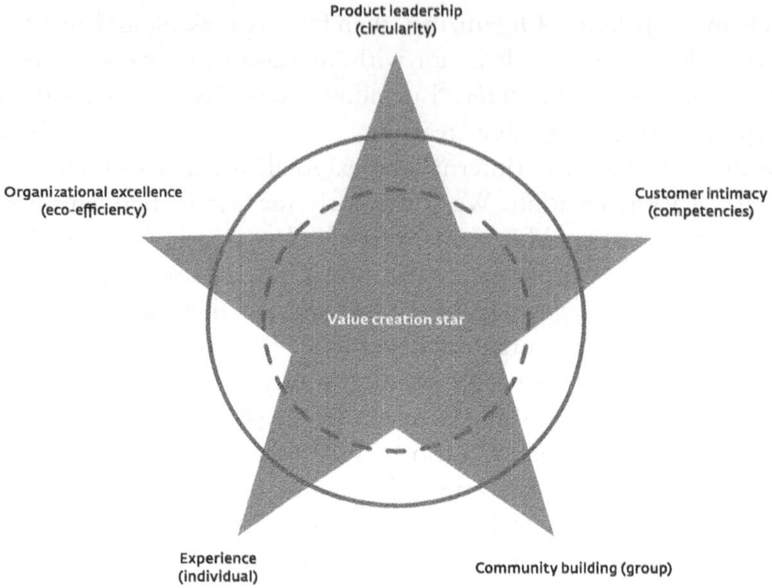

Fig. 5.3 Strategies for value creation

1. The *Product Leadership* strategy concentrates on offering ground-breaking new products. Product Leadership promises customers the best, fastest, and most novel products. Such providers distinguish themselves through technologically advanced products, creativity, rapid commercialization, and constant improvement. Their reputation, if all is good, is not based on a single new invention or an accidental hit, but on new products that are invented and brought to the market year after year. For us, a circular strategy seems to connect closely to product leadership. The essence of circulatory is to develop products and components and use raw materials in such a way that their value is maintained over a long period of time. This comes down to operating from the idea of producing products that are the *best of their class.*
2. With the *Operational Excellence* strategy, companies provide their customers with reliable products and services at very competitive prices in a very user-friendly manner. The promise here is simple: low prices with high convenience, that is, the lowest total costs. It takes a lot to keep those costs low: not least, very tight logistics and production processes to reduce costs. Such companies are not at the forefront of the market, but they are quick followers, where teething problems have already been removed from the products and services. They are clone-builders who often market their

products and services at a high volume without frills. Here, we link operational excellence to the strategy of eco-efficiency. This strategy is about minimizing such things as material and energy use, showing similarities to the cost-reduction perspective of operational excellence.

3. Companies that promote *Customer Intimacy* mainly follow a *niche* strategy: they focus on what specific customers want. Those organizations do not offer standard products or services. They believe in a *sense and respond* approach and thus offer tailor-made solutions. It is not about one-off transactions, but about building lasting customer relationships. Companies distinguish themselves in fulfilling specific customer needs, which only they are able to recognize because of their relationship with and specific knowledge of the customer. In this way, they promise the best custom-made and total solution. They continuously try to add value to the business model of their customers and therefore also think about *the customer's customer*. It is therefore important to follow that customer closely in all of his or her developments.

In addition to Treacy & Wiersema (1999)'s three well-known strategies, we believe there are two more worth flagging: Experience and Community Building.

4. As a fourth strategy, we distinguish *Experience*, which was introduced by Pine and Gilmore (1998). It is essential for Experience that the customer becomes a co-producer (a *prosumer*—a contraction of producer and consumer) in an experience. It is not the products or services by themselves that are central, but the combination of several things in such a way that the customer has an almost tailor-made experience. The core of this strategy is to provide guidance and direction, bringing elements together in such a way that an experience is created time and time again. The intangible part (the *service*) occupies a more critical position than the things that go with it (the *things*). So, the Experience Strategy is ultimately about *product as a service* (PAAS) and *performance*. An experience is by definition bound to an individual.
5. In addition to these four, we see an emerging fifth strategy, which we refer to as *Community Building*. Community building is about making or creating material and non-material connections leading to a combination of useful services and/or products for and within a specific community. This process of collective value creation is often enabled by the Internet of Things (IoT), whereby more and more devices communicate with each other, which can enable new services and products. In light of the

increasing interest in the circular economy and the organization of value retention, the IoT could be supplemented with the *Internet of raw materials* (IoM). Connecting this to groups of people, to communities, would be a genuinely new development. Think of groups of people who start an energy cooperative, buy a farm together, and hire a farmer, or of a street or neighbourhood who jointly purchase several (electric) cars and other means of transport and develop a neighbourhood mobility plan. Then community and technology form a dynamic and co-creating whole. This new phenomenon is witnessed more and more often.

As indicated at the beginning of this section, it is necessary to link these five strategies to the three principles of this book. This is not self-evident, because the notions used were formulated in an era that operated under a different economy, and therefore different business models were not actually in question. The underlying idea was one of continuous growth and making financial profit.

Yet, linking the strategies to the three principles is less complicated than would appear at first sight. We think that product leadership has a connection with circularity because it is about organizing value retention. Operational excellence can be linked directly to eco-efficiency—a core concept within sustainability. Customer intimacy can be related to inclusivity, because it asks what needs, capabilities, and wishes people have and how these can be addressed. Experience also has a connection with inclusivity and is easy to connect with individual needs to make a difference in transition processes. Community building is also linked to inclusivity but focuses on the group level. In addition to being a unique value creation strategy, community building is also anchored in this book in one of the three basic types of business models (see also Chapter 6).

Whatever choices you make to realize your plans, it is advisable to limit yourself to one leading strategy—without losing sight of the earlier-introduced principles of sustainability, circularity, and inclusivity—and at most to one supporting strategy, and to communicate these choices clearly.

5.5 Case Studies: Proposition

Case Study: WashingGreen

WashingGreen has an innovative laundry method which uses no water and reuses CO_2 representing a more sustainable option for hotels to have their linen laundered. Hotels that have their linen washed at WashingGreen have a considerably smaller carbon footprint than mainstream laundry services. This allows WashingGreen's clients to position themselves as a more sustainable hotel and to play a role as an early adopter in developing a greener hotel industry. Adopting a more sustainable laundry policy gives hotels the opportunity to make themselves future-proof while contributing to societal change.

Case Study: Happee

With our proposition, we want to offer a new playful opportunity to solve the problems surrounding waste separation and public urinating. We want to do so by putting sustainable pop-up urinals at events. These urinals are made of plastic caps. By giving the caps a second life, we show that waste is a resource and can become a valuable secondary raw material. In addition, the colourful urinals make it more attractive to pee into them, so that people no longer have the urge to urinate in public.

Case Study: Greengold

The proposition is to establish an algae farm that uses excess CO_2, as well as excess heat and energy from a waste incinerator for growing animal feed. The algae produced will be dried to form animal feed that is very rich in protein creating a viable alternative to soy. This creates a good alternative for soy, the cultivation of which is not without drawbacks. Extra value is created by substituting soy for dried algae given that soy cultivation has negative environmental effects.

Case Study: Bea the Bee

Our dream is to solve two fundamental problems—the amount of litter and the loss of biodiversity in ecosystems—through education and creating awareness. To make this dream come true, we want to make educational building kits for insect hotels which we will deploy across schools throughout the Netherlands, along with an education package on both the plastic problem and the decline in insect populations. Through Bea the Bee children are made aware of the two problems by means of an interactive education and construction kit while also actively becoming part of the solution.

Case Study: Duckweed

At the core of the business model is the reuse of captured CO_2 for the cultivation of high-quality duckweed throughout the year. Duckweed is a small plant with special properties. Under optimum growing conditions, duckweed has a high protein content (35–43%). Duckweed production is much more environmentally friendly than, for example, the production of soy, because it does not have to be grown on agricultural land. In addition, duckweed contains proteins with a better composition of essential amino acids (that organisms cannot produce themselves) than soy. This makes it potentially a good substitute for soy in products such as animal feed. Duckweed already has a high growth rate of its own and can survive in extreme conditions. When CO_2 is added, the growth process increases by a significant percentage (estimated at 33%).

5.6 It's Not That Simple

Formulating a clear and compelling value proposition is crucial in the development of a business model. It gives direction to the strategy, shows which adjustments are being made to the existing range of products and services, with whom you could take these steps, what this will yield for which party, and what impact you expect to realize. The proposition will seldom be perfect at the first attempt and will be revised several times. The process of tinkering with and revising your value proposition takes time. Only when the proposition is perfect will you find that you can easily formulate a one-liner or elevator pitch.

Do keep in mind that not all propositions have to be new or groundbreaking. PeelPioneers (peelpioneers.nl) are a young company who are the sustainable waste food collectors of the twenty-first century. Yet, at the same time, it is *back to the past* in a trendier format, as they have developed a circular solution for transforming citrus peel leftovers from fresh juice production into a secondary raw material for use in other products.

Another classic example is the proposition of Greyston Bakery (www.greyston.org). This bakery, which has been operating for over 30 years, gives people who have struggled to access or keep jobs a second chance and an opportunity to meaningfully participate in society again: 'We don't hire people to bake brownies, we bake brownies to hire people' (Greyston Bakery, n.d.).

References

Commonland (n.d.). Commonland: 4 returns from landscape restoration. Retrieved on 19.5.2019 from: www.commonland.com/en.

Elkington, J. (1997) *Cannibals with forks: The triple bottom line of 21st century business*. Capstone.

Greyston Bakery. (n.d.). Retrieved on 19.5.2019 from: www.greyston.org.

Nyenrode. (2018). Peter Bakker officier in de Orde van Oranje-Nassau [University website]. Nyenrode Business Universiteit. https://www.nyenrode.nl/nieuws/n/peter-bakker-officier-in-de-orde-van-oranje-nassau.

PeelPioneers. (n.d.). Retrieved on 19.5.2019 from: www.peelpioneers.nl.

Pine, B. J., & Gilmore, J. H. (1998). Welcome to the experience economy. *Harvard Business Review, 76,* 97–105.

Treacy, M., & Wiersema, F. (1999). Customer intimacy and other value disciplines. *Harvard Business Review, 71*(1), 84–93.

Part II

Design Stage

In the Definition Stage, you decide WHAT you are going to do. The next logical step is to decide HOW you are going to design the organisation of your business model. The five steps in the Design Stage help you to concretise the form and working method of your business model as much as possible. The first four steps are: choosing the business model archetype, understanding which parties are involved, the choice of strategy, and defining the core activities.

We have opted for this order, but it does not have to be absolute. As indicated in Chapter 1, filling in the building blocks is an iterative process. When you have completed the first four of the building blocks in this stage in conjunction with each other, it is time for the external test (the fifth step) which relates to both the Design and the Definition Stages.

6

Business Model Archetypes

Children grow; unfortunately, bicycles don't. That is why we offer a second-hand children's bike subscription, for convenience and circularity. BikeFlip offers subscriptions for second-hand children's bikes. If a child grows out of the bike, the start-up immediately offers a new, refurbished bike. When there is a problem with the user's bike, BikeFlip will repair it. *BikeFlip*, www.bikeflip.nl.

Broodfonds (Breadfunds) is a solidarity-based safety net, developed by and for entrepreneurs. It consists of groups of from 20 to a maximum of 50 entrepreneurs, who know and trust each other, where a member who becomes unwell will be supported and will receive gifts from others to live on for up to a maximum of two years. *Broodfonds*, www.broodfonds.nl.

The first B2B (business to business) marketplace to fight food waste, InstockMarket.nl is the first online wholesaler for rescued products, and has built a network of Circular Chefs. These chefs receive a daily notification with an overview of the products that must be saved from going to waste that day. *InstockMarket*, www.InstockMarket.nl.

Herenboeren is a growing civic movement and innovative approach to sustainable farming that demonstrates that the production of food can be done differently, better and, above all, more sustainably. *Herenboeren* are cooperative farms that enable citizens to share ownership of or develop their own cooperative farms, so consumers become both producers and consumers based on demand. *Herenboeren*, www.herenboeren.nl.

Roof2Roof wants to close the bitumen cycle of roofs. For this purpose, the Roof2Roof method has been developed. With this method, old bitumen roofs that need to be renovated or demolished are assessed for Roof2Roof recycling suitability. Roof2Roof processes the clean and separated bitumen roofing

J. Jonker and N. Faber, *Organizing for Sustainability*,
https://doi.org/10.1007/978-3-030-78157-6_6

material into raw materials to be used for the production of new roofing rolls. *Roof2Roof*, www.roof2roof.nl.

DutchSpirit operates in accordance with the principles of the circular economy: by charging a deposit combined with our lease concept, all suits and jackets are returned to us so that we can reuse or recycle them in a responsible manner. *DutchSpirit*, www.dutchspirit.com.

6.1 The Logic of Value Creation

The BMT provides the building blocks to develop a novel logic for a business model. In such a model the nature of multiple value creation, the way this is organized, and how transactions take shape are operationalized in such a way that it meets the proposition. Practice shows that at present business models aimed at capturing multiple value creation can be divided into three major categories: (1) platform business models, (2) community-based (or collective) business models, and (3) circular business models.

This classification is not absolute or restrictive because there are all kinds of variations and combinations. Still, it does offer guidance to work purposefully on the development of a specific archetype. When using the BMT, it is useful, therefore, to consider at an early stage which business model archetype is dominant in the realization of the intended value proposition.

The three archetypes (or basic forms) of a business model differ mainly in the way in which they create value. The mechanism through which value creation takes place is also different, while each basic form has its specific objective. Finally, each business model type differs in its infrastructural and technological requirements. In the next three sections, each archetype is elaborated on, with the factors mentioned further explained. We also present practical examples of each of these archetypes.

6.2 Platform Business Models

Much of what we own, we only intermittently or even hardly ever use. Think of the car not being used for more than 90% of the time, unworn clothes in your wardrobe, or an MRI scanner that is only operational 40% of the time. The number of examples is infinite, both among consumers and companies. So would it not be useful to make smarter use of the available overcapacity by having more people take advantage of it? That is exactly what a platform business model seeks to do: put overcapacity to use. By *brokering* access to underutilized capacity, fewer things need to be produced. The underlying idea is that making more efficient use of existing capacity reduces the pressure on raw materials and our natural environment. The exploitation of overcapacity can be realized relatively easily using what people already have, know, and are able to do. In this way, a platform can be an accelerator for more drastic forms of eco-efficiency than may be achieved through product design efforts.

The first business model archetype is a platform model which aims to make better and more efficient use of what we have through asset or performance management enabled by datafication and digitalization. At its essence this archetype is about better functional utilization: to sit on a chair more often, smarter and longer, for example, to use a car more efficiently, or to lease lighting.

Platform business models are possible due to developments such as the Internet of Things (IoT), in which everyday devices are linked to the internet, so that usage can be registered and optimized (like the smart refrigerator mentioned in Chapter 2 which can keep track of exactly what goes out per week, so that purchases are made more accurately, and waste is prevented). A strengthening factor in platform business models is (1) the increasing datafication and digitalization of materials, objects and (social) networks, and to a lesser extent—but still a promising factor—(2) the increasing use of cryptotechnology. Both make it increasingly easier to convert smart utilization approaches into a working business model. Datafication and digitalization lead in turn to the development of all kinds of new services—often typified as the trend towards servitization—delivered via digital platforms such as the IoS. The platform business model archetype can often be found under broad headers such as the performance, functional, or sharing economy (Jonker & Faber, 2015).

Once you start to look around there are plenty of examples: energy cooperatives are popping up like mushrooms, so-called *bread funds*—offering a new form of insurance—are showing unprecedented growth, and children's bike subscriptions are growing in popularity—see, for example thebikeclub.co.uk. There are plenty of examples: think of the sharing website Peerby (www.peerby.com) or frequently used examples like BlaBlaCar (www.blablacar.com), Floow2 (www.floow2.com), or, mentioned with some hesitation given all the uproar they have created, Airbnb (www.airbnb.com).

Example

Excess Materials Exchange

The Excess Materials Exchange platform is a digitally facilitated marketplace in which organizations offer excess materials and products. The platform functions like a dating site, linking supply and demand with the highest use or (reuse) value. For example, by using a QR code or RFID chip, materials are linked to a raw materials passport so that they can be monitored throughout their life cycle. The platform then calculates the best high-quality match, while considering the financial, environmental, and social values of the transaction. Excess Materials Exchange, n.d., excessmaterialexchange.com.

The value created in this business model archetype comes from facilitating transactions between two or more groups of people. These transactions can take various forms. In a standard transaction, what is of value is monetized. In other words, parties involved express the value of their product or service in money. But monetization is not necessary per se: (digital) platforms can also offer the possibility of conducting hybrid transactions. In a hybrid transaction, the parties involved in the agreement will settle the contributed *values* in different forms, for example, by setting off the use of a drill against a lift to the supermarket, or by exchanging the power produced by local solar panels into discounts on products at the local supermarket.

Furthermore, transactions do not necessarily have to take place between two parties (bilateral), but a platform can also facilitate transactions between multiple parties (multilateral). This has the advantage that a greater variety of assets can be offered. Such hybrid characteristics increase the viability of the business model, because one person is looking for mobility, the other for food, and the third sees self-produced energy as a complement to the household budget. The idea is to connect the variety of needs on a platform and turn them into transactions, or parts thereof. Platform business models are easily combined with the other two business model archetypes: community/collective and circular.

Example

The Oogstkaart (Harvest Map) Platform Model

Oogstkaart (Harvest Map) is a Dutch online marketplace for the professional reuse of various types of excess materials from the retail and construction sectors (for example glass, metal to textile, and organic material). It aims to show available materials, elements, and components, and is mapping the urban mining potential of the Netherlands. Oogstkaart supports both suppliers and users of excess materials (Oogstkaart, www.oogstkaart.nl).

6.3 Community or Collective Business Models

The second archetype is the so-called community-based or collective business model and refers to the creation of business models in multi-stakeholder thematic communities by citizens, with the help and involvement of public entities, together with companies related to healthcare, food, insurance, mobility, or energy, for example. The main principle is that a group of people, organizations, and companies collaborate on organizing one or more needs, wishes, or problems (such as generating local energy, growing food, or organizing mobility). A whole range of *organizations* can be distinguished under this archetype, from *pure* models carefully organized by citizens, to, and at the same time, cooperation of citizens with other organizations be it not-for-profit, governmental bodies, or companies. We opt to mix these various types here. After all, it remains essential that more and more people are willing to invest in their own facilities, their own neighbourhood, their own electricity, as long as this provides forms of *profit* for the various parties involved. In this process of collective organizing, people become simultaneously a consumer and a producer—a prosumer. This means that they play an active role in organizing decentralized modes of production, and therefore no longer rely solely on centralized distribution systems (think of electricity and food, but also mobility) enabled by communication and other technologies which are becoming more accessible and cheaper every day. These technologies not only make it possible to connect people in different ways but also install community apps with various functions, from lost-and-found, to the actual availability of shared cars, to managing local energy grids in a neighbourhood.

The idea of doing things together as a group of people is, of course, as old as humanity itself. This idea is also known as *the commons*. We are inspired by Ostrom (2010),[1] in addition to Restakis (2017) and Bollier (2016), who defined the commons as a (set of) shared resource(s), material and non-material, maintained or co-created by a community and governed by that same community's norms and rules. Intentionally creating and distributing collective value can be seen as a particular property of the commons. Collective and shared value creation can be seen as a process based on open contributory systems that govern work through participative practices, and create shared resources that, in turn, can be used for further developments (Kostakis & Bauwens, 2019). When the aforementioned trends in information and communication technology such as the IoT and the IoS and the idea of the commons are combined, they form a breeding ground for collective or

[1] Read Ostrom's synthesis of a life's work: Beyond Markets and States: Polycentric Governance of Complex Economic Systems (*American Economic Review*, Vol. 100, No. 3, June 2010).

collaborative[2] business models: enterprising citizens setting up energy cooperatives, smart carpooling, food co-ops, or jointly looking after local green areas. Participants invest money (e.g. locally through crowdfunding) and time (time banking), and thus arrive at a what can be labelled as a neighbourhood business model, or a community-based or even an *urban* business model. Despite these linguistic differences in labels, the essence remains the same.

Example

Windpower Nijmegen

This project concerns an energy cooperative that operates four wind turbines to the north of Nijmegen. In 2016, over 1,000 members of the cooperative invested in wind shares to finance the construction of the turbines. Cooperative members get a return from the profit from selling the electricity that is generated. Part of the proceeds also go to an environmental fund which helps realise projects in the area, such as the construction of a fibre optic cable in the hamlet that is right next to the wind farm. This ensures that the local residents, who were initially quite critical about the construction of the turbines, also benefit from the wind farm. The cooperative is now expanding electricity production with the construction of solar parks. Because solar panels mainly produce electricity when the windmills do not produce much, and vice versa, cable pooling is used. For example, one single cable is needed to connect the windmills and the solar panels to the electricity grid. (Windpower Nijmegen, www.windparknijmegenbetuwe.nl).

Key Points

Value creation in collective and collaborative business models is based on three principles:

1. **Collective and Shared Investment**: Possibly with hybrid means (time, money, energy, waste, mobility).
2. **Collective and Shared Returns**: Sharing in the revenues of the business model (e.g. the electricity generated by an energy cooperative is distributed in proportion to the investment).
3. **Multiple Value Creation**: Working simultaneously on tangible and intangible multiple values that are of value to the community or the collective at hand.

[2]The intertwined use of the words *collective* and *collaborative* can be a bit confusing. The first term refers to the commons—to a group of people linked together by (for example) principles, values, and a shared aim, in addition to maybe a physical location such as a village, neighbourhood, or project site. The second term refers to the fact that this group is deliberately collaborating to achieve this goal.

As the interests of the group of people who are part of the community take central importance, this type of business model offers the opportunity to involve a variety of people as well as their skills. This is also referred to as the pursuit of inclusivity. In collective business models, value creation is therefore linked to the formation of an active community. The value that is realized with the community business model therefore exceeds the value of the visible products or services, such as mobility, electricity, or vegetables. Despite all these different labels, the essence remains the same: a diverse group of people, often combined with institutional parties and companies and driven by various motives, join forces to organize a specific (common) function. A successful collective business model contributes to creating and sustaining communities.

Example

The Grootstal Estate

The Grootstal Estate on the border of Nijmegen in the Netherlands has been a family estate for a hundred years, where stewardship equals caring for cultural history, landscape, nature, and wellbeing. In the last century, the context has changed drastically. The rural area is now a city, vastly influencing the way the estate functions, but what persists is the search for a balance between people, ecology, and economy. For the Grootstal Estate, value creation is not only creating value for oneself, but also for one's environment, which leads to multiple value creation with a large number of (entrepreneurial) partners who are active on the estate. This takes a variety of shapes, including (among others) sheep herding, sustainable agriculture, growing a vineyard, selling the produce grown on the estate, or organizing sustainability workshops. In the spirit of the integral character of the estate, they work from their complementary strength within the whole (Grootstal Estate, www.landgoedgrootstal.nl).

6.4 Circular Business Models

The third business model archetype is based on the idea of designing and manufacturing raw materials, components, and products in such a way that they can be kept in circulation quasi-indefinitely (within the constraints of thermodynamics). The question central to a circular business model is therefore how we can preserve the value embedded in specific material(s), component(s), or product(s) such as electronics, lithium batteries, car tyres, bricks, paper, concrete and other building materials, plastic, or glass for as long as possible. Key to circularity is identifying material flows with the aim being to close material loops and realize value retention through reducing the use of raw materials and production waste that arises during the manufacturing and packaging of products, but also extending the lifespan of products through repair, refurbishment and remanufacturing such that the products can have multiple users. Moreover, circular business models may involve, for example, building materials, metals, packaging, wastewater, or (residual) heat. This can be done on a large scale, for example by using residual flows from one company as a commodity for another company (referred to as industrial symbiosis), but also on a small scale, by creating local markets for plant cuttings, peer-to-peer clothing swaps, or repair shops in a neighbourhood.

Example

Buurman

Buurman (meaning neighbour) stands for local reuse. Instead of dumping, burning, or low-grade recycling of waste, Buurman gives residual materials – particularly from the construction and built environment – a new life through their shops and workshops. The workshops are open to both groups and individuals: for example, you can participate in courses to learn more about working with reclaimed materials or rent a workbench for your own DIY projects (Buurman, www.buurman.in).

It is quite a challenge to create a truly circular business model where commodities remain in the loop for as long as possible and are of the highest possible quality. Refurbishing materials and spare parts requires additional energy, transport, labour, and often the use of additional virgin materials in order to sustain a specific level of quality. The carpet tile manufacturer Interface, for example, takes back used carpet tiles, recovers useful raw materials, and reuses them in the production system. To be able to close a material loop completely, several parties are needed in almost all cases. They will have to jointly arrive at a conclusive, circular business case aligned with a collective revenue model which in most cases will require entering into long-term relationships. Establishing and maintaining longer-term relationships is, by definition, more likely to make the realization of a circular business model a strategic challenge.

Important

The Circular Potential of Resources

Annually an estimated 92.8 billion tons of resources (not including water) are used in the global economy, equalling approximately 33.4 kilograms of resources per person per day. This total is broken down as follows: 37.8 billion tons of minerals used in construction, 28.7 billion tons of biomass used for food, construction materials, and firewood, 16.6 billion tons of fossil fuels burned for the generation of energy, transportation, and input for the chemical industry, and 9.5 billion tons of metal ores used for energy production and various metals. The global economy is only 9% circular, highlighting the significant opportunity that is currently uncapitalized (De Wit et al., 2019).

So a circular business model is essentially a description of the way in which value creation and retention are organized among parties—at a given moment, in a given context, and given the available resources. However, circularity raises several challenges with regard to materials. To maintain materials of the same quality, it is not uncommon to add a certain percentage of virgin material into the loops. In a linear economy, this is predominantly based on materials obtained from mined ores; in a circular economy, on the other hand, the emphasis is on transforming waste by-products into secondary raw materials which can be utilized as material substitutes.

Furthermore, it is not yet sufficiently known what materials are contained in existing products. Consider, for example, the concrete that is *trapped* in buildings or copper in electronic equipment. A company such as *SlimBreker* uses, among other things, the cement from the demolition of concrete, which can be used, for example, for printing houses by yet another party (Slimbreker, n.d., www.slimbreker.nl).

Up until recently the demand for the reuse of materials was much less prominent, so information was not systematically collected about the amount of materials in circulation. As a result, this complicates the planning supplies of recycled materials of a specific type and a specific quality. Building such a library of materials, the products in which they are present and their quality will, therefore, be an essential step in further closing material loops. The Madaster Foundation has taken up the challenge of developing such a library (www.madasterfoundation.com).

That said, circular business models are not only about raw materials. Retaining the embedded value of products also requires a full commitment to the maintenance and repair of goods which in turn necessitates adapting the design of products and the use of materials to enable circularity.

Moreover, some nuance is required with regard to circularity—the circular economy is aspirational and constrained by limits to thermodynamics, thus most circular business models will result in some residual and/or waste flows. However, by making processes as circular as possible, this can be considerably reduced relative to the dominant linear economic model. One example that illustrates this point is Bundles, a Dutch company who have partnered with

Miele and Koru beds to provide subscription to everything from white goods to beds (www.bundles.nl). The Bundles proposition is based on the concept of product as a service (PAAS) or product–service systems (PSS).

> It is possible to grow an economy with less impact on the environment. With less impact on resources. And with lower costs. That's good news for shareholders. But most of all, it's good news for the next generations! Stientje van Veldhoven, Minister for the Environment and Housing, The Netherlands, 'Global Entrepreneurship Summit', 5 June 2019.

Example

Increasingly we are drinking more and more fresh fruit juice. In the Netherlands alone, 250 million kilograms of peel are discarded each year (mainly orange peel). PeelPioneers extracts the components present in orange peel so that they can then be used as raw materials for making new products. The raw materials are extracted from the citrus peel in two steps. In the first stage, the essential oils that are used in food (for example) are extracted. In the second stage, the citrus pulp is retained to be used in animal feed. The ultimate goal of PeelPioneers is to achieve the fullest possible value of this former waste stream. PeelPioneers, www.peelpioneers.nl.

After you have identified the type of business model you want to realize, it is important to think about the parties you can do this with. Which collective of partners is needed, and how can you arrive at your value proposition? This is developed further in Chapter 7—Parties Involved.

6.5 Selecting a Business Model Archetype

Choosing a business model archetype might look straightforward, but it can be quite a tricky task. Often, in practice, it turns out that a single business model type is insufficient, and that a combination is required to realize one's dream or proposition.

For instance, a circular business model can be combined with a platform business model very well, by linking circularity to a so-called Product Service System or PSS (Tukker & Tischner, 2006) or to one of the many PAAS models. The Bundles case, as discussed earlier, exemplifies this combination of a circular business model and PSS. In PAAS, providing access to the function of a product through a service is central rather than owning it. Payment for accessing the product is based on the use of it which can be related to time, availability, deposit, replacement (including upgrading and refurbishment), or intensity. For example, time refers to the total time that the product is accessible to a user, like renting a car. The claim to functionality is related to use. The intensity of use is linked to having access to the function of the product. This is done, for example, when offering cloud services, whereby in addition to storage capacity, monthly data throughput also depends on the type of chosen subscription.

Similar observations also apply to the platform and collective business models. Seeking to make more efficient use of overcapacity is also central in a platform business model, which can be a combination of PAAS with the IoT or the IoS. Also, in community-based or collective business models, simplification of the settlement of mutual transactions can be facilitated on the same basis. This means the IoT and other digitalization strategies associated with platform business models can be deployed by collective business models to enable value capture and value exchanges based on different transaction modes (e.g. money/time/energy/food).

To further determine which business model archetype or combinations thereof apply to your specific dream or proposition, we present additional business model archetype classifications. Tukker (2004), for example, distinguishes between different PSS business models (see Table 6.1), which make explicit the spectrum of platform-based business model archetypes. Central to this classification is the question of where the balance is when creating value: is it more product-oriented, service-oriented, or an equal division of both?

Central to PSS business model archetypes is the choice regarding whether or not to transfer ownership of a product from the producer to the customer. PSS business model archetypes are central to Walter Stahel's (1982) framing of the circular economy whereby the producer remains the owner of the

Table 6.1 Product–service system archetypes (based on Tukker, 2004)

Archetype	Product-oriented	Usage-oriented	Result-oriented	Product–service balance
Product-related	■			Product
Advice and consultancy	■			Product
Product lease		■		Equal share
Product hiring/sharing		■		Equal share
Product pooling		■		Equal share
Activities management			■	Service
Pay per unit			■	Service
Functional result			■	Service

Table 6.2 Sustainable business model archetypes (based on Bocken et al., 2014)

Group	Strategic objective
Technological	Maximising material and energy efficiency
	Value creation from waste
	Substitution with renewable raw materials and natural processes
Social	Providing functionality instead of transferring ownership
	Stewardship
	Promoting satisfaction
Organizational	Attributing new social/environmental functionality
	Develop solutions for upscaling

product and is therefore incentivized to invest in necessary improvements as well as repair and remanufacturing to capture the benefits of prolonging the life cycle of the product.

Bocken et al.'s (2014) sustainable business model typology highlights the diversity of sustainability and circularity strategies which they group into three types of sustainable business model archetypes (see Table 6.2). This typology can be related to and overlaps with the three business model archetypes discussed here: platform, community, and circular.

Key Points

1. **Technological archetypes** are oriented towards deploying technology-related innovations to enhance resource efficiency, material substitutions and circularity.
2. **Social archetypes,** in contrast, emphasize the role of social innovation in sustainable business models. Here the question arises regarding access to rather than ownership of products and the role of the end-user and their consumption habits.
3. **Organizational archetypes** concern the re-evaluation of the role of the organization in society with regard to its significance as well as how an initiative can be scaled up and thus increase its impact.

We hope that the Tukker (2004) and Bocken et al. (2014) typologies will provide inspiration when developing Building Block #4—Business Model Archetype and working with the BMT more generally.

6.6 Case Studies: Business Model Archetypes

Case Study: SourceForge—Platform Business model archetypes

SourceForge is an online platform for sharing open-source software. Programmers can put the software that they make and want to offer as open-source on this platform for free. The website provides a wide range of software products. Next to applications for domestic use, including games, applications are also offered for the business environment. In addition to complete applications, the source code of a lot of the software is also made available. People can use these to further develop or to incorporate solutions of their choice into their programs. Earnings to keep the platform running come from advertising revenue.

Case Study: Eendenkroos—Circular Business model archetypes

In this business model, the main focus is on closing material loops and value retention of raw materials. The captured CO_2 is not the only residual stream that is reused as a resource: the manure surpluses of local farmers also get a new function in this BMT (Hofs, 2019). As a result, this business model closes nitrogen and phosphate loops and reduces costs for farmers. The manure and CO_2 are converted into high-quality duckweed. Local farmers may purchase duckweed as protein-rich food for their animals.

Case Study: Herenboeren—Community Business model archetypes

Herenboeren is a movement to encourage citizens to start a nature-driven country farm . The idea is that individual citizens buy a cooperative farm together to produce food for themselves but pay a professional farmer to manage it. Every year, members of the cooperative collectively determine what food the farm will produce in the cultivation plan. The members collect food from the farm every week. The farm also promotes contact between the members by organizing various activities such as excursions, cooking workshops, or nature activities. The community is the hub of the Herenboeren business model.

6.7 Laying a Logical Foundation

The choice of business model archetype for the BMT is a fundamental one. It allows you to decide on the main direction of your business model as later design choices follow from the business model archetype(s) selected. For example, a platform business model will always lead to a discussion about the formation of a group of customers and a group of providers. A community/collective business model automatically leads to the identification of a specific community that will build, maintain, and use the business model. A circular business model requires that you clarify which material cycle is central to the business model. Hybrid combinations of the three archetypes are also possible, assuming that one archetype is leading (Fig. 6.1).

When working through the BMT, it is valuable to sense-check the choice of business model archetype at various stages in the process given its iterative nature. Given the fundamental nature of this design choice, further fine-tuning or revision may be required. For example, an initial decision to organize a circular business model focusing on closing the loop might change and evolve into a platform business model if matching the supply and demand of materials appears to be more critical in realizing your dream or proposition. It is not always possible to get these kinds of choices right at the start. Refining comes from continually sense-checking your choices and making changes to the design as necessary.

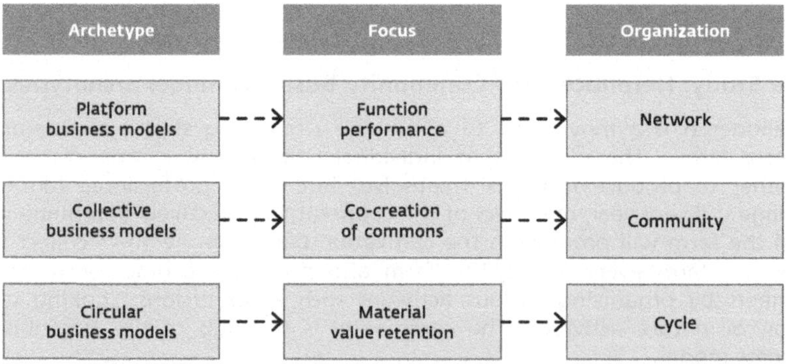

Fig. 6.1 Overview of key business model archetypes

References

Bocken, N. M. P., Short, S. W., Rana, P., & Evans, S. (2014). A literature and practice review to develop sustainable business model archetypes. *Journal of Cleaner Production, 65*, 42–56.

Bollier, D. (2016). *Commoning as a transformative social paradigm.* Retrieved on 23 July 2019 from: thenextsystem.org/commoning-as-a-transformative-social-paradigm.

Buurman. (n.d.). Retrieved on 22 October 2019 from: www.buurman.in.

De Wit, M., Verstraeten-Jochemsen, J., Hoogzaad, J., & Kubbinga, B. (2019). *Circularity Gap Report 2019: Closing the circularity gap in a 9% world.* Retrieved on 24 September 2020 from: docs.wixstatic.com/ugd/ad6e59_ba1e4d16c64f44fa94fbd8708eae8e34.pdf.

Excess Materials Exchange. (n.d.). Retrieved on 19 May 2019 from: excessmaterialsexchange.com.

Hofs, Y. (2019, October 18). *Ons mestprobleem is al meer dan vijftig jaar oud: De stikstofcrisis is één groot déjà vu.* Volkskrant. https://www.volkskrant.nl/nieuws-achtergrond/ons-mestprobleem-is-al-meer-dan-vijftig-jaar-oud-de-stikstofcrisis-is-een-groot-deja-vu~b652bf32/.

Jonker, J., & Faber, N. R. (2015). *Framing the WEconomy: Exploring seven socio-economic trends that enable shaping a transition towards sustainability* (Working Paper, p. 46) . Radboud University Nijmegen.

Kostakis, V., & Bauwens, M. (2019). *How to create a thriving global commons economy.* Retrieved on 13 June 2019 from: thenextsystem.org/learn/stories/how-create-thriving-global-commons-economy.

Landgoed Grootstal. (n.d.). *Landgoed Grootstal.* Retrieved on 19 May 2019 from: www.landgoedgrootstal.nl.

Madaster. (n.d.). Retrieved on 24 September 2020 from: www.madaster.com.

Oogstkaart. (n.d.). *Oogstkaart: Marktplaats voor professionele upcyclers.* Retrieved on 24 September 2020 from: www.oogstkaart.nl.

Ostrom, E. (2010). Beyond markets and states: Polycentric governance of complex economic systems. *American Economic Review, 100*(3), 641–672. https://doi.org/10.1257/aer.100.3.641.

PeelPioneers. (n.d.). Retrieved on 19 May 2019 from: peelpioneers.nl/.

Restakis, J. (2017). *Cooperative Commonwealth & the Partner State.* Retrieved on 23 June 2019 from: thenextsystem.org/cooperative-commonwealth-partner-state.

Slimbreker. (n.d.). *Sustainable Concrete Recycling—c2c—With the SmartCrusher.* Retrieved on 10 February 2020 from: www.slimbreker.nl/smartcrusher.html.

Stahel, W. R. (1982). The product-life factor. In S. Grinton Orr (Ed.), *Inquiry into the nature of sustainable societies: The role of the private sector* (pp. 72–104). HARC.

Tukker, A. (2004). Eight types of product—Service system: Eight ways to sustainability? Experiences from SusProNet. *Business Strategy and the Environment, 13*(4), 246–260. https://doi.org/doi.org/10.1002/bse.414.
Tukker, A., & Tischner, U. (2006). Product-services as a research field: Past, present and future. Reflections from a decade of research. *Journal of Cleaner Production, 14*(17), 1552–1556. https://doi.org/10.1016/j.jclepro.2006.01.022.

7

Parties Involved

We grow oyster mushrooms on our partners' coffee grounds. Our partners provide us with a service in return. That could be in the form of products, but other forms are also possible. *Brans Oesterzwamkwekerij*, www.oesterzwamkwekerij.nl.

In close collaboration with our stakeholders, we draw up a strategic plan every four years in which we describe how we fulfil our mission. Our strategy is a reflection of the trends we see in society and technology. *Dutch National Organization for Applied Research* (TNO), www.tno.nl.

The objective of *Boekel Energie* is to facilitate affordable, sustainable, and locally owned energy for all residents and businesses of the town of Boekel. This initiative, which has representatives from all walks of life, is seeking to set up a local sustainable energy cooperative in the municipality. *BoekelEnergie*, www.boekel.nl.

At the *Windcentrale* you become the co-owner of a turbine, with which you generate your own 100% sustainable wind energy. Everyone can benefit from the efficiency and the green power of wind turbines. Everyone can become a Wind sharer. And by everyone, we really mean everyone. *The Windcentrale*, www.windcentrale.nl.

DNB (the Dutch National Bank) wants to facilitate and stimulate sustainability in the financial sector and the economy. For that, we actively seek cooperation, for instance in the Sustainable Finance Platform and in the Network of Central Banks and Supervisors for Greening the Financial System (NGFS). This international network aims to make the financial system greener and increase the financial sector's efforts to achieve the Paris climate targets. *DNB*, www.dnb.nl.

J. Jonker and N. Faber, *Organizing for Sustainability*,
https://doi.org/10.1007/978-3-030-78157-6_7

We enable everyone to contribute to a sustainable future by investing in partnerships with new energy producers assisting those who dare to take responsibility and actively commit to creating a better tomorrow. We are also there for the switchers who are looking for new energy at a fair price. *Huismerkergie*, www.huismerkergie.nl.

New Horizon Material Balance facilitates the dismantling of buildings with the aim of harvesting as many materials as possible for reuse enabling them to supply the largest range of urban mining building materials in the world. New Horizon Material Balance is also the coordinator of the Urban Mining Collective (UMC) which consists of a wide range of partners from the Dutch construction sector, namely: Stiho, Rexel, Elektroned, Knauf, Tétris, JLL, TGN, Wavin, Douveren Brickworks, the Rutte group, NIBE, ABN AMRO, Thinkle, Kingspan Unidek, Spaces4You, Weekamp, Rensa, ZND, and Icopal. New Horizon Material Balance controls the raw material flows within the collective and brings the (joint) innovations to the market. *New Horizon* newhorizon.nl; *Urban Mining Collective*, www.urbanminingcollective.nl.

7.1 Who Is Participating?

In this building block, the central question is identifying what actors and stakeholders you want to engage with, work with, or create value for through your business model. As indicated in the previous chapter, identifying the parties that you work with is an essential, or community-based business model. Working together on (multiple) value creation is always a collective task in which value chains and networks take a central position.

The Parties building block addresses the identification and selection of stakeholders that are relevant to the realization and implementation of your business model. It is useful to make an overview of them when designing a business model. In the first place, it is about determining who they are and what interests they have or may have in relation to your business model, which in turn will help to determine what relationship these stakeholders have with your business model. Are they parties you have to deal with immediately as they are essential for your business model to work? Or are they more distant, but ultimately influence the social acceptance of your idea?

Freeman (1984) formulated the notion of stakeholders in relation to organizations. A stakeholder is any person or group of people who have a particular interest in an organization. Stakeholder theory arose in response to the prevailing, restrictive, *shareholder* perspective. The latter assumes that an organization only serves one group of people: the shareholders. Everything that happens within the organization must therefore be to advance or serve the interest of this group of investors. The rationale underlying this approach is that shareholders are the paying party and own the organization. Principal-agent theory is central to explaining behaviour within the shareholder view of organizations. The agent (read director, manager, superior) works on behalf of the shareholder (the Principal) and will carry out his or her work within the limits imposed by the Principal. Conversely, the Principal will check the agent's activities and, if necessary, step in to make adjustments.

Stakeholder theory has a broader perspective and considers the shareholder to be just one of a multitude of different stakeholders of an organization. Other stakeholders include customers, employees, local residents, the government, and suppliers. The idea is that not only can shareholders determine what happens within an organization, but that the course of an organization is plotted in consultation with these stakeholders. Some stakeholders are directly involved in decision-making. Other stakeholders are somewhat more distant and do not have a direct say, but do experience (in part) the consequences of decisions made.

Not all groups of stakeholders therefore have the same influence on decision-making. In order to better describe the influence of these groups, Mitchell et al. (1997) distinguish between (1) power, (2) legitimacy, and (3) urgency. Power refers to the degree to which a group of stakeholders can move an organization in a certain direction, through force, seduction, or imaging (Mitchell et al., 1997). Legitimacy addresses the question of to what extent a stakeholder is justified in exerting pressure on an organization, within the existing social context. Finally, urgency relates to the extent to which a stakeholder calls for immediate action (Mitchell et al., 1997). It is important for organizations to determine what each stakeholder's position is with regard to power, legitimacy, and urgency. Only then will it become clear to what extent the interests of the stakeholder concerned must be taken into account in the way in which an organization is managed.

In short, stakeholder analysis consists of identifying the actors and parties that are relevant to the realization and implementation of your business model. Numerous tools have been developed in recent decades to identify parties and determine the nature of their relationship. How you use these tools will depend on what you want to achieve. Do you want to make an initial sketch of your business model, or are you looking for a detailed blueprint?

7.2 Identifying People

In order to determine which actors influence your business model, it is important to identify which parties in your network you will proactively shape the proposition with. There are various ways to portray (potential) partners, such as a traditional stakeholder or chain analysis (Johnson et al., 2017). However, be mindful that these traditional analyses start from an individual organization that creates a value proposition. In contrast, in the BMT we want to get away from the traditional distinction between internal and external stakeholders because a core premise of our BMT is intentionally formulating and organizing the value proposition together.

For these reasons, we suggest that you do a network analysis to determine the parties you want to work with to realize your business model, for example other companies, government departments or agencies, or future users. In network analysis, you identify everyone who is or may be relevant to the business model and indicate the extent to which there is a relationship between you and the identified parties. The actors identified can, of course, be parties from your existing network, or parties that are affiliated with your network and with whom it is relatively easy to establish contact. It could also be that you can only realize your value proposition by entering into a relationship with parties with whom you have no relationship as yet.

We encourage you to keep an open mind and think broadly. Key partners could be the neighbour you do not yet have contact with or a third party in a completely different sector that can purchase or take care of a residual flow from you. In identifying potentially relevant stakeholders, try to get an impression of these potential new partners and more specifically what activities you can organize with them.

There are many ways to carry out a network analysis. It can be done very easily, for example, by firstly identifying the names of actors who are relevant to realizing the value proposition and adding them to Post-its® in a brainstorming session, and secondly, exploring how they are related.

To aid identification of actors in the first step of this process, we highlight three key approaches to mapping networks: (a) Spider Web Model (Fig. 7.1), (b) Mesh Network Model (Fig. 7.2), and (c) Cluster Tree Model (Fig. 7.3).

(a) **Spider Web model:** Start from your own position where you, as an initiator, set up a partnership and identify the related parties with you in the centre. This is a network model reminiscent of a spider in a web (Fig. 7.1).

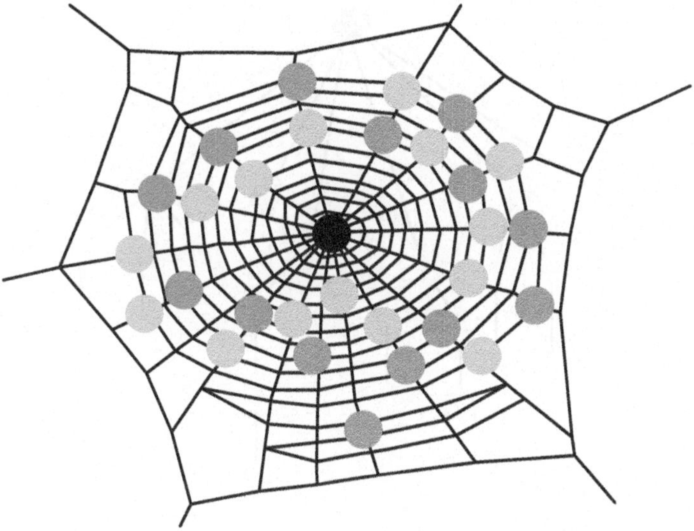

Fig. 7.1 Spider Web model

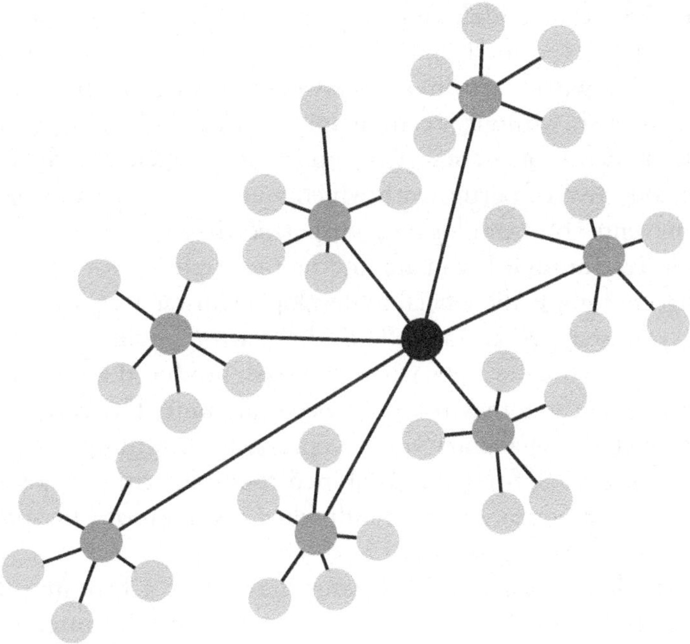

Fig. 7.2 Mesh Network model

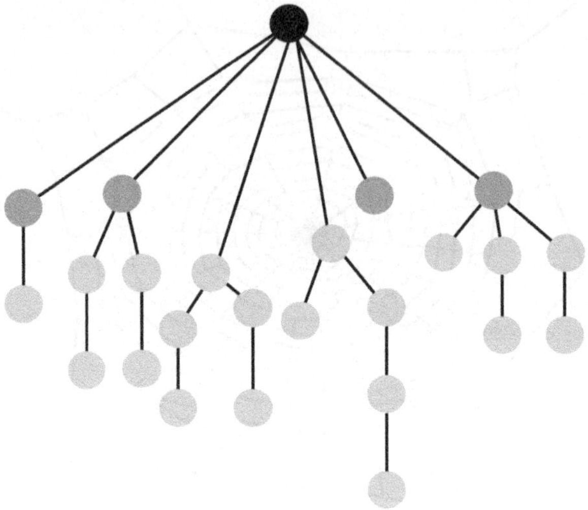

Fig. 7.3 Cluster Tree model

(b) **Mesh Network model:** When you create a value proposition with multiple parties, a mesh model (Fig. 7.2) is a good starting point. The participating parties are links in networks in which all parties are mutually connected, without a central spider in the web. However, within a broader network of parties, it is important to determine the boundaries of the collective of parties with which you realize the value proposition. This prevents you from losing your perspective.

(c) **Cluster Tree model:** If you are finding the mesh network approach challenging, it might be beneficial to develop a Cluster Tree Model (Fig. 7.3). Here, you start with yourself as the starting point of the network. What may become evident when you have produced an overview of the network is that you may not be the central point. The BMT is designed intentionally to challenge you to approach everything—including the network analysis—from the combined/multiple actor perspective rather than from just your own or an individual organization's perspective.

The identification of the parties in your network is a first step that serves as the basis for a much more extensive analysis of the interrelationships between different actors. In addition, understanding these interrelationships can enable you to investigate these actors' powers to positively or negatively influence the value proposition. Several methods are available to support these additional analyses. Here we recommend two tools to determine the possible roles and influences of the various stakeholders and parties in your network:

1. **Force field analysis:** Once you have mapped your network you can indicate the forces between parties, for example with green and red arrows, addressing the question(s) of how the parties relate to each other and whether they have a positive or negative influence on each other or on your business model idea. This process can provide insight into the roles and interrelationships of the parties and how and whether you might need to align your network to realize your value proposition.
2. **Stakeholder value analysis:** This is a more extensive method to visualize the current or intended value of transactions for each stakeholder relationship. In a stakeholder value analysis, you indicate what you exchange with the different parties in the network, for example: money, products, services, data, knowledge, reputation, access. The thickness of the arrows can indicate the relative size of the transactions. This gives greater insight into the roles and relationships between the parties involved, and how you can seek to align them. By mapping the interests of stakeholders, you ensure that interests are linked to transactions and value(s) creation. In multi-stakeholder business models, interaction, participation, and collaboration between parties are crucial. Achieving the desired co-creation requires trust, openness, and meaningful engagement between parties.

TIP

For additional examples of how to perform a force field analysis or a stakeholder analysis, look at businessmodellab.nl/en/tools (Business Model Lab, 2019).

After you have analysed which parties are relevant and how they can contribute to the realization of the goal, you can also consider how and what type of partnerships you want to enter into with these parties. Do you enter into a cooperation agreement with them? Or develop a joint venture together? Or do you set up a cooperative? At all of these key decision points, sense-check your choice of business model archetype and whether your partnership structure will influence or impact your proposition in any way.

Example

Developing a Circular Holiday Home

In the circular economy, new business models are created not only within, but especially between organizations. This has resulted in a spontaneous collaboration between four participating parties: a holiday park owner, a contractor, a finishing company, and a demolition company. Together they have developed a circular holiday home. By involving the demolition company in the design process, optimization is achieved in the chain, closed loops are created, and materials are used optimally, for example by making agreements about dimensions of sheet material so that no residual waste remains. As a result, parties not only get new cooperation partners but also share knowledge and acquire new roles in the chain.

7.3 Case Study: Parties

Case Study: GreeNet

GreeNet's dream is to reduce litter produced by train passengers. For this purpose, GreeNet has created and launched the Clean Mobility Initiative (CMI) to change the behaviour of travellers, so that they return their waste at train stations via Reverse Vending Machines (RVM). The GreeNet business model contains a large number of parties. On the one hand, this makes it very strong, but this also brings weaknesses. The network analysis method that is used to list and identify the parties is the spider in the web model.

Figure 7.4 provides an overview of all parties involved in this business model. At the core, there is GreeNet. GreeNet facilitates the CMI and ensures that

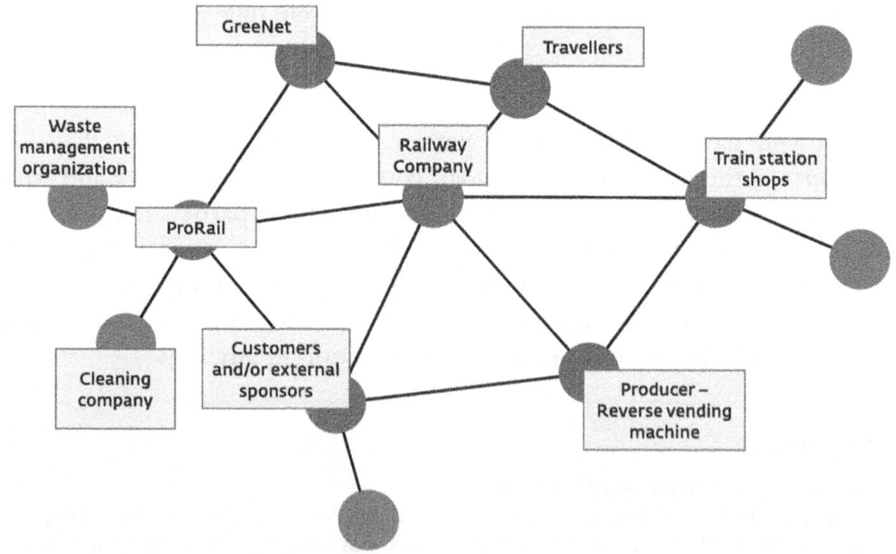

Fig. 7.4 GreeNet Network model

communication between all stakeholders runs well and that all parties involved do what they have to do. GreeNet is the spider in the web so to speak. Dutch Railways will finance the savings system and the RVM in this business model.

Dutch Railways and ProRail want to create attractive and comfortable railway stations for travellers and other users. A properly functioning cleaning process is an important priority here. The cleaning company Asito is responsible for cleaning services in the north-west and south-west as well as the north-east of the Netherlands. In addition, ICS (another cleaning company) will continue to do the cleaning at a number of the railway stations in the south of the country, with an extension to a number of stations. GreeNet wants to link the savings system to a public transport card. Transnet already has an app for the public transport chip card, so it is a simple step to add functionality by which people can keep track of their credit balance and costs.

In the future, GreeNet would like to collaborate with various stores and facilities available at the various railway stations. One could think of shops, food counters, or toilet facilities such as Sanifair or 2theLoo. The more station stores want to participate in the credit system, the stronger the value of the credits becomes. At these stores and facilities, you could pay with the credits that are linked to your public transport chip card.

We put our trust in the millions of Dutch Railways travellers who will be using the new savings system. When they hand in their plastic bottles and paper cups, they will be able to save the credits using their public transport chip card. In addition, the traveller will unscrew the cap from their PET (polyethylene terephthalate) bottles themselves, lest the bottle be refused by the RVM. A large part of the process will, therefore, be the responsibility of the travellers themselves.

For the collection of waste, a producer of the separation systems is required. It is important that the machine can distinguish which waste is deposited and put it into the correct waste bin. The machine will refuse bottles that are supplied with caps. An RVM can do this. Consequently, the choice of this type of machine was easily made.

In this context, it is also important that there is an extra compartment in the RVM for people to drop their plastic caps into. Immediately after collection, the residual waste will be shredded, so that much more residual waste can be stored in the machine. With this RVM, a monitor or tablet will be provided allowing people to indicate the choice of either price or credits, and on which travellers can scan their public transport chip card. A possible manufacturer of this is Tomra, a company which focuses on the production of this type of collection system.

We give external sponsors the opportunity to provide awards that travellers can get. This is to ensure that the big awards do not have to be financed by Dutch Railways themselves. But of course, we also give Dutch Railways the option to make awards available. We could even have these sponsors contribute to the regular credit value. The advantage for these sponsors is the prestige they get by entering into this collaboration.

After the material has been collected and separated, a lot of plastic bottles, caps, and paper cups remain. These can be picked up by parties who benefit from them. For example, the caps could be delivered to WasteBoards, while the bottles could go to producers such as Coca-Cola. These parties aim to make all drinking bottles circular by 2025.

7.4 The Art of Uniting Parties

Identifying and understanding the actors or stakeholders that are relevant to the realization and implementation of your business model is pivotal. Defining the interests, influence and interrelationships between the parties in your network primarily helps to determine the necessary connections that must be made in order for your business model to function, and in addition, understanding which stakeholders can play a crucial role in helping you to create a good fit between the business model and its environment. This fit may be necessary to receive the support needed to anchor your business model in the social context and successfully realize its ambitions.

In all of the business model archetypes discussed, it is not always immediately obvious in advance which actors may play a role in creating the necessary supporting context for a business model to thrive. This makes continual reflection on the key stakeholders and their roles in the Parties building block vital because you will need to decide which of your stakeholders you will actively engage to shape and co-create the strategy underpinning your business model. We will discuss this further in the next chapter.

References

Business Model Lab [Tools]. (n.d.). Retrieved on 20.6.2019 from www.businessmodellab.nl/en.

Freeman, R. E. (1984). *Stakeholder management: A strategic approach.* Pitman.

Johnson, G., Whittington, R., Scholes, K., Angwin, D., & Regnér, P. (2017). *Exploring strategy: Text and cases.* 11th edn. Pearson Education Limited.

Mitchell, R. K., Agle, B. R., & Wood, D. J. (1997). Toward a theory of stakeholder identification and salience: Defining the principle of who and what really counts. *Academy of Management Review, 22*(4), 853–886.

8

Strategy

Bundles use the most efficient A+++ machines. Bundles also help to wash smarter and more economically. The Bundles Buddy is a smart device that monitors your washing patterns and gives you personal advice on how you can wash smarter through programme selection, detergent and load sizes, and washing temperatures. If everyone washes smarter, together we can save a lot of electricity! *Bundles*, www.bundles.nl.

Babyexchangerie are conquering the market for baby things with a lease model. For a fixed monthly amount, you can rent everything new parents need for children up to about one year of age, such as a crib, a pram, and a baby carrier. Once the child has grown out of it, you send it back. *Babyexchangerie*, www.Babyexchangerie.nl.

FLOOW2 made visible the supply and demand of equipment, facilities, surplus stock and knowledge of employees within the Albert Schweitzer Hospital. Things not used cost money, and by making better use of what the hospital already has, these costs are reduced. FLOOW2 creates a WinWin sharing platform. *Peter van der Meer, Albert Schweitzer Hospital Executive Board*, www.floow2.com.

The Surplus Food Factory has an important point of departure: to take surplus food destined for human consumption and recover it for the same purpose. We want to save as many vegetables as possible to turn them into tasty products. *The Verspillingsfabriek*, www.deverspillingsfabriek.nl.

Cascading differs from ordinary reuse and recycling in that it changes the function and the extent to which the product is processed. A cotton T-shirt can serve as an example. When reused, a worn T-shirt is sold in a second-hand shop. When recycled, the T-shirt is shredded into cotton fibres, which

J. Jonker and N. Faber, *Organizing for Sustainability*,
https://doi.org/10.1007/978-3-030-78157-6_8

are then spun into new yarn. Cascading is the use of old T-shirts as cushion filling. *Het Groene Brein*, https://kenniskaarten.hetgroenebrein.nl.

We see great opportunities for cooperative farms that make citizens share ownership of their farms: consumers who both produce and consume. We help them develop these small-scale mixed companies that produce sustainable, healthy, and tasty food and restore lost food skills. *Herenboeren*, www.herenboeren.nl.

8.1 Mapping Out the Route

Strategy has been very briefly touched upon in earlier chapters. In Chapter 5, five traditional value creation *strategies* were explained (product leadership, organizational excellence, customer intimacy, experience, and community building) as well as five value creation *positions* over time (transformation, recycling, circularity, regenerating and restoring). These are both strategic considerations to reflect on the nature of value creation in a business model and how to address them strategically. But there is more. Therefore, in this chapter, we will dive more specifically into the nature of strategy itself and present a typology of strategies (Fig. 8.1). It is handy to have a *fresh* memory of the three earlier-introduced business model archetypes in Chapter 6 and the guiding principles that were introduced in Chapter 2 since they create the basis for what we see throughout this book as sustainable business models.

So, here we define strategy as a route towards your desired value proposition. It can be seen as a set of actions you define leading to an actionable future-oriented perspective—often with the parties you work with—with the primary goal of arriving at your proposition. In addition to the actors and

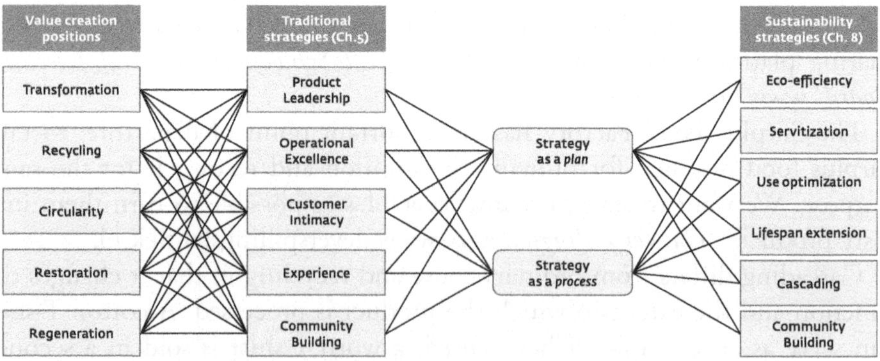

Fig. 8.1 Typology of strategy choices

stakeholders that you work with (as discussed in Chapter 7), other local factors also play a key role. Environmental factors can range from geographic conditions to material availability, natural elements, or available infrastructure. Together, these factors offer opportunities or impose restrictions on the business model you are seeking to develop.

When developing a strategy, it is important to distinguish between (1) strategy as a *plan* and (2) strategy as a *process* (Mintzberg, 1987; Mintzberg et al., 1998). In the first case, strategy is used as a design or blueprint which specifies in detail what to do, when, and under what circumstances. We often see this approach used by organizations because it gives guidance in calculating cost–benefit ratios, provides so-called benchmarks or milestones, and you can easily apply financial indicators to it. In contrast, strategy as a process is about plotting a path in general terms, in which benchmarks and performance indicators do not play a dominant role. Your strategy is rather a sketch that allows you to get where you want to be with greater flexibility. In other words, strategy as a flexible process takes into account all kinds of factors such as traffic, weather, your mood, the progress of the route and, if you wish, a lot of other elements. You broadly know where you are going, but you can easily adapt your course. Depending on your approach to strategy formulation, you can use different tools.

Whichever strategic approach you choose, you should always make it clear from the start where you are headed and be aware that you will need to make choices along the way and that your choices have consequences. The core of the strategy building block is determining the route along which you can best realize your proposition, given your stakeholders and the contextual factors. A strategy is therefore fundamentally a matter of clear, reasoned and actionable choices.

For the BMT, we distinguish six strategies that can be used, be deployed, or underpin the development of sustainable business models: (1) eco-efficiency, (2) product as a service, (3) use optimization, (4) lifespan extension, (5) cascading, and (6) community building. Each of these strategies can be used either stand-alone or in a balanced combination while developing one of the business model archetypes. To help you make clear choices we provide a brief description for each of these strategies below.

Definition

Eco-efficiency

The eco-efficiency strategy focuses on the *low-hanging fruit*, the reduction of the use of material and energy throughout the life of a product, but also increasing output using the same amount of input. This strategy is often used to reduce negative effects (such as waste, the emission of toxic substances, the use of pesticides). This strategy was launched in the 1990s by the World Business Council for Sustainable Development (WBCSD). This approach can enable organizations to reduce their carbon and wider environmental footprint, but in principle, organizations will keep doing the same things, so it does not represent a business model innovation.

Definition

Product as a Service/Servitization

The essence of the product-as-a-service strategy is to market the function of a product, rather than selling a product. For example, companies like Phillips or Urbanvolt (urbanvolt.com) selling light instead of a lamp or lightbulb, or companies selling heat instead of a central heating system and so on and so forth. PAAS can lead to dematerialization, which means making fewer *things*, while still having access to the functions. For companies that opt for this strategy, this will lead to different design choices with a focus on lifespan extension and quality, new and often more elaborate forms of service, and appropriate logistics networks. It can ultimately mean that ownership relationships of a product change. There are three common forms of this strategy (derived from the typology of Tukker & Tischner, 2006).[1]

- **Product-oriented service strategy**: This consists of the sale of a product with, for example, a (mandatory) maintenance package, or the more or less compulsory purchase of consumables that enable the product to function. Consider, for example, a printer that only accepts toners of its own brand, a car for which you can only use the batteries of that brand, or a camera for which only one kind of memory card or film can be used.

[1]The discussion on product–service systems (PSS) and business models may sometimes be a bit confusing. In this book, we explicitly position PSS as a strategic building block of a business model. A typology of PSS itself is not a typology of business models.

- **Use-oriented service strategy**: The supplier remains the owner of the product and grants access to its use through a rental or lease contract. The supplier remains responsible for the maintenance of the product. An interesting thing about this strategy is that it is important for the manufacturer to make a product that will last as long as possible, and, when it breaks down, can be repaired as easily as possible. Think of the example of Bundles working with Miele to sell consumers a subscription to washes instead of washing machines and tumble dryers.
- **Result-oriented service strategy**: Here agreements are made about the result, and not about the product. The customer pays for the purchase of a unit of the product (e.g. per print, per wash, per night), or for the functional result. Philips sells light, Auping (www.auping.com) sells a good night's sleep.

Frequently, many of these PAAS strategies are combined with a (compulsory) subscription. This could mean that the consumer is obliged to purchase a certain number of washes, units of washing powder, or boxes of toner. One step further is that such a subscription also entails the obligation to purchase electricity of one specific brand. The degree of sustainability of these different product–service system strategies ultimately depends on the extent to which it leads to an actual reduction of the production of goods (and therefore less use of raw materials) and the use of energy, water, soap, or toner, and so on. It is also interesting that the PAAS strategy tends to focus primarily on environmental sustainability (the ecological side), and that the social component is often included less. That is remarkable, because PAAS requires, in addition to hardware, extra input from people.

Definition

Use optimization

The use optimization strategy builds on the premise that many assets and products (chairs, buildings, cars) are not fully utilized. We also call this unused capacity *idle capacity*. We make, organize, and arrange a lot that we do not use and then discard it. That is a waste of time, energy, creativity, raw materials, or the transport involved. Organizing a (digital) platform that provides a catalogue of this idle capacity and connects it can lead to optimization of use.

Definition

Lifespan extension

The essence of the lifespan extension strategy is maximizing the value retention of a product. Extending service life—sometimes referred to as lifespan extension—starts with the design of a product and is guided by, among other things, choice of material, *design for repair*, and *design for recycling.* Essential to this strategy is to design products and the components they are made with so that they can be used in a second, third, fourth, or *nth* cycle of use with as little loss of properties (and therefore value) as possible. Lifespan extension is considered a central strategy in the circular economy (Bakker et al., 2015).

Example

Extending the lifespan of pruning shears

Felco has fully committed to preserving the lifespan of its pruning shears. All pruning shears parts are replaceable, right down to the handles. The shears have been designed in such a way that users can replace the broken parts themselves (Felco, www.felco.com).

Definition

Cascading

Cascading involves the joint design of a loop with multiple parties. By creating the cascade together, you also create a business model together. The essence of cascading is the maximum use of materials and/or residual flows between these parties. One type of cascading is conversion: the conversion of residual flows into new raw materials (e.g. the conversion of sewage sludge into biogas). Another form is substitution. This form focuses on the replacement of materials and raw materials by more sustainable alternatives (e.g. lignin from roadside grass as a binder in asphalt). The crux of this strategy is that it is not achieved without cooperation between the parties.

Definition

Community building

Finally, the community building strategy is about consciously organizing joint value creation for and within a community, often focused on facilities such as energy, care, or food (Jonker & Faber, 2015). Such a community can be an area or a neighbourhood, but also an entire village. The central assumption is that in every community, there are all kinds of *capabilities* or capacities that are either not utilized at all or do not come into their own. This strategy is based on making better use of those social and institutional capacities. What does it take to give a neighbourhood energy autonomy? That is not only a financial issue (where does the money come from?) or a technical issue (with matters such as an appropriate energy mix, a smart grid, and perhaps the use of cryptotechnology), but above all a management or control issue. As a neighbourhood, could we set up an organization with our people? And can people who work for that company be paid or partially paid with, for example, electricity, or mobility, or food?

A Short Reflection

A number of the strategies mentioned above primarily focus on the resource, or, in other words, the material side of sustainability. These strategies are ultimately about reducing the use of raw materials and the negative impact that transformation and the use of these raw materials have. For example, producing and using a car has a significant negative, material, and ecological impact, and a pair of jeans has a major impact during its use because of the repeated washing and the energy and chemicals used in that process.

This means that these strategies are particularly useful for those sustainability issues where the raw material challenge is at the centre. Consequently, they are less meaningful if there is a more social or ecological sustainability issue at stake. Attempting to reduce the amount of raw materials does not necessarily lead to more inclusion of people, nor does it *automatically* lead to the restoration of biodiversity. If this is your actual intention, you will have to make a conscious choice to take aspects from the various strategies and, if necessary, supplement things. The kind of strategy formulation which requires *tinkering* with strategy is referred to as *strategic bricolage*. Be mindful that strategic bricolage will affect and determine the impact of your business model and the different types of value you create (see Chapters 11 and 12). It can lead to juggling with indicators and various types of impacts and your task will be to make sure it remains workable.

8.2 Tools

A number of the tools we presented earlier are, with some adjustments, also suitable to be used again here (see, for example, Chapter 3—Motive and Context, and Chapter 4—The Dream). Below, we outline a selection of tools which align with the two distinct approaches to strategy formulation: (1) *analytical tools* which support strategy as a *plan*, for example SWOT and DESTEP, and (2) *conceptual tools* which support strategy as a *route*, for example brainstorming, mind mapping, and gaming.

Strategy as a Plan: Analytical Tools

The most straightforward advice here is to start with one of the well-known tools such as a SWOT, DESTEP, Porter's strength analysis, McKinsey's 7S model, Lewin's driving and restraining forces or similar strength and weakness analysis (just searching the internet provides a range of ready-to-use instruments). Combine tools for external and internal analyses and apply these as systematically as possible. Preferably work visually (e.g.

using Post-its® on large A0 sheets), and do this together with the team, the colleagues, or other parties (see Chapter 7—Parties Involved) that are involved in the business model you are developing. You can also explore working with dynamic digital tools, examples of which can be found on the internet. A good and recent example is the eight-step business model portfolio (see: www.managementimpact.nl/artikel/een-businessmodelportfolio-analyseren-8-stappen) based on the work of Aversa et al. (2017).

However, whenever you choose to work with ready-made tools, be mindful that all tools and frameworks are based on certain logic(s) and will therefore have their own particular perspectives and blind spots (perhaps not always immediately obvious at first glance). One perspective might reflect the dynamics in the environment, while another is about competitiveness or the match between your core activities and the changing requirements in the environment. And perhaps even more importantly, the bulk of these tools emerged in the context of a linear economy over the past 50 years. The majority of them have an organization-centred perspective and thus tend to adhere to a straightforward cost–benefit analysis. After all, only very recently has greater importance been attached to sustainability, multiple value creation, inclusivity, and value retention by organizing circularity, let alone a regenerative or restorative economy. While there are emerging tools which promise to include these aspects of strategy, on closer inspection these wider concerns are largely treated superficially.

Strategy as a Route: Conceptual Tools

This strategic approach gives much more freedom to think from a certain point of departure about the specific point on the horizon you are aiming towards and how you want to get there. The current Dutch government has taken this approach through their Big Hairy Audacious Goal (BHAG) and stated ambition for the Netherlands to be a 100% circular economy by 2050. But that also applies to propositions (see Chapter 5—Proposition), such as 'No more single-use plastics in Dutch supermarkets by 2030' or 'What changes in legislation, business operations, and the chain are necessary to stop the practice of *chick culling* by 2025?'

All these horizons are perfectly defendable, but they require a hefty and above all new, often unknown, and collective organizational effort that involves all kinds of aspects (including fiscal, legal, organizational, material, moral, and international). When you think a little more about it, you will soon discover all kinds of more profound problems behind these problems.

When you have tackled one issue as well as possible, a new problem will appear. It is not without reason that we call them *wicked problems*.

To make progress in solving these kinds of complex issues, you have to start from scratch. A white sheet of paper, literally, but also mentally. Can we forget for a second what we know and what we can do and start thinking from scratch about how we want to solve an issue? This requires a collective mindset. Because it is difficult, if not impossible, to work without a shared vision of the future towards solutions for that future. In practice this means brainstorming, exploring the seemingly impossible and creating scenarios about how the world could be—intentionally seeking to co-create and nudge a different future into being. Of course, while there are a whole range of brainstorming techniques, the essence of these is always to start with a blank canvas, be it a sheet of paper, or a physical or digital whiteboard. Ideally this kind of strategy formulation process is conducted in person whereby it is easier to facilitate interactions and ensure that everybody is engaged, has an opportunity to voice their perspective(s), and has genuinely bought into the collective vision and strategy developed. If online forums and tools are a necessity, it is even more important to take care to ensure that all participants are actively engaged in the process.

You will probably need to combine brainstorming with mind mapping. Fortunately, today there is a wide range of digital tools that can enable group ideation processes, such as (but not limited to): Popplet (creating mood boards), Stormboard (online whiteboard), Brainsparker (the inspiration for brainstorming techniques), Flock (group chat 2.0), Slack (group email), and Mindmeister (group mind mapping). The examples listed above can be found at tallyfy.com/brainstorming-tools.

8.3 Case Studies: Strategy

Case study: WashingGreen—eco-efficiency + life extension strategies

The WashingGreen B2B business model is ecologically more efficient than conventional washing in various ways. Firstly, no water is used in the CO_2 washing process. WashingGreen is, therefore, more efficient in water consumption than conventional washing. Secondly, WashingGreen is more energy-efficient than conventional washing machines, due to the fact that the LCO_2 (liquid carbon dioxide) washing machines require less energy than conventional washing machines. Thirdly, as the linen does not get wet in the CO_2 washing process, no drying process is required, contributing to considerable savings in energy costs. Fourth, this business model also incorporates the lifespan extension strategy: CO_2 washing is considerably better for the fabric because no drying process is involved and as a result, the fabrics last longer.

Case study: GreenGold—cascading + use optimization strategies

GreenGold's value proposition is to establish an algae farm that uses excess CO_2, as well as excess heat and energy from a waste incinerator to grow animal feed. They have chosen to use cascading as the underlying strategy to realize this proposition. The cascade is reinforced with an element from the *use optimization strategy*. Cascading involves jointly designing a loop with several parties: in this instance, it relates to the CO_2 cycle. The cascade in this case is realized through a conversion of residual energy and CO_2 coming from other industrial processes (such as the incineration of waste) to grow algae, with dried algae as the end product. The dried algae are then sold as a very suitable component in animal feed. A key partner of GreenGold processes the algae into animal feed and resells it. In this way, multiple forms of value are created in a cascade, and new resources arise based on residual flows—dried and/or ground algae as a component of animal fodder—resulting in a reduction of methane gas, for instance with cows.

Case study: GreeNet—community building strategy

Please bear in mind that the proposition of GreeNet is to address the litter problem at railway stations. It is suggested that a community building strategy be used to arrive at developing the proposition. This chosen strategy is about consciously organizing joint value creation for and within a community of all stakeholders involved. Keeping the trains and stations clean brings about a significant expense to be addressed by all stakeholders. Evidently it involves the passengers as well. Travellers can use a vending machine to hand in their litter (plastic bottles and paper cups) and will receive a small refund in exchange. The purpose of this is to involve travellers in the collection of the litter so that they realize that waste is a resource that can be converted into a product of value.

Case study: Plastic-eating mealworms—cascading strategy

The aim of this project is to close the loop by cleaning up plastic-residue streams by using mealworms that eat and digest the residues. To achieve this goal, the initiators of the project work alongside several parties that together form a loop. Think of waste-collectors, mealworm farmers, and residue users. Together they aim for the most efficient use of materials and residual flows between the various parties. As a result they operationalize a cascade strategy employing recovery of waste streams, conversion, and substitution.

Case study: Happee—strategy mix

The basis of Happee's business model is to produce attractive-looking mobile urinals for use at festivals made from recovered and recycled bottle caps. The product is a sustainable and viable substitute for existing mobile urinals; however, Happee faced several strategic choices. Firstly, related to the merit of the product: here a use-oriented service strategy is applied by leasing the urinals, while Happee, as the producer, remains the owner of the urinal. The second strategic component extends the lifetime of the raw material—the plastic caps (lifespan extension strategy). By melting the plastic caps, these caps retain their value. Thirdly, a cascading strategy is also deployed: the urine that is collected in the urinals is transferred to the municipal water board, which then purifies urine and converts it into drinking water and other resources. The fourth and final strategy concerns community building. By placing attractive urinals at the festival and collecting urine with appropriate publicity as *fun* but also as a *sustainable thing*, Happee creates social awareness of the importance of separating waste. It goes without saying that the proper use of the urinals will result in a cleaner environment.

8.4 Everything Is Context

To realize your business model, you can choose from or combine the multiple strategies described in this chapter (eco-efficiency, product as a service, use optimization, lifespan extension, cascading, and community building). Which of these strategies or combinations thereof you choose depends on the specific circumstances and context in which you are seeking to realize your business model and the underlying value proposition. After formulating your strategy, it is time to think about the implementation of it which we refer to as choosing *core activities*.

References

Aversa, P., Haefliger, S., & Reza, D. G. (2017). Building a winning business model portfolio. *MIT Sloan Management Review, 58*(4), 49–54.

Bakker, C., den Hollander, M., van Hinte, E., & Zijlstra, Y. (2015). *Products that last: Product design for circular business models* (2nd ed.). TU Delft Library.

FELCO. (n.d.). *Reserveonderdelen FELCO SA*. Retrieved on 19 May 2019 from: www.felco.com/us_en/service/index/spareparts.

Jonker, J., & Faber, N. R. (2015). *Framing the WEconomy: exploring seven socio-economic trends that enable shaping a transition towards sustainability* (p. 46) (Working Paper). Nijmegen: Radboud University Nijmegen.

Mintzberg, H. (1987). Crafting strategy. *Harvard Business Review, 7*, 66–75.

Mintzberg, H., Ahlstrand, B., & Lampel, J. (1998). *Strategy safari: A guided tour through the wilds of strategic management*. Free Press.

Tukker, A., & Tischner, U. (2006). Product-services as a research field: Past, present and future. Reflections from a decade of research. *Journal of Cleaner Production, 14*(17), 1552–1556. https://doi.org/10.1016/j.jclepro.2006.01.022.

9

Core Activities

Ahrend is the only manufacturer of cradle-to-cradle chairs in the Benelux. This means that we use materials that can be reused time and again, use renewable energy, and respect diversity. […] During the design of vitalizing workspaces, we always aim to close the cycle with our products. That's why we also like to maintain ownership of the products and assist users with our services. We call this *Furniture as a Service*. In this way, we ensure that the circular economy becomes a reality. *Ahrend*, www.ahrend.com.

Tesla's home battery integrates with solar energy to utilize the infinite power of the sun and reduce dependence on fossil fuels. *Tesla*, www.tesla.com/nl.

Felyx is a successful scale-up, offering shared electric scooters as a new and disrupting urban mobility concept. *Felyx*, https://felyx.com.

Sustainability is in our DNA, which is why we believe sustainable business operations are important. In 2019, we were the first supermarket in the Netherlands to open an energy-neutral store. More and more of our trucks are also running on LNG (Liquid Natural Gas), which emits far less CO_2, and more than 90% of our residual flows are recycled into new raw materials. *Lidl*, https://corporate.lidl.nl.

Innovating with waste flows to create fascinating circular products, TRIBOO is the circular office furnisher. *TRIBOO*, www.triboo.nl.

We are expanding the system of separate waste processing at stations and on trains. We are also researching how we can already reduce waste at the time of purchase with more possibilities for reuse. *Dutch Railways*, www.ns.nl.

iPhone Kliniek has specialized in iPhone and iPad repairs for many years. *iPhone Kliniek*, www.iphonekliniek.nl.

J. Jonker and N. Faber, *Organizing for Sustainability*,
https://doi.org/10.1007/978-3-030-78157-6_9

Refurbished devices are devices that are pre-used and are, after an overhaul by our experts, like new again. This way they get a second life. The products that are refurbished usually come from the business community and trade-in programmes. They are extensively checked, tested, cleaned, repaired, replaced, and upgraded whenever necessary. With a refurbished device you are not only environmentally conscious, but it also saves you a few pennies in your wallet. So: hello nice sustainable product and possibly that new pair of shoes with the money you saved! *LEAPP*, https://leapp.nl/pages/refurbishment.

Railway sleepers are used in the construction of railways. We use the oak variants, which logically have a well-lived appearance. We clean the wood thoroughly in advance and convert it into tabletops. *Oak & Steel*, www.oaknsteel.nl.

Europe is at the head of aluminium recycling and this position is something that Alumeco wants to keep contributing to. This contribution includes a thorough sorting of our waste metal, which is collected in containers and sorted by types of alloy, ready to be recycled. This careful waste sorting actually ensures that aluminium can be reused repeatedly to produce the same types of products. In this way, optimum use of aluminium is achieved. *Alumeco*, www.alumeco.nl.

Generating energy from waste is sustainable and offers many benefits. In addition to the energy and reducing the amount of waste, the combustion residue is also used effectively. Road construction, in particular, can benefit from this residue. More than 85% of this combustion residue is now being put to good use. Energy from waste appears to be here to stay. *Duurzaamheidskompas*, https://duurzaamheidskompas.nl/blogs/energie-uit-afval/.

In Germany, ReFood collects around 500,000 tons of food waste every year. From these raw materials, they generate electricity and heat in their own biogas plants for currently some 50,000 households, replacing energy from such sources as nuclear power plants and coal. *Refood*, www.refood.nl/nl/rf-nl/groene-energie/.

9.1 The More Specific the Better

Now it is time to specify what you are going to do. Which core activities will you undertake alone or with others to achieve your goal through the chosen strategy or mix of strategies? These can be both technical and organizational activities. Given the wide variety of companies, business models, and the context in which they operate, it is impossible to present a comprehensive list of activities. However, bear in mind that the core activities should align with the chosen strategy (or strategies), enable the realization of the overall goal, and ultimately be coherent within the proposition.

In an existing company, it is about evaluating/re-evaluating existing activities, adding new activities, or discarding activities that no longer sufficiently match your new objective(s). With a new venture, you have more freedom in devising new activities, without having to take into account the potential constraints that may accompany existing business operations.

The activities that are needed to initiate a change or to start a new business model (such as training people or purchasing resources) we will refer to as the *starting* or *initial activities*. The activities you undertake after the business model sets off we will refer to as the *operational core activities*. These are always available and are a central part of the daily management of your business model. Companies can profile themselves well through a social issue or problem that they adopt if there is a logical connection with the *core activities* of the company and the problem concerned. If this is not the case, there is a chance of *greenwashing* (Hollander & Gadella-van Wersch, 2017).

Important

Sustainable business operations

Companies and organizations have an ever-growing need to integrate sustainability into their *core activities.* Sustainability principles are therefore an important motive in determining the business strategy. They are integrated into medium-term policies and objectives and the development of practices and procedures. By ensuring sustainable business operations, companies are better able to meet the demands of stakeholders, initiate change, and create long-term value. *Luca Crisciotti* (2016), *CEO DNV GL*, www.dnvgl.co.uk.

The *core activity* concept emerged in the last century after many companies developed into conglomerates of companies, often with very different activities (Prahalad & Hamel, 1990). The idea of a core activity is that a specific part of the business activities can be seen as the speciality of the company: what it is really good at. Other organizations are better at handling matters that fall outside of this speciality.

9.2 Core Activities Framework

The American environmental programme of the 1970s introduced the now-familiar sustainability activities: reduce, reuse, recycle. Although the origin is not entirely clear, most sources refer to the launch of these concepts during the first *Earth Day* in 1970 and they can potentially be attributed to *The Environmental Handbook* by Garrett de Bell (1970).

The *reduce, reuse, recycle* trinity has evolved over the years. For example, a whole *family* has been built up of what is commonly referred to as RE-strategies (REs). Some authors propose a family of ten REs (see, for example, Potting et al., 2017), which we modify slightly and extend, to incorporate the circular bioeconomy considerations, and present as 13 REs. While it is easy on reflection to quickly expand the list to about 30–35 strategies, this would lead to an unworkable framework.

Key Points

The REs of circularity

Below we outline a list of 13 REs that we consider core activities within strategies for the development of sustainable business models, building on and extending Potting et al. (2017).

Refusing raw materials or products that are harmful to people and the environment, or that make it difficult to reuse a product at the end of its life in whatever form.

Redesigning products and components so that they can be repaired and the materials can be recovered at the end of the life cycle.

Bio-based Redesign (Substitution) is the commitment to develop and valorize renewable raw materials to replace fossil fuel-based virgin raw materials. For example, potato peels can be used to make cellophane, and rejected fruit to make fruit leather (Fruitleather Rotterdam, www.fruitleather.nl).

Rethinking whether the use of the product can be intensified, for example, by sharing assets (such as machines, buildings, vehicles).

Reducing the use of raw materials and energy in production and use.

Reusing the product, for instance by finding another user or application.

Repairing defective products without replacing crucial parts.

Refurbishing a product by updating products and parts, so that it can be put on the market again.

Remanufacturing products by harvesting key components or cores to create equivalent products guaranteed as new.

Repurposing the components of a product for another application. Examples are the bike paths in the Dutch cities of Giethoorn and Zwolle that are made of plastic, or Remade Industry that transforms discarded police uniforms into an overnight bag, backpack, or barbecue apron (Remade Industry, 2019).

Recycling products to recover raw materials for use in new products. The technological challenge lies in the production of secondary raw materials

with the same properties as *virgin* materials. In an ideal scenario this means that the same products can be made without the need to add virgin raw materials. Ioniqa, for example, recovers the materials from PET bottles so that they can be perpetually recycled, so to speak, into PET bottles (Ioniqa Technologies, n.d.).
Recovering refers to capturing energy from products at the end of their life cycle when all other REs have been exhausted.
Re-converting[1] of waste into raw materials with another application. For example, converting CO_2 into methanol (fuel), raw materials for medicines, or as a growth accelerator in agriculture.

Over the past 50 years there has been a recurring debate in strategic management regarding the nature of the relationship between strategy and core activities. Is strategic management concerned with the question of setting a route a strategic choice? Or is it about things that we should not do, or should do differently? In other words, is it a strategy or an activity? In the latter case, these questions could also be regarded as a core activity within a strategy. For the sake of clarity, we make a choice here in which we describe and elaborate on the strategies in Chapter 8 and see the REs as core activities within them. To clarify this, we have also linked strategies and core activities to the three types of business models (see Chapter 6—Business Model Archetypes).

Because you work from a specific goal (see Chapter 5—The Value Proposition) and selected strategies (see Chapter 8—Strategy), it is useful to state which (core) activities are necessary to realize sustainable business models. As our aim is the creation of multiple values, here we distinguish ourselves from conventional business administration where core activities are often solely identified in such terms as processes, competencies, and technology.

That does not mean that these conventional structures are no longer important. Rather, we focus on those core activities that are a first step towards the concrete operationalization of the sustainable business model that is being scoped. This means that if we opt for *Refuse*, for example, we indicate which raw materials can no longer be used or which processes are no longer permissible. We can also take this a step further, such as by indicating that we no longer consider certain types of waste (heat, CO_2) acceptable. Whatever the considerations, choosing them explicitly leads to demonstrable interpretations of the core activities and is thus a first step towards the measurable indication of those core activities (see Chapter 11—Impact) (Fig. 9.1).

[1]Of course, *Conversion* is not a real *RE*. But if we formulated it as an *RE* that would cause confusion, we would have to use *Remake* or *Reuse*, and that, in turn, would also lead to confusion.

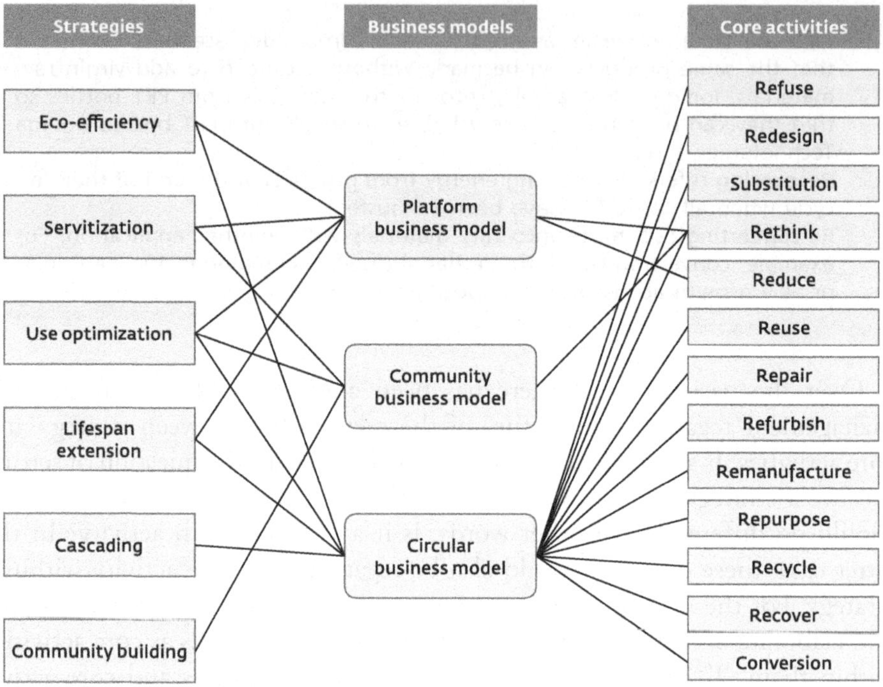

Fig. 9.1 Combining strategies, business models, and core activities

9.3 Case Studies: Core Activities

Case study: GreeNet

GreeNet's dream is to reduce litter produced by train passengers. For this purpose, GreeNet has created and launched the Clean Mobility Initiative (CMI) to change the behaviour of travellers, so that they return their waste at train stations via Reverse Vending Machines (RVMs). An RVM is a machine in which travellers can return their waste, just like the machines for returning empty glass or plastic bottles in the supermarket. Here the technology has been extended so other types of waste can be returned as well. The actual pilot mainly focuses on the return of plastic bottles or paper cups. This smart machine scans the material and separates it into various independent mono-streams of waste. The ease of the return process is a crucial factor in making the project work.

Travellers are incentivized to return their waste to an RVM through a savings system. After returning the bottles or cups, the traveller has two choices: receive a fixed amount of GreenCredits, or the chance of a prize. The Green-Credits can be used for such things as discounts on mobility (public transport), consumer goods such as coffee, or to pay for the use of public services like a public toilet. There is also the potential for Dutch Railways to offer travel credit, upgrades to first-class or use of public bikes. Other companies can also contribute to the CMI initiative by offering tickets for the lottery.

Case study: WashingGreen

WashingGreen provides an industrial linen laundry service to the hotel industry using CO_2. WashingGreen purchases fair trade linen from their linen suppliers. This linen is then chipped, given a barcode, and transported to their customers with a CO_2-neutral means of transport. Hotels use the linen and can indicate when a dirty load of laundry needs to be collected via the WashingGreen app. At key points in the process the linen is scanned—so the hotels know where the linen is located and WashingGreen knows how many washing cycles the linen can go through before it must be recycled. After the washing process using CO_2 the linen is sorted, with suitable items going back to the hotels, or reused or recycled by one of WashingGreen's partners.

Case study: Rotterzwam

Rotterzwam, an oyster mushroom farm in Rotterdam, the Netherlands, believes in a society where material loops are closed, resource usage is optimized, and food is produced locally. They cultivate oyster mushrooms on locally collected coffee grounds, which they sell to restaurants and supermarkets in the Rotterdam area. Rotterzwam's philosophy is not only to emphasize locally produced vegetable proteins but also to stimulate the ease with which residual flows are used to produce mushrooms locally, regionally, and internationally.

Rotterzwam opened its nursery to the public in May 2019. Here they convert 6,000–7,000 kg of coffee grounds into 1,200–1,400 kg of oyster mushrooms every month. Core activities of Rotterzwam are the logistics of collecting coffee grounds daily (using 100% electric transport), to ensure stability of supply in the oyster mushroom cultivation process, and last but not least to establish the nursery as a circular economy experience centre. The ambition is to share knowledge and experience through guided tours, business networks, and workshops at their new nursery. These three core activities together lead to a business model that yields both economic and environmental benefits (www.rotterzwam.nl).

9.4 A Running Score

Thus far in the BMT methodology, you have completed the Definition Stage and most of the Design Stage. It is OK to take a break now, take the dog for a walk, go for a workout or a swim, or have a drink. In fact, a night's sleep does not hurt you every now and again. Our advice is to proactively get some distance from your pet project and actively try not to think about your BMT.

Once you have had a break from your BMT, come back with a fresh pair of eyes and take another look at how you have completed the seven building blocks of the BMT so far and how each building block relates to one another. If necessary, fine-tune and adjust your choices. The fifth and final stage of the Design Stage/Phase now awaits you—the next step is to take what you have in front of you and go through the steps of Building Block #8—External Test.

References

Crisciotti, L. (2016). Duurzaamheid wordt onderdeel van kernactiviteiten [Sustainability becomes part of core activities]. Retrieved on 21.2.2020 from: www.duurzaam-ondernemen.nl/duurzaamheid-wordt-onderdeel-van-kernactiviteiten-conclusie-groot-internationaal-onderzoek-onder-bedrijven/.

Fruitleather Rotterdam (n.d.). Retrieved on 19.5.2019 from: www.fruitleather.nl.

Hollander, H., & Gadella-van Wersch, C. (2017). *Duurzaamheid is passé: 8 ingrediënten voor succesvol en toekomstbestendig ondernemen.* Business contact. http://mgtbk.nl/1jr3ln.

Ioniqa Technologies. (n.d.). Retrieved on 19.5.2019 from: https://ioniqa.com/applications.

Potting, J., Hekkert, M. P., Worrell, E., & Hanemaaijer, A. (2017). *Circular Economy: Measuring innovation in the product chain.* PBL.

Prahalad, C. K., & Hamel, G. (1990). The Core Competence of the Corporation. *Harvard Business Review, 68*(3), 79–91.

Remade Industry (2019). Retrieved on 19.5.2020 from: https://remadeindustry.com/.

10

External Test

The Cradle to Cradle Institute assesses products for material quality, material reuse, the use of renewable energy and CO_2 management, water management, and social justice. To maintain the Cradle to Cradle certificate, we must continue to work on improving our products on these criteria. *Brabantia*, www.brabantia.com (Can we use this certificate? In other words, is it legal?).

Doubts arise. Do we actually know this specific market and target group well enough? How do potential customers experience our story and our products? Do we strike the right chord with our services or what we tell about them? What are the customer's priorities? And also, which brand name should we carry? Not unimportant either! *Klantkenners*, http://klantkenners.nl/portfolio/de-nieuwe-business-propositie-toetsen (Looking for valuable feedback).

The proposition was not clear and stimulating enough, so together with the client, we had another go at it. We then asked decision-makers and potential customers in the industry to think along with us (critically). The research has led to a stronger proposition, concrete next steps, and new enthusiasm within the team. *Klantkenners*, http://klantkenners.nl/portfolio/de-nieuwe-business-propositie-toesten (Looking for valuable feedback).

When deciding on the ultimate value proposition, it is necessary to also compare your proposition with the propositions of your most important competitors. Of course, you want to be 100 per cent certain that you distinguish yourself sufficiently from the rest. Your distinctiveness is one of the most important elements in why a customer says yes to *you* and not to your *competitor*. *RedFoxBlue*, www.redfoxblue.nl/blog/waardepropositie-hoe-ontwikkel-je-ze (Does it already exist?).

J. Jonker and N. Faber, *Organizing for Sustainability*,
https://doi.org/10.1007/978-3-030-78157-6_10

Now you have a value proposition which you think could be promising. As a final step, you will test everything you have come up with. It is important to start this at an early stage so that you can also make adjustments earlier when your product or service is not appreciated by customers as much as you had expected. *Rob Blaauboer*, www.frankwatching.com (Looking for valuable feedback).

However, a proper test of the idea for all these aspects is quite a job, which will take up quite some time. Many people with an idea do not take this time to do it. They prefer starting with the development of the product or service right away. But that is not always the best thing to do. By investing in this stage, you save yourself … quite a lot of time and money. Furthermore, you save yourself much negative energy, because you will not be flogging a dead horse (for too long). *Pedro Nijssen*, www.pedronijsen.wordpress.com (Looking for valuable feedback).

10.1 Seek Confrontation

The external test is the final building block of the Design Stage of the BMT. Here you will test the viability of the new company, business activity, or intervention. That said, some of you might find it useful to take the external test immediately after formulating your proposition given that the steps in this building block enable you to interrogate your business model further. For some entrepreneurs and intrapreneurs it can be extremely beneficial to ask others for feedback on your idea at the very start or even before the Design Stage/Phase.

TIP

Talk (from the very beginning) about your ideas. Go outside! Tell your friends, explain your ideas to your neighbour—talking about your idea will help to make it more concrete and to clarify to yourself where you want to go with the idea.

Knowing that you have already gone through almost two stages of the BMT so far will hopefully give you direction and inspiration. The BMT, by providing a framework and guide for your business model development process, should add new meaning to situations, things, relationships, or organizations in your network. Often an idea is good or new because it combines two (or more) components in a smart, unusual, or *new* way, and characteristically you would not usually expect them together. Think of the combination of sweet and sour in cooking (chutney), using waste as payment (plastic, for example) to access WiFi, or tackling litter by putting it in RVMs that reward you with credits of some kind (telephone, food, transportation, etc.) for doing so. These novel combinations should make you raise your eyebrows (or maybe more) because you see that they offer new opportunities.

Good ideas can lead to a different opinion, a change in behaviour, a new or modified product, or a different working method, as long as the idea is recognized, intuitive, clearly articulated, and of its time. There is a certain logic underlying all good ideas, although it may not be entirely self-evident at first. Bringing it all together into an attractive and catchy whole with the right words and accompanying images is not always easy in practice. That is why right now, at the final step of the Design Stage/Phase, you consciously seek out scrutiny of your idea. See what it is worth. Let people shoot holes in it. Yes, it might be very painful when people step on your beautiful and cherished idea with their clumsy feet. See this as an important rite of passage you need to navigate which is necessary if you want to realize your business model. Take comfort in the fact that this process will ultimately strengthen your idea. Many good ideas fail at the Definition Stage/Phase, let alone implementation. External testing is essential to giving your idea and subsequently your new venture the best shot at navigating the so-called valley of death.

If you want to, you can test your business model idea against all kinds of criteria (DareToo, n.d.). Just to show you what is possible, we provide three sets of what could be called *reflective questions*. If you do not have much time, perform your check on the basis of the very concise set of seven questions below. If time allows, go to the expanded set of five questions in Sect. 10.3. And if that is still not enough we have added a checklist from a bank (see Fig. 10.1) to show what kind of questions they raise when you come in to ask for funding for your idea. So be aware that there is some redundancy in what we are doing.

Questions

- *Need in the market*: Does your target group need your idea?
- *Financial feasibility*: How much should be invested and what is the expected return?
- *Technical feasibility*: What technology do you need? Is it feasible to get?
- *Legal feasibility*: Does your idea conform to existing laws and regulations?
- *Ethics*: Does your idea disadvantage groups of people? Or does it harm the environment?

- *Timeframe*: How much time does it take to implement your idea, and do you have that time?
- *Relevance*: Is your idea still relevant in the market at the time of its introduction?

The bottom line comes down to talking to as many people as possible about your business model idea now that it is sufficiently scoped/formulated. Find people who can comment critically but also constructively on your innovative way of working and who—if necessary—can put you in touch with the right people in their network to realize your plans. For a quick alternative with a fresh, open mind, you can also discuss the BMT with other critical practitioners and take it a step further. You then have a type of a peer-review technique called *entrepreneur for entrepreneurs*. Selecting the *critical other* needs to be done with great care. You do not necessarily look for those who agree with you: you are looking for fresh and honest feedback on your idea. Either way, leave your drawing board and head outside.

10.2 Testing Is Applied Research

Performing this step of external testing with a certain amount of objectivity is akin to a form of applied research. Research here means two things. You have

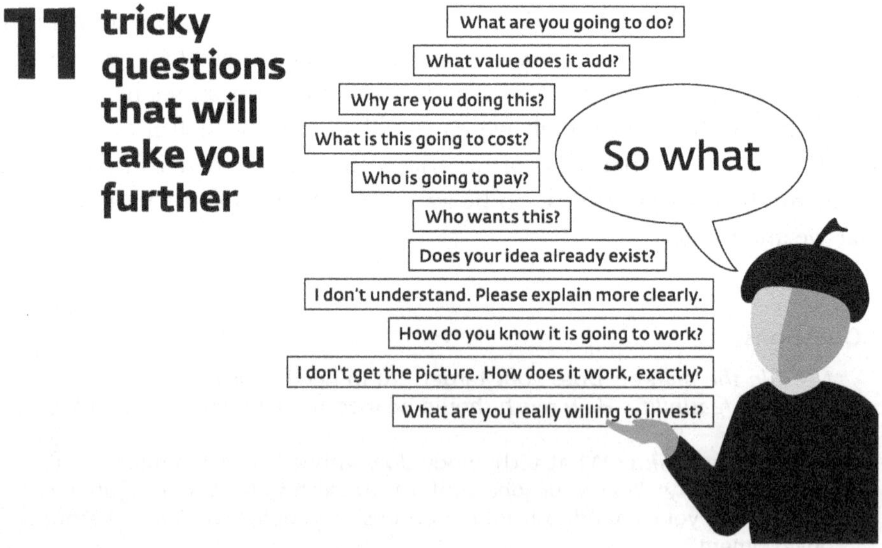

Fig. 10.1 11 tricky questions that will take you further

an idea and you confront it with the other ideas and beliefs that society has. Or you attempt to create a concept from all kinds of insights, technological developments, trends, and observations, often mixed with a little gut feeling.

In both cases, it means looking for facts. These can be carefully collected and (critically) analysed statements, but also quantitative data (numbers) as long as it is all quality information. So steer clear of the *science is just an opinion* trap. Anecdotal makeshift evidence is not enough to express significance. Stick to the facts.

When you are looking for feedback (because that is what it is), prepare well. Think of the questions you want to ask (five to seven would be fine). Look for people you know or hope will respond critically and constructively. This often takes (a lot of) time. Be well aware of it and do not rush. Tell your respondents what you want and what you need. Record your conversations (ask for permission). Do not get angry when people say things you are not happy with. Listen carefully and be patient. If necessary, make a report per interview (one A4 page with the main points of each interview is often sufficient) and send it for validation to your respondents individually afterwards.

Preferably seek a minimum of ten interviews with a variety of people (e.g. different age groups, nationalities, job types, life experience) so you can get a diversity of perspectives on your business model. Listen back to all the interviews at home and organize them by topic. Take some distance and find the common thread. But also ask people you trust and who can work diligently to reflect on the feedback with you. It might be useful to work on an A0 sheet to write down your experiences/observations with Post-its® or stickers. Visualizing your analysis makes it easier to discover patterns: what are the main issues, what are the side issues, and how could you solve them or address them through modifications? If possible, suggest a follow-up conversation with each of the people you initially interviewed for feedback to reflect on your analysis of the collective feedback you've collated (without taking too much of their time).

10.3 Minimum of Five Checks in an External Test

Ready-made tests for business model ideas are hard to find. What you need to check will depend on the way you have put together your business model, and on what you specifically want to test. Here we recommend that you consider at least five aspects when you are in the *testing* step of the BMT.

1. **Does it already exist? What is your USP?** The first check to perform is to check whether your idea already exists. How unique is your idea, and how can you substantiate a claim regarding novelty? Check from the start of working with the BMT whether what you have come up with is not already out there, and if it exists elsewhere how can you differentiate yourself? Google or surf one of the many wikis. Go to forums or to the library (whether physical or digital). Spread an invitation to your networks. Clarify your USP (Unique Selling Point)—how does your activity differ from the others? Are there similar activities that you can learn from? What are the successful elements of similar activities that can help you optimize your intended business idea? The fact that the idea already exists, in part or as a whole, does not have to be a problem or an obstacle. If your idea has been successfully implemented elsewhere that can be an indication that it is viable. The question becomes how you can differentiate yourself or do it better.

   Sustainable initiatives often focus on sharing knowledge and ideas to stimulate cooperation. Together, parties can achieve more than they can independently. The most pronounced form of knowledge sharing is *open-source* development.

   An example is the electric car manufacturer Tesla. Its mission is to accelerate the development of sustainable transport. To this end, Tesla has made its patents available (Schmidt, 2019), which will also allow other car manufacturers to speed up the production of electric cars and help Tesla realize its dream.

TIP

You can also use the *Rotterdam Method*. This method consists of insistently asking the question *Why*? three times: *Why, Why* and *Why*? It is the simplest method of interrogating an idea.

2. **Is it legal?** The second check you perform is whether the activity conforms to existing laws and regulations. If you have an innovative business activity, it remains to be seen whether the existing legal framework provides for this. Laws and regulations are usually based on past insights and experiences; they represent the interests of the established order and thus of mainstream practice. If the regulation proves to be an obstacle, you have a range of options. One possibility is to look for a different interpretation

of the legislation and explore the manoeuvring space. A second option is to look at rule-free areas or investigate how others have dealt with similar obstacles. A third option is not to wait for changes to the legal framework but to *anticipate* and start the activity while informing relevant local authorities as appropriate.

Example

Struvite waste as a raw material?

For water companies, struvite, a residual substance that remains after filtering sewage water, is a large part of their waste stream. This material is rich in phosphate and would therefore be a good raw material for all kinds of phosphate-based applications. An important one is an application in fertilizers for agriculture. Various water companies are therefore contemplating disclosing struvite as a raw material. However, external testing has shown that Dutch law imposes restrictions here. Struvite is recognized as waste, and Dutch regulations do not allow the use of this residual flow as an input for manure that will be used in the production of food.

3. **To which economy do you contribute?** The third check is a difficult one, but one that matters a lot. You may have largely developed a smart, perhaps even brilliant idea, but in which economy does your business model fit? Or to put it even more clearly: to which economy does your idea contribute? Are you committed to recycling or circularity, or do you dare to take it a step further and focus on a regenerative or restorative economy (see Chapter 5 when discussing the developments around value creation)? Is it possible to further develop your current idea so that it fits into the new economy? In essence, this check requires you to ask yourself the question: how does your business model contribute to the transition? It is also worth asking your interviewees, because they may have reflected deeply on your idea.
4. **Unintended consequences**: The fourth check focuses on unforeseen effects (the unwanted impacts) which are referred to as *unintended consequences* in systems thinking. It may be that your initiative makes a significant contribution to the wellbeing of people, but that it simultaneously harms biodiversity. Not all impact is equal: one impact will be stronger than another. You will pay more attention to this in the Result Stage when you develop the impact analysis (Building Block #9). In this check, you are actively trying to seek out possible blind spots, things which unintentionally create negative impacts that you may have missed before.

Only if you regularly turn your focus off, can you turn it on again later. If you do not, you run out of fuel, and your brain is no longer able to distinguish between relevant and irrelevant stimuli. *Mark Tigchelaar* (24 May 2019)

5. **Valuable feedback**: During conversations about your BMT with third parties, you are likely to receive valuable feedback, which may be counter to what you would like to hear. Relax and really listen. Try not to be defensive when people say things you would rather not hear! Just let them bring it on. See this as an opportunity to perfect your proposition and business model idea. If you intentionally value all feedback—good, bad, or indifferent—this fifth check is more like a bonus and can lead to all sorts of positive side-effects. Perhaps through these conversations you will be referred to other people, which will help you to increase the number of partners in your network, or you are pointed to subsidy schemes that could support the initial stage of your business model. If someone is willing to invest their time in engaging with you and giving you feedback on your idea, take their feedback in good faith—treat them as critical friends, which all entrepreneurs need.

10.4 Case Studies: External Test

Case study: WashingGreen: Does it already exist?

The WashingGreen business model is a combination of two different and existing business activities. Firstly, washing with LCO_2 is a concept that is still in its infancy. Several companies in Belgium and America already wash with LCO_2 machines, but there are not yet any companies that do so in the Netherlands. LCO_2 machines can already be bought from the www.alibaba.com website. Compared to conventional washing machines, they are still expensive and limited in size. Secondly, although LCO_2 is not being used on a large scale in the hotel industry in the Netherlands, there are large laundry companies that offer a large-scale laundry service and linen lease for hotels throughout the country. By combining these two existing business activities, a new concept is created, which is a sustainable LCO_2 laundry service with LCO_2 for the hotel industry.

Case study: CO_2 Trade: Is it legal?

In recent years, many types of online platforms have emerged to bring supply and demand together and connect people (CBS, 2018). In the Netherlands, there are the first community platforms for CO_2, such as www.co2bank-utrecht.nl. These intend to match companies and/or individuals aiming to offset carbon emissions to companies that can store CO_2 (e.g. agricultural entrepreneurs planting food forests and/or increasing humus content in the soil—which also has a positive impact on fertility, water retention capacity and biodiversity).

When developing a platform it must take into account privacy legislation, rules regarding the use of cookies, and compliance with consumer rights. Since 2018, the General Data Protection Regulation (GDPR) applies. In addition, from 2019, there are European rules for online platforms, to avoid abusing their position vis-à-vis dependent companies (European Commission, 2019). There is a risk that online platforms can act harmfully by changing general terms and conditions without explanation, lack of transparency, and termination of the service without motivation (European Commission, 2019). Be aware that that is not all, since there is also growing criticism of the use of energy and thus pollution.

Case study: GreeNet: Which economy do you contribute to?

GreeNet seeks to encourage the recycling of waste, specifically plastic bottles, closing a loop. The collection of plastic bottles using an RVM will not be enough to solve the full extent of the plastic problem. That said, the major contribution that GreeNet will make to the economy is creating awareness among citizens who travel on Dutch Railways. Due to the enormous reach of Dutch Railways, GreeNet has the potential to engage with many people and make a difference in the Netherlands in terms of awareness-raising in relation to sustainability and viewing waste as a resource.

Case study: Waste app: Unintended consequences?

The aim is to extend the business model focusing on the collection and processing of waste plastics with an app. This extension will make people aware of what is happening with plastic waste and thus inspire them to separate plastic waste properly through a reward system. However, there are always unintended consequences which need to be actively sought out. For example, the app/system could be hacked, or people could start using more plastic to save points. This approach taps into app users, which excludes several groups of people. Younger children or older people may not have access to the app or understand how the app works. For an indication of the recyclability of the product, we also depend on information from the manufacturer. This is a bit like a butcher inspecting his meat: the manufacturer may be tempted to indicate a higher recyclability level because this is good for business. In reality, the recyclability can be lower. Recyclability is also not always easy to calculate, especially for packaging that consists of several parts. Therefore, to reduce the risk of this unintended consequence we need to consider how we can create an incentive for manufacturers to be honest about their data.

Case study: CO2FAB4U: Valuable Feedback

During the development of their business model, CO2FAB4U met with people with expertise in various fields. They were given plenty of feedback. This often meant that the components of the business model had to be reviewed. During the judging process of the evaluation of their business modelling course, they were asked several critical questions. The feedback from experts and questions from the jury ultimately helped in putting together a business model that was as realistic as possible. Also, due to the help of the specialists, but also through their own assessment, they sometimes had to adjust their plan. For example, they discovered that PET and PEF are very similar, but that they cannot be recycled together. There must be a PEF mono-stream in order to be able to recycle it. One of the specialists suggested that it might be an option to provide PEF for closed events, which is an idea that they have included in their final plan.

10.5 Has Your Business Model Survived the Test?

Going through the External Test steps may mean that you need to partially adjust some elements of your business model before you move on to the Result Stage of the BMT. If necessary, go back to previous stages and review and work through the building blocks again. So be it. The difficult (but also the great) thing about feedback is that you don't know what you don't know in advance. One thing is clear though, once you do know—take advantage of it! There is no point in developing something that no one is waiting for or no one will use.

Another thing to remember is that every version of your business model in this stage is a permanent beta. See this stage as the car wash (see Jonker, 2014), in which you adjust and refine the BMT several times. That said, it is really important that you do not wait to start your new business model until you have had all the interviews, and you have a perfectly filled out BMT. Your new company, business activity, or intervention is always evolving.

References

DareToo. (n.d.). Retrieved on 26.12.2019 from: www.daretoo.nl.

European Commission. (2019). *Report on climate-related disclosures*. Retrieved on 24.9.2020: https://ec.europa.eu/info/sites/info/files/business_economy_euro/banking_and_finance/documents/190110-sustainable-finance-teg-report-climate-related-disclosures_en.pdf.

Jonker, J. (2014). *New business models; Working together towards value creation*. Academic Service.

Schmidt. (2019). Tesla's free-to-use patents are all about sustainability—And strength. *The Driven*. Retrieved on 24.09.2020 from: https://thedriven.io/2019/02/04/tesla-patents-free-to-use-sustainable-strength/.

Tigchelaar, M. (2019). We maken onszelf letterlijk dom door telkens onze aandacht te verplaatsen. *NRC Handelsblad*. Retrieved on 25.5.2019 from: www.nrc.nl/nieuws/2019/05/24/we-maken-onszelf-letterlijk-dom-door-onze-aandacht-telkens-te-verplaatsen-a3961499?fbclid=IwAR1c6-5bg4Zv_ayQ3Ur-S75_jtn1IiY3jgL-lHhq8kZIFsfUftVOD-7h2F4.

Part III

Result Stage

In the previous stages, you have thought about and worked on WHAT your business model entails (Definition Stage) and HOW you organize your business model in such a way that it creates value (Design Stage). You then tested your business model idea with third parties (external testing). The next step is to work out the impact of your business model and which values will be created as a result—this is the Result Stage.

The central focus of the last two building blocks of the BMT is the question of how you can measure the results of your business model idea. This Result Stage helps you to expand upon two crucial parts of your business model: (1) the impact that the business model has on the (broader) social, ecological, economic, and material environment, and (2) the revenue model (or hybrid revenue model) in which it is made clear which values are created for whom—going beyond looking exclusively at financial returns. In our view, impact and multiple value creation go hand in hand: they are integrated, hence it is even possible to frame this as *integral* value creation.

11

Impact

The Quorn company, which makes meat substitutes from mycoprotein, shows the CO_2 impact of its products. The production and transport of a kilogram of Quorn mince result in 1.3 kilograms of CO_2 equivalents, while beef mince produces 27 kilograms of CO_2, fish 3.6 kilograms of CO_2, and tofu 3.5 kilograms of CO_2. This information shows that a meat substitute is a more sustainable alternative to meat. To be sure that the calculated impact is correct, Quorn collaborated with the Carbon Trust Organization. *Quorn*, www.quorn.co.uk/about-quorn/planet

We have replaced the lids of strawberry, grape and cheese boxes, and more, with a thin layer of foil. That saves almost half a million kilos of plastic per year. *Albert Heijn*, nieuws.ah.nl/over-verpakkingen-bij-albert-heijn

The four wind turbines along the A15 generate energy for over 7,100 households in the region. *Windpark Nijmegen-Betuwe*, huismerkenergie.nl

Did you know that jeans are, on average, €33 too cheap? That is because all kinds of hidden costs are not included in the price. These hidden costs include, for example, pollution of the surface water by toxic dyes. They also include […] underpaying employees in clothing factories. Employees cannot live a decent life on their scanty wage, as a result of which their children often do not receive a proper education. *True Price*, https://trueprice.org

Investing has always been about striking a balance between risk and return. For companies, sustainability has truly become a major element of risk management. This is also because the risks of climate change are increasing. It is, therefore, an increasingly important part of the entire investment picture. *Hans Slomp, Fund Manager Actiam, ASN Bank*, www.asnbank.nl

Roadside grass yields around 140 m^3 of biogas per ton, which means that about 87 million m^3 of green gas can be produced from a million tons. This is sufficient for 55,000 households. *Groengas*, https://groengas.nl

J. Jonker and N. Faber, *Organizing for Sustainability*,
https://doi.org/10.1007/978-3-030-78157-6_11

An average inland vessel (ship) with a propeller consumes around 200,000 to 400,000 litres of fuel per year. The 7,000 inland vessels of the Dutch fleet use approximately 2.1 billion litres of fuel per year. In addition to this fuel consumption, there is also room for improvement in the area of air emissions such as sulphur (SO_2), nitrogen (NO_x) and particulate matter (PM10). *Duurzaambedrijfsleven*, duurzaambedrijfsleven.nl

11.1 Speaking of Impact

This chapter unpacks Building Block #9—Impact, which seeks to determine the impact that your business model idea will have on the broader social, ecological, economic, and material environment. We have found, especially during the development and trialling of the BMT, that this building block is often challenging for BMT users. Nevertheless, this building block is crucial in a sustainable business model. After all, the Result Stage is about translating impact (Building Block #9) into value(s) creation (Building Block #10). And here we mean multiple value(s) creation rather than only financial value, which is the focus of most linear business models.

It is important to clarify the impact of your business model. This can be in a general sense, but also focused on specific stakeholders, a raw material, or a specific context. Even the most *advanced* companies can find this complicated. It is quite challenging to indicate whether and to what extent impact is part of a strategy and core activities. In short, there is a lot to be done.

Impact is about the short- and long-term effects of your sustainable business model. What are the positive and negative consequences of your business model, now and in the future? You can measure the effect of your business model in three successive stages: the concrete output of your production or services (the direct result), the outcome (medium-term environmental effects), and the impact (lasting long-term effects).

Example

The Fruitmotor Cooperative (De Fruitmotor)

The Fruitmotor Cooperative processes leftover fruit from fruit growers from the Betuwe (a region in the heart of the Netherlands where a lot of fruit is grown) into ciders and juices. The revenues from these products are used to increase the sustainability of the Betuwe fruit cultivation. Fruit growers and other supply-chain partners, as well as interested citizens, can become members of the cooperative. The Fruitmotor's output—the juices and ciders—are for sale in shops and catering establishments within and outside the region. The outcome is that fruit growers can invest annually in sustainability thanks to the revenues from what used to be considered a waste product. The intended impact is an increase in biodiversity, enhancement of the landscape, and improvement of soil, air, and water quality (De Fruitmotor, www.defruitmotor.nl).

In the development of your business model idea and starting a new venture you are likely to have already thought about the ultimate impact you want to have. You can think of impact as the concrete translation of your Dream (Building Block #2) through a Proposition (Building Block #3). What will truly change significantly when your dream is fulfilled, and what does this mean for the design of your business model? It is important to formulate your intended impact as specifically as possible. It is also worth anticipating what you as a start-up, or as a company, may be held accountable for and within what timeframe. After all, making the impact you want often takes time. For a sustainable business model, it is necessary to determine which positive impact you aim for, whether there are possible negative impacts, and how these two interrelate. Reflecting on your impact and seeking to measure your impact right from the start will enable you to continuously monitor whether you are still on your intended track as your idea evolves or your venture grows.

11.2 Quantifying Impact

To determine the impact of your business model idea, we recommend you choose a number of relevant indicators—these will also enable you to measure and monitor your ongoing impact. We suggest you identify indicators primarily for yourself and the partners with whom you realize the business model; after all, you stand for the product or service with which you will seek to make a difference. Secondarily, identify indicators for customers, governments and other parties to show the relevance of your business model. Transparency and clarity regarding the impact of your business model will enable you to approach investors. But you also do this exercise because there are *silent* parties such as nature that you may affect—which are important to be aware of.

Extensive, but also complex sets of indicators are, for example, the EU indicators for circular economy (Eurostat, n.d.a) and the UN SDGs (Eurostat, n.d.b)—see www.ec.europa.eu/environment/sustainable-development/strategy/monitoring/index_en.htm. One widely used indicator, for example, is reducing CO_2 emissions—this can be planned, measured, and monitored.

The main point is that you translate the wide array of indicators that exist into a set of indicators that fit your business model, such as the examples for the carpet tile manufacturer Interface in Fig. 11.1. The more concrete and measurable your indicators, the easier it will be to communicate your impact with other parties.

We recommend that you use a common method like SMART to test your indicators. SMART stands for Specific, Measurable, Achievable, Relevant, and Time-bound. A brief explanation is presented below that you can find in the public domain (Wikipedia), but there are dozens of variants and elaborations in circulation if you want to know more:

Key Points

- *Specific*: Is the objective of the indicator in question unambiguous?
- *Measurable*: Under what conditions is the desired (measuring) goal achieved? The indicator must, therefore, be able to indicate (1) where you currently are and (2) what the intended goal is.
- *Achievable*: Is the indicator achievable for all relevant stakeholders, but also, for example, for the natural and biological environment?
- *Relevant*: Is the indicator relevant in relation to the goal you want to achieve? Make sure not to narrow down the goal too much so that the validity of the indicator is maintained.
- *Time-bound*: When (in time) must the identified measuring target be reached? The question is also whether the indicator shows the current situation fast enough.

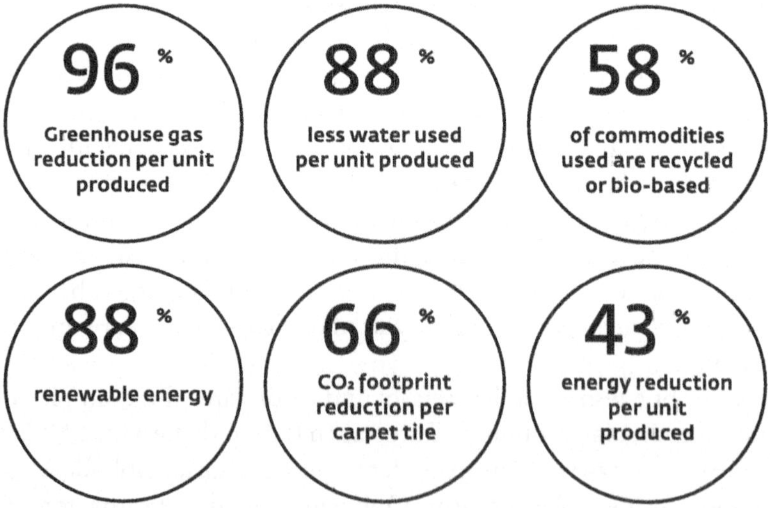

Fig. 11.1 Impact indicators—Interface

After you have defined the indicators, you determine the measurability of those indicators, as well as the method you will use to report on them. Keep a keen eye on the practical feasibility, as well as the costs involved in measuring and reporting. Also, consider when your impact will become visible and measurable. What impact can and may you be judged on in three years? In five years? In ten?

Of course, you want to have a positive impact with your business model, but it is important to also identify the possible negative impacts. You use the same indicators for this. Perhaps it will turn out that the impact is neutral: then the long-term effect of your business model will be neither positive nor negative.

If it turns out that your business model could lead to an actual negative or neutral impact, take a good look at the design of your business model. Can you reverse the expected negative impact? Can you perhaps compensate for the negative impact? If the negative impact seems insurmountable, it makes sense to go all the way back to the Design Stage of the BMT.

Example

How to Overcome a Negative Impact?

In the *Groene Woud*, the triangular area between the Dutch cities of Eindhoven, Den Bosch and Tilburg, the local government authorities have encouraged individuals and companies to plant old varieties of tall fruit trees. The trees were made available free of charge because they enhance the cultural landscape and biodiversity. After a number of years, there was an abundance of fruit. After many fruit snacks and stomach aches from the apple pies, the apples and pears were put on the roadside in a crate for others to help themselves. But even then the harvest was still too abundant, resulting in food waste as a negative impact. To address this negative consequence, an initiative was developed to enable people to use mobile juice presses at several locations in the area to create juice (which can last for up to two years before it needs to be consumed) and therefore avoid food waste (Het Groene Woud, www.hetgroenewoud.com).

It can be difficult to quantify the impact of an organization or a business model idea. A good start is to brainstorm by going through the previous building blocks to think about relevant indicators. What is the difference you want to make as an organization? Which parties can you cooperate with to achieve this? Which activities will contribute to the realization of the chosen strategy? Use the answers to these questions to choose appropriate impact indicators and start formulating your impact statement. It can still be adjusted and updated afterwards. As an organization, do you mainly want to increase your social impact? Which social indicators apply then? How can you take a first step towards making this impact quantifiable?

Tip

It is useful to expand on your (intended) impact in a statement. For example: 'We choose a platform business model because ...' or 'This business model has a social impact because it directly contributes to the social inclusion of ...'.

11.3 Case Studies: Impact

Case Study: WashingGreen

WashingGreen provides a concept for the hotel industry to wash linen with LCO_2. Water is essential for the conventional laundry process. It is used as a *solvent* for the detergent and as a means of transport for removing dirt from the wash. However, the use of water is superfluous when washing with LCO_2. This means a reduction in water consumption of 100%. This process simultaneously reduces energy consumption and the CO_2 footprint, and thus the operational costs.

Case Study: Litterati App

Picking up litter is what Dirk Groot of the Zwerfinator does (see zwerfinator.nl). That does not sound very exciting, because everyone can do it. But the different and smart thing in this case is that Groot maps all the waste he collects in the Litterati app. Everyone can see where companies or stores leave their waste. Groot confronts companies with this data and asks for a solution. For example, he collected a particularly large amount of plastic wrappers from Antaflu cough drops and shared this discovery with the producer. And it worked. From 2020 the company will wrap the drops in paper (www.voordewereldvanmorgen.nl an initiative of the ASN Bank).

Case Study: Jumbo Supermarket

Founded in 1921, Jumbo has grown into the second largest supermarket chain in the Netherlands and has also opened its first stores in Belgium. In 2021 they

Fig. 11.2 Impact reduction—Jumbo Supermarket

have a market share of 21%, 687 branches, and over 60,000 employees. Being a company of this size brings serious responsibilities when it comes to packaging. To address this they have developed a companywide reduction programme to reduce their waste and plastic footprint. Their aim is to reach a 20% reduction in packaging waste by 2025 through using 20% less packaging material, 100% recyclable packaging (which is often also reusable), plastic packaging consisting of an average of 35% recycled and/or bio-based plastics, less fossil materials, and cardboard or paper packaging made of recycled material as much as possible, or else 100% FSC-certified, as well as offering more sustainable choices. Figure 11.2 shows how Jumbo addresses the various packaging areas.

'Jumbo is fighting packaging waste by packaging less and better and by minimizing our waste flows' (www.jumbo.com).

Case Study: Eendenkroos

It was decided that a selection of ecological indicators for the process of growing duckweed would be used based on the *ReCiPe* model from the *Life Cycle Analysis* method, because they are specifically suitable for measuring and formulating ecological impact (National Institute for Public Health and the Environment, 2019). The selected indicators are the degradation of tropospheric ozone (the greenhouse gas emissions CO_2, methane, and nitrogen), human toxicity (health risks), water and land use and terrestrial ecotoxicity (decrease in biodiversity), and fossil/renewable fuels (energy consumption). These indicators are applied to the following points in the production process:

the recycling of CO_2 and the use of manure from local farmers as a nutrient for duckweed, and the transport of manure and duckweed from the growing location. They are also used to gain insight into the desired ecological results: the use of duckweed as a substitute for soy in animal feed.

Case Study: Bread Bags

How simple can it be? You all know them: the plastic bags you put your bread in at the supermarket. Marie-José de Zeeuw from IJsselstein devised an alternative with her citizens' initiative *BROOD-nodig* (Dutch for *much needed*): a bread bag made of cotton, which will last for a long time. In this way, she wants to put an end to single-use plastic packaging. Already after two years around 5,000 bags have been distributed among 80 shops and 30 municipalities. De Zeeuw says that her initiative will save around 500,000 plastic bread bags per year (www.voordewereldvanmorgen.nl, an initiative of ASN Bank).

Case Study: Mealworms

The core activity of our business model is the cultivation of mealworms as an addition to animal feed. As a result, we contribute to the reduction of CO_2 emissions (because of less feed) and less deforestation due to soy cultivation. More than 90% of the soy that we eat is *hidden* in meat, eggs, and dairy. We also create new jobs by stimulating mealworm farms. In addition, we satisfy a growing protein requirement through the cultivation of mealworms. The world population will grow from 7 to 9 billion in the coming decades. The protein requirement in the world is even expected to increase by 60–90%. Based on the number of tons of mealworms sold and the nutritional value they have, we specifically want to calculate how much soy has actually been replaced. Through our activities, we expect to contribute to 7 of the 17 SDGs set by the UN: (2) No starvation, (3) Good health and wellbeing, (9) Innovation, (12) Responsible consumption and production, (13) Climate action, (15) Living in rural areas, and (17) Partnership to achieve goals.

Case Study: Krijg de Kleertjes

Every parent knows how fast children grow and that it is almost impossible to keep buying clothes that fit. That is why four mothers set up *Krijg de Kleertjes*: a network in which parents can exchange children's clothing—not only physically, for example at someone's home, but also online. In this way, parents do not have to buy expensive new clothes again and again. That saves a few pennies, but it is also a lot better for the environment. At the end of 2017, *Krijg de Kleertjes* calculated that after five years the network had reused an estimated 10,000 kilograms of clothing, saving enough CO_2 to drive around the globe 12 times (www.voordewereldvanmorgen.nl, an initiative of ASN Bank).

Case Study: Bea the Bee

This case revolves around the recycling of plastic waste in order to develop education packages about DIY insect hotels which are sold to schools. To determine the impact of insect hotels and the education package, we have chosen the following indicators: (1) The weight of plastic recycled, (2) The number of insect hotels sold, (3) The number of people (children, parents, local residents) reached with this message. The education package has an impact on children and stimulates them to actively look for naturally occurring materials that they can fill their DIY insect hotel with. The educational materials that are supplied with the hotel, and the possibility of putting theory into practice immediately, creates awareness among children of both the plastic problem and how they can contribute to fighting the decline of insects. Ultimately, we would like to know the number of bees and insects that will benefit from the insect hotels, but we are unsure whether measurement is actually feasible.

11.4 Assessment and Impact Reporting

Indicators are increasingly linked to measuring and reporting methods, which are frequently internationally established. These methods often present their own sets of sometimes complex indicators that one is often required to use. This means that there may already be an assessment or reporting method that you can (or perhaps even must) use, whether in part or in full. The (compulsory) application of established reporting methods could mean that conflicts arise between indicators that you have chosen yourself and indicators in the assessment and reporting methods that, for example, are used by a government. This context makes it all the more important to investigate what you could be held to account for in your own business model well in advance. Some examples of commonly used assessment and reporting methods are shown in Table 11.1. These may help you determine whether you can use any existing reporting methods.

Table 11.1 Examples of impact assessments and reporting methods

Measurement methods	Instruments
Impact	**Life Cycle Analysis** www.rivm.nl/en/life-cycle-assessment-lca/recipe www.pre-sustainability.com/ www.youtube.com/watch?v=cYOC8_jJcII
	Social Return on Investment www.socialvalueuk.org www.avance-impact.nl/nl/publicaties www.avance-impact.nl/av2015/content/uploads/2016/02/Impact_First_longread-definitief-bijgewerkte_afbeelding.pdf
Reporting methods	**Global Reporting Initiative** www.globalreporting.org
	Reporting 3.0 reporting3.org
	ISO 26000 mvonederland.nl/iso-26000/wat-is-iso-26000
Integrated Reporting	integratedreporting.org/

Applying these methods individually or in combination with each other remains challenging in practice. After all, novel and sustainable business models are developed within the existing, highly monetized society. Your new or modified business model will, therefore, always face financial requirements, and associated accounting and reporting systems. Not infrequently, this means that your efforts to create other values with your business model are eventually evaluated from a linear accounting perspective. Here we strongly advocate for the use of multiple indicators (not just financial indicators) so that you are not forced to monetize by definition. We are talking about clean air, promoting biodiversity, or, at a higher abstraction level, striving for a restorative and regenerative economy, not to mention promoting happiness.

11.5 Keep It Simple

We have come to the end of a challenging chapter addressing an important building block: Impact. While it is relatively easy in the process of selecting indicators to keep refining by adding things, before you know it you will have created a maze of indicators and sub-indicators. The question remains as to whether you or your team actually understand precisely what those indicators measure, whether measurements are feasible in practice, and how these indicators are related. Identifying proper and useful indicators and measuring and monitoring them is easier said than done. For those of you who want to explore the complexity of indicators in greater detail, we refer you to the European Commission's Sustainable Development Indicators: www.ec.europa.eu/environment/sustainable-development/strategy/monitoring/index_en.htm.

Whatever you do, stick to the motto *Keep it simple*. Fewer indicators is more, as long as they cover the key impacts you want to demonstrate. For additional orientation, also look at how other companies or projects have dealt with this question. Then develop your own indicator dashboard, and first and foremost test it. So this is an additional external test after Building Block #8—External Test, and may cause you to revisit earlier steps and building blocks in the Design and Definition Stages. So be it—the BMT is intentionally an iterative process.

References

De Fruitmotor. (n.d.). *De Fruitmotor*. Retrieved on 19 May 2019 from: www.defruitmotor.nl/.

Eurostat. (n.d.a). *Indicators Eurostat: Which indicators are used to monitor the progress towards a circular economy?* Retrieved on 19 May 2019 from: ec.europa.eu/eurostat/web/circular-economy/indicators.

Eurostat. (n.d.b). *Indicators Eurostat: SDG indicators: Goal by goal*. Retrieved on 19 May 2019 from: ec.europa.eu/eurostat/web/sdi/indicators.

Het Groene Woud. (n.d.). *Sappig – Puur, (h)eerlijk sap…uit Het Groene Woud | Het groene woud*. Retrieved on 19 May 2019: from www.hetgroenewoud.com/initiatieven/sappig—het-groene-woud-vruchtensapp.

Het Groene Woud-ei. (n.d.). *Home – Het Groene Woud-ei*. Retrieved on 19 May 2019 from: www.groenewoudei.nl.

National Institute for Public Health and the Environment. (2019, June 16). *LCIA: Het ReCiPe model*. www.rivm.nl/en/life-cycle-assessment-lca/recipe.

12

Value(s) Creation

Thuisafgehaald—a home cooking peer-to-peer meal service—is in business with the aim of creating a better world. Our social goal comes first, but we apply business principles in our approach. We define profit in broader terms than just financially. Our profit consists of the social and sustainable added value that we offer to society. *Thuisafgehaald*, www.thuisafgehaald.nl.

Granny's Finest is a slow fashion label that contributes to the social participation of senior citizens. With all our products being handmade from natural, reused, and certified materials, we work on greater social cohesion, preservation of craftsmanship, and a sustainable world. This makes you feel good. *Granny's Finest*, www.grannysfinest.com.

We at *Gasunie* are in the business of extracting and distributing natural gas. For each of the six forms of capital (financial, manufactured, intellectual, human, social & relational, and natural), our value creation model shows how we use these to achieve our strategic objectives. It also visualizes the values we create through our core activities and what impact these have. *Gasunie*, www.gasunie.nl.

Next to taking care of people and the environment in the countries of origin, we also take a critical look at our packaging, the production process, waste, and transport. By working closely with the producers, we not only improve our coffee and tea but also the living and working conditions of the workers. *Simon Levelt*, www.simonlevelt.nl.

Taxi Electric is actively recruiting drivers among […] people over 50. We offer any service-oriented and friendly driver a chance to come and work for us. Never before has nature faced such hard times. Therefore, we drive solely

J. Jonker and N. Faber, *Organizing for Sustainability*,
https://doi.org/10.1007/978-3-030-78157-6_12

electrical vehicles charged with green electricity. That is our contribution to a healthy city. *Taxi Electric*, www.taxielectric.nl.

De Nederlandsche Bank [the Dutch National Bank] states that the financial sector is also confronted with social and environmental risks. The sector can play a key role in working with true value and true pricing: monetizing external costs and being aware of multiple value creation. This not only concerns financial developments and results but also ecological and social effects. *National Network MVO (Corporate Social Responsibility—CSR), The Netherlands*, www.mvonederland.nl.

The three pillars (People First, Living our Values, and Develop for the Future) reinforce the most relevant topics for our people: (1) an environment in which everyone can grow, perform and succeed, (2) an environment where people feel they belong and have their voices heard, (3) an environment where people can develop themselves to be fit for the future. Ultimately, we want to create a fulfilling employee experience and become an employer of choice. *Arcadis*, www.arcadis.com .

12.1 Everything Is a Transaction and Has Value

With this chapter, we have arrived at what we consider to be the most challenging building block of the BMT, Building Block #10—Value Creation. A business model provides a logic for value creation (see Chapter 2) that is translated into a proposition (see Chapter 5). Transactions in turn are the operational acts that demonstrate an appreciation of the value created between parties, while also realizing it. For this reason, they are also considered the actual moment to *settle* within a value creation process.

A key assumption is that you normally pay for what you buy. Consequently, we can say from this perspective that our society is designed based on an endless flow of transactions—large and small, day in and day out—which we usually complete financially. However, while not mainstream yet, in addition to financial settling, other forms of settling may be more appropriate under certain circumstances depending on the nature of the value(s) being created.

Here we make an explicit distinction between the *value bearer* and the *transaction medium*, for example, money and the transaction itself. Money is a unit of account, a medium of exchange, or a store of value. In contrast, a transaction is an action between parties.[1] In the dominant prevailing economic context, a transaction translates as a payment in cash or the receipt of money.

We construct our existence with transactions. We do this constantly, consciously and unconsciously, sometimes with lots of meaning but at times inconspicuously, and also over varying time spans (long- and short-term). Transactions are translated into daily activities, such as buying a loaf of bread, paying for a haircut, a car, a house or the electricity and water you use at home. Those transaction processes continue throughout our day—often just between two parties, sometimes with multiple parties.

All this leads to a dynamic mix of transactions between people (C2C), between people and governments (C2G and G2C), between people and companies (C2B and B2C), between companies themselves (B2B), between companies and governments (B2G and G2B), and between governments (G2G). We call this economy. So, there are transactions in all shapes and sizes, with large and small impacts. Because it is not always clear what the transactions are and how these can be used in the context of sustainable business models, it makes sense to rank them in order. Therefore, in this chapter we present a typology of transactions and related PSS strategies, which in turn we link to the concept of multiple (hybrid) values (e.g. sales, take-back, deposit, rent and use). What we want to explain as clearly and as unambiguously as possible is how multiple value(s) creation can be achieved within and through a broad variety of transactions.

12.2 Speaking of Transactions

Anyone who thinks superficially about the word *transaction*, certainly in an organizational or business environment, quickly interprets that concept as an agreement in which goods, whether or not in combination with services, are exchanged based on monetary valuation (in mutual comparison). This exchange contains both a valuation and, often, a change in ownership. This turns transactions into the operational acts that demonstrate an appreciation of the value created between parties, while also realizing it. As outlined earlier, this can be done bilaterally between two parties, or multilaterally between several parties.

[1] It is worth noting that there are many other meanings attributed to the word *transactions,* for example law (notably criminal law), IT, trade, and sociology, which go beyond the scope of the BMT and therefore we will not expand on here.

For transactions to run smoothly and efficiently, we need to regulate and organize them together. Based on a long history, a dominant monetized transaction system has come to exist. We express our appreciation of a good or service through a sum of money. A transaction is the exchange mechanism that regulates the valuation of a good or service between parties. In other words, it is the sum that changes hands in exchange for a product or service. It also means that we pay for what we want to have but also to meet the demand of the other party. After all, we buy a loaf of bread (after which we own it), but we also purchase the services of the hairdresser, after which we *own* a haircut. These are of value because we can satisfy our appetite or look better. Transactions are the foundation of revenue models, regardless of the nature of those transactions. However, the transaction does not reveal the value exchange (or its nature) itself, nor whether the exchange is just and correct. This raises the question of whether everything can or should be expressed in monetary terms.

Transactions and Externalities

The common implicit logic of business models leads to a valuation of transactions that is monetized, which almost automatically leads to revenue models. By doing that, we express what we find of value in money. This is certainly practical, but at the same time, it means that values that are excluded from the revenue model do not count and thus actually disappear. Monetizing only partially expresses appreciation. There remains a part that is not or is insufficiently valued, or does not need to be valued. This phenomenon is known as an *externality* or *externalizing*. An externality is any form of value (or loss of value) that is disregarded in financial transactions and therefore does not count (see, for example, Buchanan & Stubblebine, 1962). Many *unsustainable* business models are based on externalizing costs. This means that underpayment of labour or the destruction or pollution of nature is not included in the (final) price. So, we have an economy based on partial pricing. We do not pay what a product or service really costs at the checkout. But someone, or, eventually, nature has to pay that price in the end. Solutions such as *true pricing* (see www.trueprice.org) try to do something about this.

Inclusivity and Hybridization

The almost fully automatic monetization of transactions in society leads to social and economic exclusion. After all, people who do not have access to money cannot participate in economic transactions—they are excluded from the system. We believe that inclusivity can be enabled by developing business models and subsequently transactions whereby multiple kinds of value(s) are exchanged simultaneously—not just financial ones. We call this *hybridization* of transactions and thus of revenue models. However, the possibilities of arriving at a different settlement in a transaction, let alone a settlement based on more than one value, are limited in the current institutional context. Despite these institutional blocks, other settlements are not inconceivable. Many alternatives are possible... why not pay with a mix of money and time, car use and cooking skills? These *hybrid transactions* enable participants to deploy multiple transaction mediums simultaneously. Consider, for example, the exchange of time, energy, mobility, care, food, or even accommodation.

Thinking in terms of financial transaction instruments is insufficient if we are to address environmental and social externalities. Alternative, more comprehensive systems are needed, for example hybrid transaction systems, in which different transaction mediums can be used both simultaneously and in combination without prior monetization. Such a system makes it possible to trade with multiple values now and in the future. Moreover, a hybrid transaction system could enable participation in society for a large group of people who currently operate on the periphery.

A hybrid system promotes, among other things, a local, direct and participatory form of economy, and thus fosters inclusivity. It also makes it possible to deploy and utilize competencies and overcapacity. In the context of the BMT, this means that you have the opportunity to design your business model underpinned by hybrid transactions. Not everything needs to be expressed as money in revenue models and transactions. But what does that mean in practice? Next we will present this idea as a typology of transactions and revenue models.

12.3 Typology of Transactions and Revenue Models

Business and revenue models are often spoken of as if they mean the same thing, which is not the case. As discussed in Chapter 2, business models describe how an organization or a community creates value and for whom. Revenue models on the other hand are part of value creation and show for whom it is generating values. In this book we focus on the generated multiple values, which may be hybrid in nature. We make a distinction between *traditional* (monetized and thus single-value) revenue models and *new* revenue models generating multiple values simultaneously. Traditional revenue models only address monetary turnover, and refer to turnover and margin based on financial transactions. Traditional revenue models offer the opportunity to work smarter and more efficiently to reduce costs or to increase the market share and, consequently, the turnover.

The most conventional form of financial transactions involves either buying a product or renting a service (temporarily). When purchasing a product, the transfer of ownership is central. Think, for example, of buying a meal, a bike, or a toaster. In contrast, renting the provision of a service is central. For a certain fee, you can use a service for a pre-agreed period of time, and ownership remains with the lessor. Examples are renting a holiday home, power tools for the garden, or a lane at a bowling alley. Tukker (2004) has arranged these traditional transactions in his overview of product–service systems—see our discussion of platform business models in Chapter 6—Business Model Archetypes. In Tukkers' (2004) model a key difference is how ownership of products is organized. In *product-oriented business models*, the transfer of ownership is central to the transactions. *Use-oriented business models*, on the other hand, are based on the principle of lease and rent whereby the revenue is linked to a payment for a certain period of use. Finally, in *result-oriented business models*, the ownership of the product stays with the party that makes functionality available, with earnings linked to a unit of use.

In addition to these conventional revenue models, we believe that other new revenue models can underpin the business models developed by using the BMT. We distinguish two new revenue models: (1) cascade models and (2) hybrid models.

The first group of revenue models concerns cascade models. The essence of these models is that the value(s) are stacked in a loop. The various parties in this loop make mutual agreements as to how they distribute cumulative value creation among themselves.

Then there is a group of revenue models in which the transaction medium(s) are hybrid. In such revenue models, the link with money is abandoned as much as possible—and, if possible, completely. This means that you can pay with more than just money (simultaneously and in combination), or within a specific community you could agree to stop paying with money at all. This variation would offer several tax benefits, one of which being that transactions which do not involve money cannot be taxed. Either way, these different revenue models together form the basis for a typology, of which the basic structure is shown in Fig. 12.1.

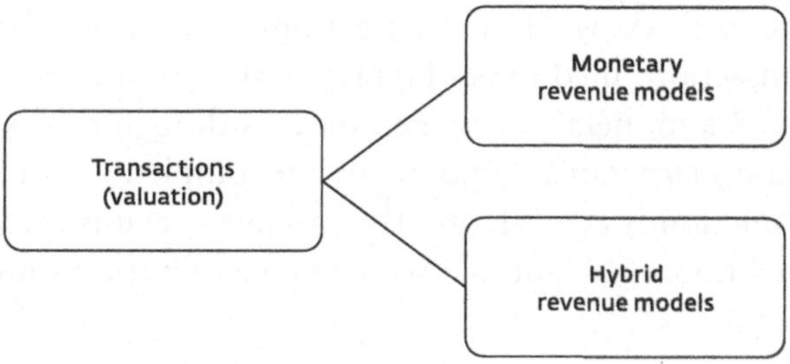

Fig. 12.1 Revenue model typology

To Have or Not to Have, That is the Question

The basis for further elaboration of a typology of business models is actually fairly simple: to have or not to have. In concrete terms, this means that a transaction can either involve ownership transfer or focus on the use of a function of a device or installation. So, you buy a car (and then it is yours with all rights and obligations), or you lease a car (where you also have rights and obligations but not the ownership). This distinction divides monetary transactions and (non-monetary) hybrid transactions.

Conventional revenue models show how monetary revenue is generated. In turn, monetary transactions show a wide range of types of revenue models. The oldest known model involves the transfer of ownership. When such a transaction generates more or another type of turnover (which is possible with a cascade model because more monetary transactions are added to one product), it is also possible to speak of a new revenue model.

Here we present an illustrative summary:

- Sale of product, part, or raw material; transfer of ownership
- Transfer of ownership (sales) of equipment for a specified period (with a buy-back guarantee)
- Sale of a product with a buy-back (or take-back) guarantee); temporary transfer of ownership
- Sales of product and related services (maintenance, advice, insurance, repair, training); transfer of ownership with rental component
- Transfer of ownership of equipment for a specific period with related service
- Sales of a total solution including service; transfer of ownership with a rental component.

Hybrid transactions show how transactions take place based on non-monetized transaction mediums. Hybrid transactions, therefore, do not necessarily *embed* a monetary revenue model, although this is possible. This leads to a preliminary (and undoubtedly incomplete) overview in which selling of the function is central, and the producer retains ownership.

Below we mention a few out of a whole range of business models based on PAAS:

- Sale of use, access to a product or function; rent per period, per performance
- Sale of performance or function of the product; rent per function of the unit
- Sale of an (integral) device
- Use by means of a deposit or security; rent per product
- Cascade model: stacking of earnings, mixed or otherwise
- Exchange based on hybrid values; simultaneous use of multiple transaction instruments.

Combining the nature of different transactions with the possibilities of using products, services, or a combination of both in a business model creates a rich spectrum of both monetary and hybrid transaction models. We have attempted to express this visually in Fig. 12.2.

The last section in this overview also gives an impulse to characterize the nature of the value. We propose a five-way division that ranges from the traditional zero-value (the usual depreciation model), through residual value (the ambition of the circular economy), through deposit (which is actually a

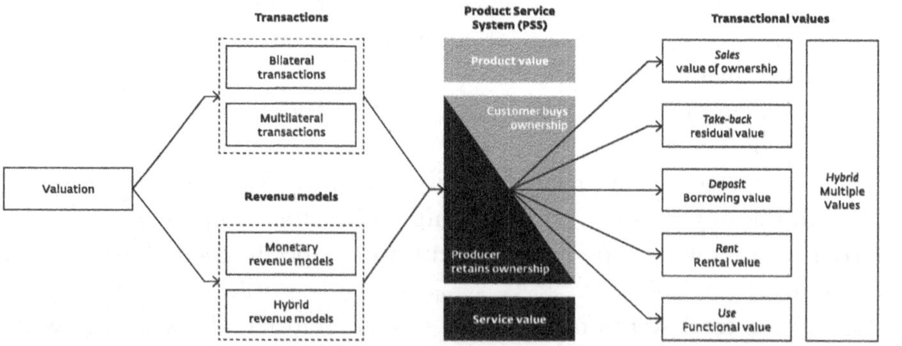

Fig. 12.2 Typology of the link between transactions, service, and multiple values

form of loan value) to functional value (the core of PAAS), and ultimately to multiple values in the context of hybrid transactions.

12.4 Bartering, Time Banks, and Hybrid Transactions

Experimenting with non-monetary transactions does not come automatically or naturally as we are so used to monetary transactions. That said, people do enter into transactions (assigning value to items or services) with each other *without* using money. Moreover, when we reflect critically on our daily lives, there are many things that we hardly use, or maybe no longer use at all which we would be willing to give or share with others without necessarily always receiving something in return. A car that sits parked in front of the house unused, a great bike that sits unused in a shed, or having surplus food and no fridge/freezer space, or what about being able to use someone else's garden for an occasional afternoon if you do not have a garden yourself? This list is endless. However, it does require that you know who wants what, what is available, and vice versa.

We already engage in these forms of hybrid transactions organically through our families and close social networks. And therein lies the rub—given the developments of the IoT, the IoS, the exponential growth of apps, and, last but not least, developments around the use of algorithms, systemizing hybrid transactions beyond our social networks is becoming increasingly possible.

Bartering and Beyond

Exchanging goods or bartering is not new. People have been exchanging goods for other goods for centuries, long before money was invented. It is a form of deal-making, but a key disadvantage is that such bartering can only occur between directly involved parties, and trusting who you are trading with is key. For instance, you have a bike that someone else wants to use for an afternoon, and, in return, they take a look at the website you want to build—you are likely to want your bike returned, and sound advice regarding how to build your website to be satisfied with the deal, making trust important.

A slightly more abstract concept of bartering are so-called *time banks*. Here, after someone has worked for an hour, they choose to get paid in hours that are deposited in their account which they can then use to pay someone else in hours. In this case, everybody's time is valued equally and the transaction unit is *one hour* which can be traded for different services or things—see www.timebanking.org/what-is-timebanking or https://ssir.org/articles/entry/the_time_bank_solution.

The notion of a *community currency* resembles the time-bank concept. These community currencies are at the heart of so-called Local Exchange Trading Systems (LETS). These types of transaction systems are also referred to as complementary currencies. Meanwhile, there are several of them in use. Examples are the WIR Bank in Switzerland, founded in 1934 (www.wir.ch), the Noppes in Amsterdam, or the Bristol or Lewes Pound in the UK (bristolpound.org and www.thelewespound.org). Since 2013, the Cyclos software developed by the STRO (Social Trade Organization) has been available to support communities to develop their own currency at both a local and larger scale (see www.cyclos.org/banks).

Hybrid Transactions

But no matter how charming the colourful collection of possibilities such as bartering, time banks, and community currencies may be, it is usually limited to a charming neighbourhood or regional initiative for and by a relatively small group of people. The dominant economy, meanwhile, remains shaped by money and organizations. Virtually everything we do (or cannot do) depends on whether we have money. Not having much money results in exclusion from economic and social interaction. Both alarming levels of household debt and energy poverty still remain a reality for too many people.

At the same time, we want society to pay more attention to sustainability—to a circular economy. Yet, sustainability, circularity, and inclusivity seem to be three ideals that are challenging to link. However, what if we connect and operationalize these ideals through the idea of *Inclusive* or *Social Banking*? This form of banking is based on a transaction system in which people *pay* with hybrid transactions, with which they create their own (local) economy (Fig. 12.3).

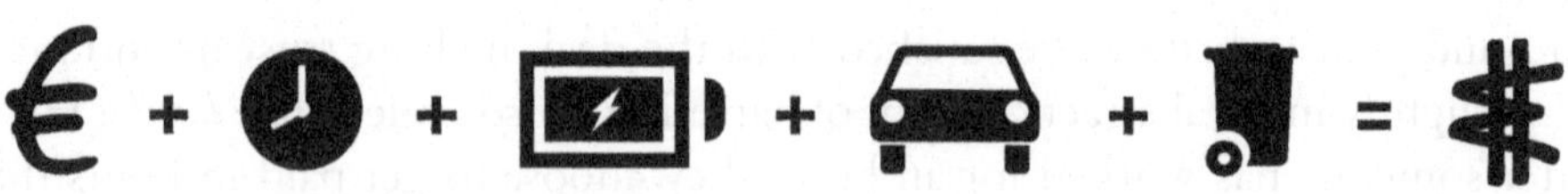

Fig. 12.3 Hybrid transactions

Definition

A hybrid transaction system can be defined as a platform in which transactions are in principle not based on monetized assets, but on, for example, time, points, mobility or energy. People can determine the value of their assets peer to peer (sometimes also called the *process of P2P valuing*) and use them in a transaction that they can design and execute themselves. It is an alternative to the traditional money system, which is based exclusively on monetary transactions between parties.

The idea of hybrid transactions is that other types of value besides money (time, waste, an unused car etc.) can be used and exchanged. This means that people who have enough money can use their time, assets, or skills in exchange for assets that they need. This can enable the inclusion of groups of society that are otherwise excluded from doing transactions.

Using a hybrid transaction system can also lead to a better use of assets, because these assets are not sitting idle or under-utilized. Making use of someone's unused car in exchange for apples from your apple tree leads to more efficient use of existing assets and less waste of perishable products. Furthermore, when you can create more transparency of the assets available in a community, there is less need to buy a product for yourself (think about standing tables for parties, electric screwdrivers, or a book that you can rent, swap or exchange with your neighbour).

This will ultimately mean we can produce fewer things, leading to a positive impact on environmental sustainability and resource use. Thinking about hybrid transactions also leads to interesting new business models, for example local PAAS platforms, selling the use of the product instead of the ownership (functional economy), or local entrepreneurs who can exchange their knowledge and services (cooperative and sharing economy).

All in all, a better allocation of assets, skills, and knowledge by hybrid transactions leads to a more circular and inclusive community. Of course, the question remains of whether and how to implement such a system. For that reason, experiments involving setting up a system around moneyless transactions can be conducted. To better understand how this could work, the following links are to various sources such as a book and two YouTube videos explaining the concept: bit.ly/2J5ZpMe; bit.ly/2VnBDlD; bit.ly/2GGsie9. The overall argument/idea is that hybridizing our transactions is possible and can contribute to the development of a resilient sharing and platform economy based on the principles of the commons. What the exact possibilities are and what impact can be achieved through hybrid transaction systems needs to be further demonstrated in practice.

12.5 What Is the Business Case of Your Business Model?

In addition to the concepts of business models, revenue models, and transaction types, another key term you are likely to encounter is *business case*. It is also common for these terms *business models*, *revenue models*, *transactions*, and *business cases* to be lumped under one umbrella, which can become somewhat confusing. A business case is commonly defined as a financial model demonstrating that a business model is financially viable without additional external funds such as sponsorship, grants, or subsidies. This infers that actually, everything that really matters in a business model can be translated into money, and other forms of value(s) do not count.

The BMT has a different approach. For a sustainable business model, a conclusive business case means that the nature of the transactions is related to the intended impact. It is possible to conceive of business cases based on social considerations that are not financially viable. Such business cases and the associated business models may continue to depend on external support (such as subsidies) to realize social impact. Here you can easily conclude that some business models and their transactions do not generate money, but that they have a right to exist due to their demonstrable social value. This implies that transactions can lead to multiple values—financial outputs being one of them—but also to a broader range of values, such as a liveable environment, mobility, and food.

Important

Instock Market

In the Netherlands, some 2.5 million tons of food are wasted every year throughout the entire food chain. As a result, all agricultural land, water, energy, and CO_2 emissions for production are lost. This has a huge impact on our earth. It's time for change! The United Nations' Sustainable Development Goals have a clear target: halve food waste by 2030. To achieve this, many solutions are needed. One is to facilitate chefs in the catering industry to be able to choose products that would otherwise go to waste (www.instockmarket.nl).

How Do You Shape Transactions in Your Business Model, and What Do You Exchange?

What type of transaction model will you be using within your business model, and why do you make that choice? Is it all about money, or have you developed a model that also includes other values? Sometimes a business model based on money is not workable, while another transaction model offers a solution. Is it possible, for example, to provide part of the funding (per transaction) and financing (long-term investments) with the help of a time bank, energy exchange, waste collection, or the shared use of resources? These are intentionally provocative and challenging questions. After all, our default is to express our transactions in cash almost automatically because it is convenient, but there are other possibilities…

It is also important to reflect on how the type of transactions you deploy will shape your intended impact: can you change the nature of the transactions within your business model in order to stimulate and valorize the impact you want to create? And what additional values and appropriate transactions do you still need to develop your business model further? This approach gives direct insight into how value is added to your business model, using the impact that you will bring about. For example, is it possible to execute part of your activities by exchanging generated electricity for something else? Of course, you need to work out what transactions will look like in such a case, and what technology (maybe blockchain) could support your business model.

12.6 Case Studies: Value(s) Creation

Case Study: Bus tickets or food in exchange for waste—Curitiba (Brazil)

In 1991 the Brazilian city of Curitiba did not have sufficient budget to build a recycling plant, so the local government thought of a way to change the situation. They launched two programmes: (1) Waste that is not waste and (2) Green exchange. The city created a local currency to reward citizens for separating organic and non-organic waste and taking it to the waste stations. In exchange for this service, citizens received an amount of local currency that could be used to buy bus tickets, food, and educational books. The impact on the city was no litter, access to education, and public transport for poor families, which, in turn, created new employment options. The programme resulted in a higher employment level, a cleaner city, a guarantee of food, and social inclusion. https://wwf.panda.org/wwf_news/?204414

Case Study: Bus tickets in exchange for plastic bottles—Surabaya (Indonesia)

In the city of Surabaya in Indonesia, the government has initiated a programme to recycle plastic bottles and increase public awareness. A one-hour bus ride costs three large bottles or ten plastic cups. More than 15,000 passengers are currently using this initiative. They travel for free every week in exchange for collecting plastic and enabling its recycling. www.phys.org/news/2019-08-trash-tickets-indonesia-plastic-bus.html.

Case Study: Exchanging waste for 15 minutes of WiFi connection—Thinkscream (India)

The Thinkscream company created a solution to the waste and internet connectivity problem in India. The smart waste bin provides a WiFi connection in exchange for waste. The moment waste is thrown in the waste bin, a sensor activates the WiFi router. The waste bin offers a code for users to log into the WiFi network. In exchange for waste, users can then use the WiFi connection for 15 minutes. www.youtube.com/watch?v=Jd-54aB5B3M.

Case Study: Exchanging waste for food—Mexico City (Mexico)

A new trade market in Mexico City is helping residents exchange their waste for food vouchers to combat the growing waste problem in the city. The local government subsidizes the local farmers who sell the food and sells the collected waste to recycling plants. In this way, the government hopes to change the population's behaviour and raise awareness of waste recycling. https://edition.cnn.com/2012/06/19/world/americas/mexico-city-barter-scheme/index.html.

Case Study: Plastic bottles in exchange for a bus or metro fare—Atac (Italia)

In Rome, travellers can recycle plastic bottles in exchange for a metro fare. Each bottle has a trade-in value of five cents. By putting it in a deposit machine, they get a discount on a metro ticket. To obtain a *free* metro ticket of €1.50, they have to deposit 30 bottles. www.reuters.com/article/us-italy-pollution-plastic/rome-offers-free-metro-travel-for-plastic-recyclers-idUSKBN1WG3BZ.

Case Study: Exchanging plastic bottles for public transport fares—Incom (China and Norway)

Incom is a Sino-Norwegian partnership that was initiated to promote RVMs and waste recycling solutions. The exchange device scans the barcode of the packaging, identifying the material and weight. The machines are installed in Beijing at such places as public transport locations, supermarkets, and schools, where in exchange for recycled goods, people can earn money to use on public transport in China. www.en.incomrecycle.com.

12.7 Conclusion

If this chapter shows—and teaches us—anything, it is how difficult it is to make multiple value creation concrete. We shape our society based on a never-ending stream of transactions—large and small, day in and day out. We go to the bakery, buy bread, sell a car or a house—some with short-term impact, others with far-reaching consequences, both negative and positive. The nature of these transactions reveals the values we consider important.

Over the past two centuries, we have increasingly left the organization of value creation to companies. Over the years, companies have focused almost exclusively on money as the central and only medium of exchange. In the resulting business models, many costs and revenues (ecological, social, etc.) are excluded. This has created a very lean, rather shabby transaction model based on monetizing. Anything that cannot be converted into euros does not count and is therefore not counted. We need to change this.

The transition requires a generation of both new business models *and* underlying transaction models. We therefore need hybrid transaction models that allow for multiple forms of value creation. Using the dominant medium of exchange unknowingly, and maybe even unwillingly, creates path dependency. As long as money is the dominant medium of exchange, we will lapse into existing monetized routines and behaviour. The goal of sustainable business models is not to generate classic *profit*, but above all, to create a world that makes sense and has value: a world based on what we call collective and shared values where multiple value(s) creation is pursued.

References

Buchanan, J. M., & Stubblebine, W. C. (1962). Externality. *Economica, 29*(116), 371–384. https://doi.org/10.2307/2551386.

Tukker, A. (2004). Eight types of product–service system: Eight ways to sustainability? Experiences from SusProNet. *Business Strategy and the Environment, 13*(4), 246–260. https://doi.org/10.1002/bse.414.

13

Alternative Routes

13.1 Alternative Routes Through the BMT

This book is designed to support you to work through the ten building blocks, which are grouped into the Definition, Design and Result Stages, from left to right and top to bottom. The underlying idea is to develop a business model from scratch by following each step in the BMT system.

From our experience you can easily spend a couple of weeks doing this (but it could take longer depending on the nature of your idea). Not because you spend every hour of every day working on it (although you can do so), but because you also have to take the time to let your business model-to-be sink in. Crucial to the process is looking at your BMT from different angles, getting people to give you constructive feedback on your idea, and, last but not least, getting distance from it and coming back to it with fresh eyes. Taking your BMT through several iterations will help to improve your business model idea step by step.

And remember, you are rarely unique. Somewhere, someone or a group of people is working on the same idea in the same way, or maybe just a little differently. Find out where these people are, contact them, and discuss your ideas. Share your knowledge—on your own, you may be faster, but together you can achieve much more.

J. Jonker and N. Faber, *Organizing for Sustainability*,
https://doi.org/10.1007/978-3-030-78157-6_13

TIP

As we said before, the BMT is by no means the only canvas available. For further inspiration, take a look at www.designabetterbusiness.tools/search?q=canvas. On this site, you will find a large number of other canvasses that may be useful. But be careful not to get waylaid by this search. Constantly ask yourself if the principles underlying a certain tool will help lead to the creation of a sustainable business model.

That said there are many other possible *routes* through the BMT, and next we outline five possible alternatives: (1) Idea-driven, (2) Proposition-driven, (3) Network-driven, (4) Impact-driven, and (5) Competence-driven. To provide you with some inspiration, we will briefly elaborate on each of these five routes with examples. Please note that the texts used for the examples presented are taken almost verbatim from the websites of the various institutions and companies bar slight modifications to improve the readability of the texts. This is intentional because these examples were selected to demonstrate how organizations apply a particular approach in practice. In addition to including the primary source for the example, we also looked for a matching YouTube clip that explains the project (Table 13.1).

Table 13.1 Alternative ways to use or *routes through* the BMT

Approach	Starting Building Block	Comments
Idea-driven	**#1 Motive and Context**	Start from a 'great' idea you have identified to solve a certain issue, around which you further develop the business model.
Proposition-driven	**#3 Proposition**	The value that you want to create for a specific target group is paramount here in the development of your business model.
Network-driven	**#5 Parties**	The network of parties that already exists is the basis for the further development of the business model.
Impact-driven	**#9 Impact**	The impact that you want to achieve is key for the development of your business model.
Competence-driven	**#7 Core Activities**	The things you are really good at are central in the development of your business model.

13.2 Idea-Driven

The idea-driven approach enables you to work through the ten building blocks step by step from top to bottom and left to right—reflecting the format of this book. Starting with a *great* idea you have identified to solve

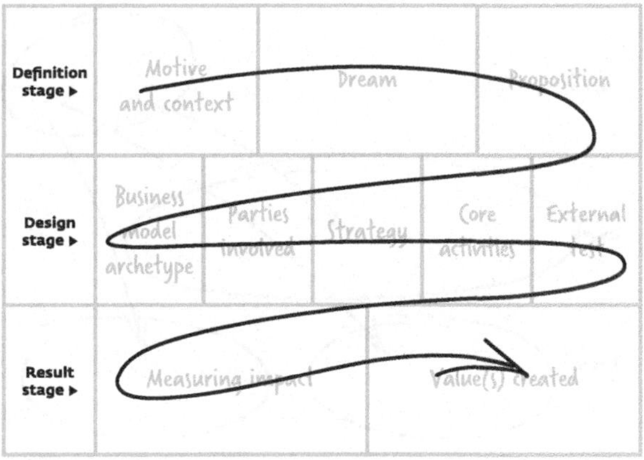

Fig. 13.1 Idea-driven

a certain issue you can use the BMT to systematically go through all the steps to develop a new business model (Fig. 13.1).

Case Study: Seaweed for packaging—Ooho (United Kingdom)

Ooho is a company that has developed the Notpla technology, a material made from seaweed and plants. The material is used for packaging which is edible or biodegrades in four to six weeks. The company is currently building an on-site manufacturing machine to use the Notpla technology for the production of sustainable packaging. From 2021 onwards, the company will lease these manufacturing machines to companies that produce single-use plastics such as nets or sachets. The home-compostable Notpla contributes to a plastic-free world without microplastics.

Website: www.notpla.com
Youtube: www.youtube.com/watch?v=Pj6Q-YCcA3s

13.3 Proposition-Driven

The proposition-driven approach is based on the value that you want to create for a specific target group. The revision of an existing idea, or even an entire business model, is central (Fig. 13.2).

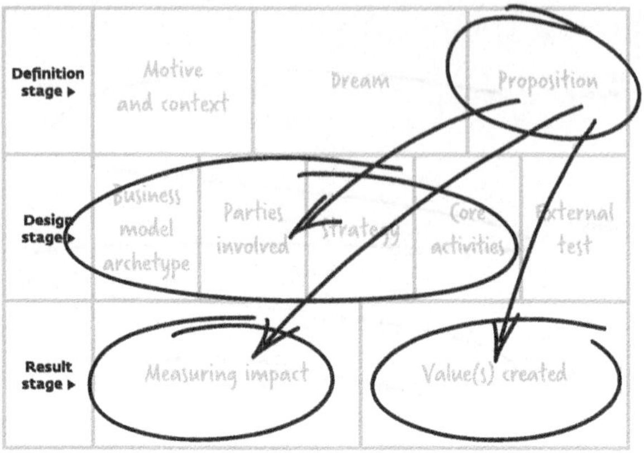

Fig. 13.2 Proposition-driven

Case Study: Recycling sportswear—Adidas and Stuffstr (United Kingdom)

Adidas has launched a new recycling initiative in the UK, entitled *Infinite Play*, in which customers are incentivized to pass on their old sportswear instead of sending it to landfill. Social enterprise Stuffstr, the London Waste and Recycling Board (LWARB), and QSA Partners organize the service which allows customers to trade worn or unused Adidas gear for e-gift cards and Adidas Creators Club loyalty points. By using the Adidas app, the Stuffstr system allows customers to sell back their unwanted clothing for store credit, regardless of condition, creating a closed-loop solution for the fashion industry.

Website: www.stuffstr.com

Youtube: www.youtube.com/watch?v=2LUkcfWE4UQ

13.4 Network-Driven

The starting point of the network-driven approach is a network of parties that want to work together on sustainable innovation with their different (but complementary) core competencies. Here the function of the BMT is to gain insight into the context and the (intended) network associated with it while being mindful of the fact that networks are ubiquitous: many companies want or need to work together.

You develop a BMT for your ideal network. To do so in the Design Stage, you can start with Building Block #5—Parties. Logical as this may sound, it may not be enough. Presumably, you want to involve your existing partners in your business model, but also attract new partners. You may need

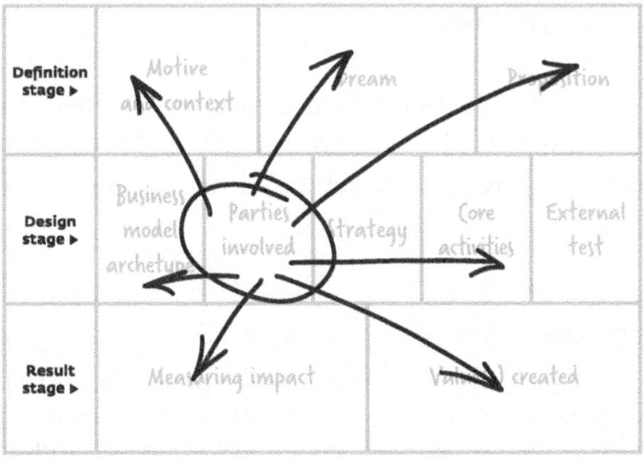

Fig. 13.3 Network-driven

to use an additional instrument to find out what competencies are present in your network and what gaps you need to fill. It may, therefore, be useful to perform a separate network analysis if you adopt this route through the BMT (Fig. 13.3).

Case Study: Net-Works

The central theme of *Net-Works* is making beautiful things out of waste. Net-Works allows residents to collect discarded fishing nets that cause many problems in the marine ecosystem. They are then sold back through a global supply chain, giving these devastating, broken fishing nets a second life as beautiful, durable carpet tiles. The Net-Works programme was driven by a need to do business in an inclusive manner. An inclusive company is a profitable company that creates jobs in low-income communities, either directly or by including a development group in the value chain. Working closely together, stakeholders create a robust business solution that has a positive long-term impact on fresh and saltwater ecosystems, while at the same time providing financial opportunities for some of the world's poorest people. It has a socio-economic and an environmental impact. The Net-Works initiative, which emerged from an unlikely partnership, shows that when the business world, environmental organizations, and communities innovate together, positive and sustainable change can result. To date, the programme has collected 66,680 kilograms of discarded fishing nets and generated enough income for 230,667 meals for local families.

Website(s): www.net-works.com
www.interface.com/APAC/en-AU/about/mission/Net-Works-en_AU
Youtube: www.youtube.com/watch?v=DX6Uidpg3VM&t=5s

13.5 Impact-Driven

The main focus of the impact-driven approach through the BMT is on creating a certain impact. The function of the BMT will therefore support the development of a business model based on a predetermined idea about impact (Fig. 13.4).

Case Study: Dopper

Crystal clear water. In every ocean, from every tap. Isn't that what we all want? Bad news. Every year, 8 million tons of plastic waste ends up in our oceans. This plastic waste does not degrade. Ever. It just breaks down into smaller and smaller pieces. Every minute, a massive amount of plastic ends up in our oceans. And in that very same minute, one million single-use plastic water bottles are sold. Meet the reusable bottle that eliminates the need for single-use water bottles. With a Dopper bottle, you have no excuse to buy single-use water bottles. Doppers are produced sustainably. And yes, most Doppers are made of plastic. But this plastic can be used again and again. Our bottles are available in a variety of materials, colours, and models. And when you don't want it anymore, it can be fully recycled! So whatever style you have, and whatever way you drink your water, there is a Dopper to suit you. Our bottles make the difference. Each bottle sold contributes to our projects, from education programmes and research to inspirational campaigns. What do we do? We inspire. Our worldwide campaigns are spreading the message to stop plastic pollution by encouraging drinking water from the tap. And we are creating, step by step, a movement of change-makers.

Website: www.dopper.com

Youtube: www.youtube.com/watch?v=EUrJECVdw8Y

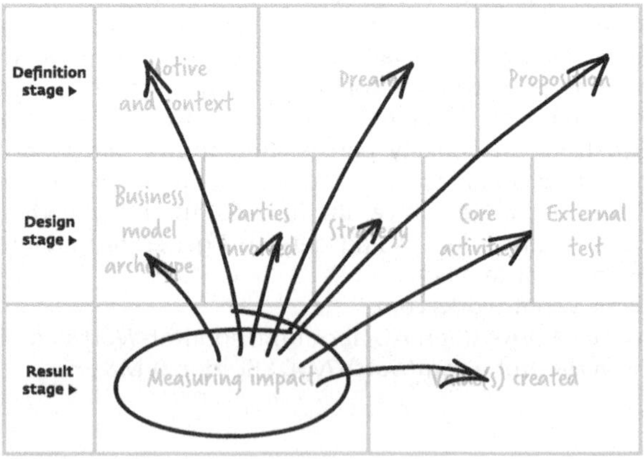

Fig. 13.4 Impact-driven

13.6 Competence-Driven

In the competence-driven approaches available, core activities are key. What can be organized with the already developed core activities in the pursuit of sustainability? Here the function of the BMT is to develop new business models from an existing core activity (Fig. 13.5).

Case Study: Aquafil & Tarkett

Paris, France and Waalwijk, The Netherlands, 21 November 2019—today. Tarkett announces that it is closing the loop on commercial carpet tiles in Europe thanks to a pioneering partnership with Aquafil. This is the result of an intensive collaboration over recent years, going beyond the traditional customer and supplier relationships. Today, the two companies present this significant step towards a circular economy at Tarkett's carpet tile facility in Waalwijk, The Netherlands. Its unique recycling centre creates two streams of materials that can be recycled and transformed into high-quality resources for new products. Tarkett has developed breakthrough technology at its Waalwijk facility. It is now able to separate the two principal components of carpet tiles—yarn and backing—while retaining more than 95% yarn purity.

'Technological innovation now makes it possible to multiply the life cycles of building materials. Together with Aquafil, we are accelerating our circular economy journey and leading our industry's progress in carpet recycling', says Fabrice Barthélemy, Tarkett's CEO. 'This is a fundamental step forward in maximizing the value of materials and preventing carpet tiles from being incinerated or sent to landfill. Truly closing the loop on flooring is a key driver of Tarkett's strategy to preserve natural resources and protect the environment'.

Giulio Bonazzi, Aquafil's CEO, comments: 'We are delighted to help Tarkett with the last mile of its journey to close the loop on carpet tile production. We must urgently transform the way products are designed, produced, and

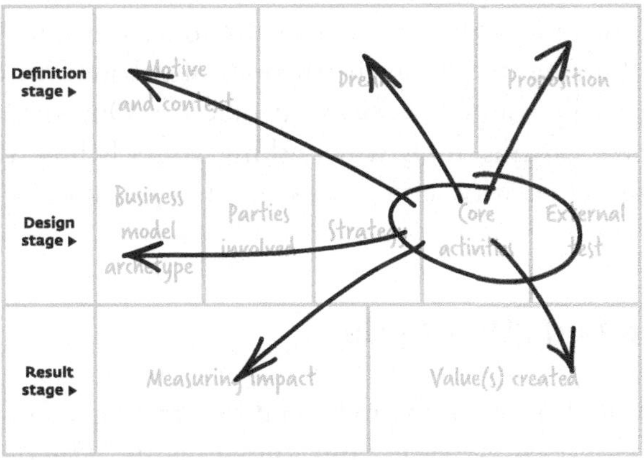

Fig. 13.5 Competence-driven

consumed. Through our collaboration with Tarkett, we will strengthen our commitment to realizing this vision by increasing the reutilization of yarns and helping to design out waste'.

Website: www.aquafil.com/newsmedia/tarkett-and-aquafil-close-the-loop-on-carpet-tiles-a-key-step-towards-circular-economy

Youtube: www.youtube.com/watch?v=uMqVZqmTQI0

13.7 What Route Do You Take?

Do the five routes through the BMT cover all possible routes? No, of course not. Think of the BMT as a box of building blocks for adults from which an endless number of combinations can be made. Ultimately, it is important for all users of the BMT—students, entrepreneurs, and intrapreneurs alike—to determine the most suitable approach or route through the BMT based on your own context and situation. If, for whatever reason, certain building blocks are particularly challenging, additional tools may be required to crystallize that part of your business model.

This point is illustrated by the fact that each of the individual building blocks can themselves be expanded on further. Take, for example, Building Block #2—Dream, and consider using tools and frameworks that are available to support working out your venture's Mission and Vision. Or take Building Block #9—Impact, about which there is still so much more to say, including regarding impact assessment. If you explore impact assessment in greater detail you will soon find yourself in a lively discussion involving both practitioners and academics, each proposing various frameworks and tools. This also applies to developing an understanding of networks (Building Block #5—Parties). Since there are already so many tools available, we have intentionally not elaborated deeply on the theoretical debates in this publication, because we primarily wanted to focus on practice. Our key concern is that you look at these existing tools while asking yourself how they contribute to sustainability, circularity, and inclusivity (see Chapter 1—Speaking of Transition).

Using a Modified PDCA Cycle

That said, there is also something to be said for creating a modified Plan-Do-Check-Act/Adjust (PDCA) cycle (also known as the *Deming Circle* or the *Shewhart Cycle*) and using it to *work* your business model idea. Originally, the PDCA approach stems from the world of quality management. However, the four main steps, (1) Plan, (2) Do, (3) Check, (4) Adjust, can also be applied in the BMT context because the content of these four steps is empty. It is the user's task to operationalize these steps by using, among other things, the earlier-introduced principles, choices regarding the three types of business model, and elaborating on the impact you would like to create with your business model.

14

The Art of Doing

14.1 From the BMT to a Working Business Model

And there you are: in one hand, you have your well-developed brilliant idea for a new company and in the other this book. The purpose of the BMT is to help you turn your idea into a viable project or organization—in whatever form. But where do you start? To be honest, it does not matter where you start, as long as you start somewhere. Pick up the BMT canvas once more and see which of the ten building blocks you think might be easiest to fill in. Sometimes starting is the hardest part—just start with that one building block and work from there, and the rest will follow naturally.

To illustrate this, we will look at two cases of an active/real project's business model using the BMT. Firstly, the KipCaravan project (which is a mobile home—a caravan—for chickens) in the Brainport Eindhoven Metropolitan Area of the Netherlands. Secondly, the Sun at School NSV2 (Zon op School NSV2) project in the city of Nijmegen, the Netherlands. KipCaravan involves low-scale egg production in several locations and the project's BMT is presented below having been worked through in a step-by-step manner from top to bottom and from left to right (Fig. 14.1). The Sun at School NSV2 project involves several parents of pupils at a primary school in Nijmegen who organized themselves to put solar panels on the school's roof. This project used the *round* or *doughnut* version of the BMT in contrast to walking through Building Blocks #1–10 (Fig. 14.2).

J. Jonker and N. Faber, *Organizing for Sustainability*,
https://doi.org/10.1007/978-3-030-78157-6_14

Fig. 14.1 Chicken mobile home case

Fig. 14.2 Sun at School case

14.2 KipCaravan Project

KipCaravan involves low-scale egg production in several locations and the name literally means *chicken caravan/mobile home*. Watch this YouTube video for an overview of the project: youtu.be/VW1QdbWmax4.

Building Block #1—Motive and Context

At a Brainport Eindhoven Metropolitan Region entrepreneurial networking event seeking to connect entrepreneurs in different parts of the region (city versus countryside), a competition was launched. Two entrepreneurs accepted the challenge that same evening. They combined their expertise (poultry farming and multiple value creation—new business models), and the concept—chickens travelling in their small-scale mobile barn (Project KipCaravan, n.d.)—was born. Context is also found in the desire to abandon the compelling cost-leadership strategy of the agricultural sector. The entrepreneurs concerned were tired of producing ever more eggs at an increasingly lower margin.

Building Block #2—Dream

The social enterprise was born out of passion: a poultry farmer's dream. He saw a mobile poultry house in Austria while on vacation and decided that if there were ever an opportunity, he would farm poultry in the same way. The farmer wanted to start keeping poultry again, similar to his parents' mixed fruit and poultry farm.

Building Block #3—Proposition

Essential to this idea is that the chickens are taken to the feed instead of the feed (from abroad) being brought to the chicken. The chickens roam freely under (fruit) trees and produce eggs and meat from food from nature and residual products (lost fruits and grain). The eggs are sold directly in the egg drive, which accompanies the mobile chicken barn. The chickens always travel with their KipCaravan to a new free-range area (fruit farms not owned by the poultry farmer but that he is welcome to let his chickens roam on). The media quickly picked up on this and headlined that the farmer goes on holiday with his chickens. After this, the farmer said: 'Of course, my chickens also deserve a holiday'.

Building Block #4—Business Model Archetypes

When choosing from the three archetypes, a circular business model fits best in the light of the contribution to a circular agro-food system, combined with elements from a community model.

Building Block #5—Parties

Initially, the approach was to purchase a ready-made KipCaravan, but because the existing systems were not sufficient, a KipCaravan was tailor-made with the specific wishes for the concept. The KipCaravans are made by a former agricultural entrepreneur with a handyman business on his former farm.

The poultry farmer's partner is a volunteer involved in a regional product shop. The concept also provides workers (who are patients with an intellectual disability) with an apprenticeship and daytime activity. With the help of the Brabant Outcomes Fund of the Province of Noord Brabant (a Social Impact Bond funded by several charities and Rabobank Foundation), a performance contract has been established for further development of the concept.

Building Block #6—Strategy

Using the direct sale of eggs and valorizing residual products from fruit farms as a feedstock for their chickens, the entrepreneurs want to produce in a future-oriented manner, with the business model taking into account societal issues such as reducing (food) waste and reducing its CO_2 footprint. In other words, a cascading strategy is applied.

Building Block #7—Core Activities

The two core activities are the production of free-range eggs and daytime activities for people with intellectual disabilities.

Building Block #8—External Test

It is a unique approach to free-range chicken rearing. The concept complies with all laws and regulations, which are limited because of the small-scale keeping of animals.

Building Block #9—Impact

The impact of the concept is more substantial than had been anticipated. The entrepreneurs were pleasantly surprised on several counts during implementation. For example, the animals have demonstrably better animal welfare: they grow older, keep their feathers longer, and lay more saleable eggs. Other impacts are a lower CO_2 footprint, more biodiversity, projecting a positive image of the agricultural sector, and the involvement of people who are distanced from the labour market. Possible negative impacts on animal health and safety have been investigated. Measures are taken with the expertise of the poultry farmer (all requirements from the regular sector apply).

Building Block #10—Value(s) Creation

The Kip Caravan concept has several transaction forms. The first form of transaction is conventional and simply based on money. The sale of the eggs covers operational costs. The second form of transaction is based on labour. Patients of healthcare institutions enjoy a novel and meaningful form of daytime activity at the Kip Caravan project as an *assistant farmer*. The third and final transaction form is aimed at generating local tourism: governments are making land available in exchange for attractive activities for people to do.

14.3 Sun at School NSV2 (*Zon Op School NSV2*) Project

The Sun at School NSV2 project involves several parents of pupils at a primary school in Nijmegen, the Netherlands, who organized themselves to install solar panels on the school's roof. This project used the *round/doughnut* version of the BMT in contrast to walking through Building Blocks #1–10. What follows is the order of building blocks that the project participants followed.

Note: You will not find the Sun at School order presented anywhere else in this book. This case illustrates that every project simply follows its own logic, with its own route through the BMT.

Building Block #1—Motive and Context

Just before the bell rings, the parents are waiting in the schoolyard for the children to run outside. They talk to each other, arrange babysitters and playdates for the children, and discuss today's news.

Building Block #3—Proposition

One of the parents observes that the sloping roof of the school building would actually be ideal for solar panels. There is no shade, there are no dormers or chimneys, and there is ample space. Other parents agree, but no one has any idea how to approach this and whether it is worth it.

Building Block #9—Impact

At the request of one of the parents, the school's headmaster finds out how much electricity the building actually uses. This turns out to be much more than expected: the lighting, computers and interactive whiteboards consume as much as 30 households on average: that is 30 × 3,500 kWh. The school uses grey electricity without any green/renewable power. Therefore, solar panels could have a positive impact on the energy bill, the image that parents have of the school, and—even if only a little—climate change. The roof is so large that, in theory, the solar panels could generate one-third of the electricity needed for the school itself. The initiators think that this is sufficient impact to warrant moving forward and start to work out a plan.

Building Block #5—Parties

During a pleasant meeting with some parents, they realize that the people who walk around the schoolyard are not just fathers and mothers. The parents have the most diverse professions and have extensive networks at hand. All kinds of talents that are needed to go from a plan to a project are there—they just have to be mobilized. There is a notary in the sandpit who can help set up a foundation. There is a lawyer at the bike shed who understands liability. A marketer plays soccer with her daughter, and a financial specialist has children in the same group. An illustrator wants to make a colouring page showing the school with solar panels. Everyone knows someone else who can also help.

Building Block #7—Core Activities

The group of initiators further develop the plan to get solar panels installed on the roof. They invite some local suppliers of solar panels and the technology involved to join the meetings. Technically it seems to be perfectly feasible. However, because the school, as a large consumer, purchases electricity together with other schools, it is not automatically possible to supply excess power to the grid. The ability to supply excess power to the grid is a key requirement because the projected solar energy production will be at its peak during the summer holidays when the school uses the least.

Building Block #6—Strategy

The student council thinks it is a good plan and wants to think about fundraising. The headmaster is already enthusiastic, but the school board has not yet been informed. The initiators decide to send an email to the board and approach the municipality to ask if there are any subsidy programmes. Pleased with themselves, they enjoy a glass of wine together.

Building Block #4—Business Model Archetype

By making good use of the diversity in the community, an effective way of working emerges. An initiative group oversees and manages the various aspects of the project, while others work on specific components. A project of this size cannot exist without several leaders.

Building Block #2—Dream

In the schoolyard, the solar panel plan creates a nice dynamic. The people involved dream of an energy-neutral school with class workshops on sustainability and the transition towards renewable energy. Some parents get so excited that they want to use their car to build a smart grid with the school. Moreover, they all share the ideal of a green school that will prepare the children for a sustainable future.

Building Block #8—External Test

The enthusiasm of everyone involved is almost dashed when it turns out that the school board is not in favour of the plan. This is a big downer. All kinds of objections are raised: is the roof strong enough? What if returning power to the grid is not possible or no longer allowed? Who will be responsible if those panels are blown off the roof? Who actually becomes the owner of the installation? The initiative group must go to great lengths to investigate and refute all objections one by one.

Building Block #10—Value(s) Creation

The financing of the system is quite a puzzle. There will be a jumble sale, a benefit drink, and a sponsored run. Parents can buy €50 certificates, with a return of €1 per year and a term of five years. The municipality does not provide a subsidy but does mediate with another funder. The school board eventually gives in and finances the rest. The expected savings on electricity costs go into a fund from which the certificates plus the return will be paid later. A separate foundation is established in which parents, the municipality, suppliers, and the board are represented.

Building Block #9—(Second Iteration) Impact

The project is a great success. The panels are installed and officially put into use with a big school party. Children give workshops on energy saving to parents and the mayor. The local press is present. The panels work well and provide clean power. However, the main impact is in the strengthening of the school network. Suddenly, many more parents know each other, and the children are proud of their solar panels. The project is still being talked about in the district and the city—an unexpected and positive impact on the community.

Building Block #3—(Second Iteration) Proposition

In retrospect, the combination of sustainable energy with crowdfunding and sustainability education is very obvious—particularly at a primary school, where the community meets every day. Why was this not thought of much earlier? It is interesting to ask why it took so long for all these elements to come together.

What the above story makes abundantly clear is that the *Road to Rome* is certainly not a straight line. It both starts and ends with a Proposition. Certain building blocks recur, with impact being perhaps the most important one. It is terrific to see how this process is one of construction, co-creation, and reflection. How, as a result, a group of people connected to the school by their children suddenly join forces and achieve a result that they might not have imagined beforehand.

14.4 The Secret to Success

These examples are, of course, shown in simplified versions. In reality, the steps for the development of, for example, KipCaravan were not completed one by one in a logical and predetermined order. In that respect, a BMT is like a waterbed: pushing on one side will cause something to happen on the other. The trick is to design all the building blocks in such a way that they come together as a logical puzzle. The interpretation of the building blocks is different for every project and every company, and there is no best order in which to stack the building blocks. The more you think about your business model, the more refined the information included in each building block will be. That is perhaps the essence of doing business: having the courage to start without a ready-made recipe. And in retrospect, if your project is successful, you may wonder why you did not recognize earlier that everything fits together so logically and smoothly. And when others ask you that question, you can answer that 'Everything makes sense in hindsight, doesn't it?'

References

Mobiele Pluimveestal Brabant Outcomes Fund [YouTube]. Retrieved on 24 September 2020 from: www.youtube.com/watch?v=VW1QdbWmax4&feature=youtu.be.

Project Kip Caravan (n.d.). *Fladderfarm mobiel*. Retrieved on 9 February 2020 from: www.brabant.nl/subsites/brabant%20outcomes%20fund/media/video/a76ad940db8c478fb64187eb4d5ee2a0.

15

Epilogue

We live in a time of social transition. Institutional arrangements that have been carefully built up in recent decades are under heavy pressure. People no longer colour within the lines. Students take to the streets in protest. Common answers and arrangements are no longer sufficient. Everywhere in society, cracks are appearing. Elected representatives of the people both devise and advocate a reality armed with polarizing facts. The COVID-19 pandemic has highlighted how our *normal* ways of doing things can be upended in a matter of weeks or months.

The only answer to these developments is to organize differently—on our own and with others. That means saying goodbye to linear economies—which are a safe and familiar way of working that we know and have mastered, but which have dark sides we can no longer ignore. Because continuing to abuse the earth, combined with a rising population, will ultimately lead to confrontations: about climate refugees, exhaustion, pollution, weather changes, declining biodiversity, floods, droughts, severe forest fires, and so on. Almost every day we see the effects of this in the news: we can read the background in newspapers and learn more from an ongoing stream of scientific reports, policy briefs and memoranda—the stream of information is endless and is growing exponentially.

Observing this development from a distance, it appears something much more fundamental is at stake. We organize collectively and collaboratively to achieve a broad range of created values which we could not realize individually. That is a timeless argument because all through the history of mankind we have shown that together, we can achieve more. But what is of value changes over time. So now, once again, we are consciously and unconsciously

J. Jonker and N. Faber, *Organizing for Sustainability*,
https://doi.org/10.1007/978-3-030-78157-6_15

trying to discover what these new forms of value creation could look like. This is what transition is all about. We use this word because it fundamentally questions the way we organize ourselves in today's world. There is no manual or standard way forward for this process of (re)discovery—only trial and error. Neither a national government nor Brussels have ready-made answers.

We have argued in this book that the search for new forms of value creation and the *triple transition* necessitates different business models: new business models that create multiple forms of value. This has been described using principles that draw attention to both the social and the ecological side of value creation in business models. As long as the nature of transitions and transactions is not revised, we will remain caught in existing routines and behaviour without being aware of them.

When we superficially *green* what we have, nothing really changes. Doing things differently implies behavioural change, and this may perhaps be the biggest challenge and greatest barrier to achieving a transition to a different, sustainable, circular, and inclusive economy. This book deliberately does not address this issue, however relevant and interesting it may be. Elaborating on the role of behaviour change would lead to a workbook within a workbook, given the nature and size of the change management discourse. It is nonetheless an intriguing question of how the BMT could be used as a change management tool.

15.1 New Models of Organizing

Working with truly new business models will necessitate different organizational relationships: more horizontal and digitally facilitated within networks. The current distinction between citizens and companies is likely to partially disappear or fade away. People are suddenly not just citizens, but also entrepreneurs and self-investors, because they start a solar park or set up a car-sharing system. Call it DIY entrepreneurship, which leads to home-generated electricity, managing an orchard together, or setting up a time bank in the neighbourhood combined with a smart grid: the possibilities really are endless.

However, to realize this, the established order must be tackled first. In the past two centuries, we have increasingly left the organization of value creation to organizations. Over the years, these have functioned almost exclusively with a focus on money as the central and only medium of exchange. In the business models that arise, many costs (ecological, social etc.) are excluded. This has created a very lean transaction model which prioritizes monetization above all else. Anything that cannot be converted into euros is not counted and therefore does not matter.

We need organizations to be jointly responsible for the life cycles of products and services, and thus the organization of the preservation of raw materials. If we want such ecology to work, it is not enough to hold the individual organization accountable for a slightly different, somewhat more sustainable, somewhat less polluting performance. Instead, the focus needs to be on how a configuration of parties bears shared responsibility for the life cycle of a building, a highway, or a raw material (e.g. plastic, concrete, or wood). This requires a different way of thinking and organizing, which is not incorporated into many business models. After all, the existing legal, fiscal, and organizational structure is entirely geared to individual companies that function in a linear value chain. Doing this differently requires a change in people's minds, but also (perhaps first and foremost) a change in the institutional structure.

The major challenge this poses is to shape value creation differently from conventional business models. The ambition is to achieve value creation that is simultaneously sustainable, circular, and inclusive. Working on this means revising (1) the nature of value creation in existing models or creating a new model from scratch, which leads to (2) a different organization of the value proposition with no one organization being central, but various parties taking responsibility over time, and (3) working with a wider range of transaction mediums (e.g. hybrid transaction systems), possibly facilitated by digital technology and developments such as cryptotechnology. The BMT is a framework intentionally designed to support you to develop new business models that are simultaneously sustainable, circular, and inclusive. If we want to get anywhere, to build up momentum and volume, we are talking about something radically different: about system change, about new ways of working, about creating and sharing what is of value.

> We can either have ourselves held hostage by a theoretical debate about how everything has to change, or start using the resources we already have today to combat exhaustion. This way we buy time and at the same time we can start the real transformation. *Ingrid Visseren-Hamakers* (10 May 2019)

15.2 Change Is Always Challenging

Working on new business models is ultimately a change management challenge. New models are not invented in a vacuum, but within the existing social and economic order. It is not without reason that we call this the *established order*. Based on all possible considerations and historical developments, that order has been established, and all potential parties are interested in keeping it that way. Proposing to irrevocably change that order creates resistance. But that is what the previous statement was advocating with such things as value creation, sustainability, biodiversity, and social inclusion. In a society where everything of economic importance is based on monetized transactions, drawing attention to including more than one value is something that just does not fit. We came across a summary of why change is so difficult (PWC, 2019). Below we present a slightly adapted synopsis of the key obstacles to change.

Key Points

Obstacles to Change

- **Obstacle 1—Breaking away**: Organizations have a hard time breaking away from existing organizational and institutional structures: everything is designed and aligned accordingly, including the institutional environment (both internal and external).
- **Obstacle 2—Earning potential**: The earning potential of a new business model cannot be demonstrated (in advance). Hence, companies struggle with the assessment of risks that a switch to a different model would entail.
- **Obstacle 3—Locked-in**: The core business *lock-in*. As an organization, we are what we are doing and can do, and our processes, procedures, competencies, and skills are geared towards this; it is hard to think outside of that box.
- **Obstacle 4—First-movers' uncertainty**: The so-called *first-movers* dilemma is an (intuitive) *break* with established and ongoing practices for many managers and directors. Being the first results in considerable uncertainty. For start-ups, it is slightly different since they are used to living with uncertainty compared to established businesses.
- **Obstacle 5—Technological disruption**: Technological disruption and new competition certainly influences the *first-mover* dilemma but is not often associated with sustainability, circularity, and inclusivity.
- **Obstacle 6—Emerging strategy**: In the process of working with an emergent strategy approach, key is gradually integrating new developments and events as they occur. As a result, a strategy develops and changes from day to day. In this process, new plans often do not pay attention to the business model.
- **Obstacle 7—No time available**: Organizations do not reserve time to work on transition and transformation. The day-to-day affairs absorb much, if not all, of the time. Really working on change requires a significant commitment and investment of time.

It is not particularly complicated to expand the number of obstacles even further (think of the aforementioned change management issues for citizens and companies), but this list gives a helpful indication of why trying to transform a business model can be met with a lot of resistance. For those who want to stay awake at night reading, consider also ecosystem thinking, value networks, cross-sectoral collaboration and so on. This certainly creates a more complete, but also a more complex picture of the nature and scale of the transformation. In this context, it is not surprising that existing organizations are mainly concerned with improvements and not with transformation, let alone transition, because questioning what they are maintaining with their work could threaten the established order.

15.3 The Six Elements of a Successful Business Model

Sometimes you come across research that is close to your own research—that is connected in some way. This observation certainly applies to the work of Kavadias et al. (2016) published in the Harvard Business Review. They conducted an in-depth analysis of 40 totally different companies—from Airbnb, Ikea, and Dell, to Lego, Rolls-Royce, and Uber—that have potentially launched a disruptive business model but have not done so with the intention to contribute to sustainability, circularity, and inclusivity. Some of these business models profoundly changed their industry, while others looked promising but ultimately failed. The authors searched for the recurring characteristics in these business models and identified six of them. Luckily, each of these characteristics has been discussed in the previous chapters. No company showed all six characteristics, but there was a rule of thumb: the more characteristics any one company had, the more chance they had of a successful business model.

So here we would say that to have transformative potential, business models must contain at least three of the following six characteristics:

Key Points

1. **A more personalized product or service:** Many new models offer a combination of products or services that are much better suited to the individual and the direct needs of customers than generic ones. Technology often plays a role in this: see our earlier comments regarding the IoT and the IoS (see Sect. 6.2 in Chapter 6) and how these developments enable customization.
2. **Closed-loop processes:** Many business models replace a linear consumption process with a loop, in which used products are reused (see our previous discussion on the RE-strategies in Chapter 8—Strategies). If the business

model is supported by an appropriate revenue model, this reduces total resource costs.

3. **Asset sharing:** Some innovations are successful because they provide the possibility of sharing valuable assets as we have seen earlier in Chapter 2 on Business models. Sometimes assets can be shared in a supply or value chain leading to a kind of forward and backward integration. Asset sharing usually takes place through two-way markets (often online) that create value for both parties: I get money for sharing my spare bedroom, and you get a cheaper and perhaps nicer place to stay. Sharing also lowers entry barriers in many industries because the entrant does not need to own the assets in question—he only has to act as an intermediary.
4. **Use-based or service-based business models:** In some models, the customer does not have to purchase the product or service, but only pays for the actual use leading to the so-called pay-per-use transaction models (see Chapter 12). Customers benefit from this because they only pay when the products or services deliver value to them. We find this totally normal when using a train or plane. The interesting development here is that this concept *sprawls* into business and into everyday life. So, we get washing-as-service, neighbourhood sun-based (central) heating, or even the service of looking through a window as part of a broad range of services that in turn create new services, given the fact that endless combinations are now possible. The company benefits because the number of customers is likely to grow.
5. **A more collaborative and horizontal ecosystem and a connection with community thinking:** (see Chapter 6—Business Model Archetypes) Some innovations are partly successful because new technology improves cooperation with partners and supports a better distribution of risks. That, in turn, enables cost reductions. But what it also allows for is using products and raw materials more efficiently. This was previously referred to as eco-efficiency and value retention.
6. **An agile and adaptive organization:** Innovators sometimes use technology to abandon traditional hierarchical organizational forms and move to organizational models that enable real-time adaptation to changes in needs. This often results in added value for users and also leads to more flexibility at lower costs. We discussed this in terms of the transition from a vertical to a horizontal organization as well as working with flexible networks (see Chapter 7—Parties Involved).

Each of these six elements in Fig. 15.1 has links to long-term trends in both technology and developments. For example, more personalization in the value proposition is a response to the fragmentation of customer preferences and the resulting demand for a more diverse offer. This personalization is enabled by sensors that collect data from cloud-connected devices. This data is analysed by big data solutions and converted into services—recommendations and alerts—that are different for each user.

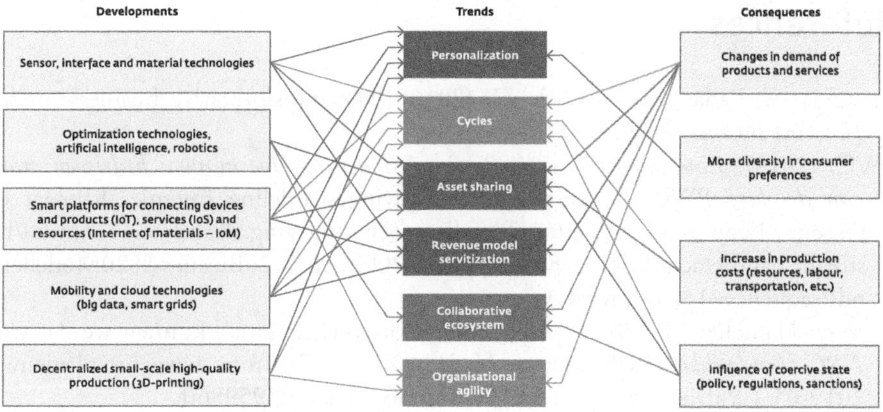

Fig. 15.1 Characteristics of successful business models (Inspired by Kavadias et al. [2016])

15.4 Final Word

Back to the present and the challenge of shaping transformation and transition through a new generation of what we have called sustainable business models. People, organizations, and government authorities are looking for ways to create value in a collaborative and collective way.

The BMT offers existing companies a lens and a framework which enables them to explore innovation opportunities which contribute to social and ecological issues and ultimately make them more successful as an organization. There are many ways this might come about. Just take a look at how organizations such as Ikea, Patagonia, and Interface experience these changes in their day-to-day practice.

The BMT also gives inventive, entrepreneurial people the opportunity to develop their own innovative business model. Sometimes these ventures—especially at the start—will be amateur. But concepts will develop over time despite mistakes being made, because we live in times where efforts to create a *New Economy* are welcomed.

People and organizations in society are tinkering with finding ways that this can be done in a dominant institutional and regulatory context. Of course, the success of this new way of organizing—which prioritizes multiple forms of value creation—is still fragile. Yet, at the end of the day, it yields a picture of a generation of new frontrunners who set the contours of a transition towards a different economy with new business models. Mainstreaming sustainable business models is by no means a given, but there is hope that over time sustainable business will become the new normal.

References

Kavadias, S., Ladas, K., & Loch, C. (2016). The transformative business model. *Harvard Business Review, 94*(10), 91–98.

PWC. (2019). *Eindrapport Groene Business Modellen: Hoe kunnen bedrijven ermee aan de slag?* PWC—Departement Omgeving—Afdeling Energie, Klimaat en Groene Economie. https://archief-algemeen.omgeving.vlaanderen.be/xmlui/bitstream/handle/acd/229984/Eindrapport%20Groene%20Business%20Modellen.pdf?sequence=1&isAllowed=y.

Visseren-Hamakers, I. (2019). Afzien van economische groei, kunnen we dat wel? *NRC Handelsblad.* Retrieved on 24 September 2020 from: www.nrc.nl/nieuws/2019/05/10/afzien-van-groei-kan-een-economie-dat-a3959860.

Appendix A: Quick Scan

This appendix contains a Quick Scan consisting of nine questions that make it possible to perform a baseline measurement of where you stand when it comes to sustainable or circular entrepreneurship. This Quick Scan is intended for entrepreneurs who already have a business proposition and who want to make their business operations more sustainable.

Add up the number of times you answer 'Yes' to the statements in Table A.1:

6–9: Start working on the BMT

3–5: Keep on reading and see what the BMT can mean for you

0–2: Be curious about what the BMT can mean for you!

Table A.1 Quick scan

Statements	Yes	n.a.	No
I fear that the customer base will become more mobile in the future. With two mouse clicks or two swipes on a phone my customer can reach competitors, and that is why I want to be socially relevant and thus future-proof my company more effectively.			
I find CSR, sustainability and circular economy vague terms. They are container concepts – everything fits in. I want to make it concrete, but I do not know where to start.			
I really want to contribute to society and I think I do everything necessary for this. Making my business operations more sustainable sometimes also gives me financial benefits. I want to make my contribution visible and increase it, but I am not sure how to do it yet.			
Raw materials are becoming increasingly scarce. That is why I want to use as few raw materials as possible and reuse where possible. Sustainable alternatives are welcome, but I do not have enough knowledge about this.			
In principle, when I need materials, raw materials or services for my company, I purchase them locally.			
I don't work in isolation: I like working with other companies or people to offer my customers the best possible solution. This cooperation can also be with a colleague/competitor.			
My company's assets are sometimes also available to other companies, associations and foundations.			
Within my company, I employ people whose job prospects elsewhere are poor.			
Together with our staff, we are looking for smart ways to separate waste.			

J. Jonker and N. Faber, *Organizing for Sustainability*,
https://doi.org/10.1007/978-3-030-78157-6

Appendix B: Glossary

Ableism

A type of discrimination in which able-bodied individuals are viewed as normal and superior to those with a disability, resulting in prejudice towards the latter. The modern concept of ableism emerged in the 1960s and '70s, when disability activists placed disability in a political context (Encyclopædia Britannica, 2013).

Archetype (of a Business Model)

A type or form of business model. Business models come in different shapes and sizes. This includes a chain business model, a cycle business model, a community business model or a platform business model. Different situations require different business model archetypes with their own appropriate form of value creation.

Big, Hairy, Audacious Goal (BHAG)

An audacious 10–30-year goal to progress towards an envisioned future (Collins, 2021).

J. Jonker and N. Faber, *Organizing for Sustainability*,
https://doi.org/10.1007/978-3-030-78157-6

Business Model

A business model describes a possible *logic* of value creation—how value is created. It consists of a number of building blocks, including (1) the value proposition, (2) the organization model including the parties involved, and (3) the revenue model. The logic of value creation is driven by a strategic choice (see Strategy) in an institutional environment, taking into consideration available resources and (core) competencies.

Circularity (1)

The heart of the circular economy is the pursuit of value retention, by organizing cycles (see Loops) around raw materials, materials, semi-finished products, and end products. The existing economy does not always lend itself to circularization. Certain things are consumed by eating them, burning them or using them in another way. Circularization goes beyond focusing on recycling, as it is part of a system approach that starts with Redesign, Life-cycle Management, Repair, Refurbishment, Substitution and Conversion. A transition is needed to achieve circularity (see also Transition).

Circularity (2)

A circular economy is an economic system based on minimizing the use of raw materials by reusing products and parts of those products, and by keeping high-quality raw materials in circulation. It is a system of closed loops (see Loops) in which the value of products and/or raw materials is preserved as much as possible, renewable energy sources are used, and systems thinking, from an organizational or management perspective, takes a core position.

Commons

The commons is a concept that is closely associated with the Community (see below). Bollier (2016) and Restakis (2017) define the commons as '[a] (set of) shared resource(s), material and non-material, maintained or co-created by a community and governed by the same community's norms and rules'. In this context, the shared resources and the standards and rules governing their use must be inextricably linked and together form the commons. Aiming to collectively create value and distributing and sharing it can be seen as a unique quality of the commons.

Community

Within the context of business models, community refers to a group of people (citizens and other parties), who consciously arrive at and share a form of collective value creation. This includes energy cooperatives, car-sharing networks and regional peer-to-peer food distribution systems.

Context

The relevant environment in which a business model operates. Realizing the promise of a business model always occurs within an institutional, material and social context, as well as at a certain point in time. Context and timing have a direct impact on success.

Conversion

The core of conversion is to turn a particular raw material (such as CO_2, plastic, or roadside grass) into another, new, raw material. For example, the release of lignin from elephant grass that can be used as a binder for asphalt, or CO_2 that can form the basis of fuel.

Core Activity

This describes the most important (primary) activity of an organization. The term is broadened here and therefore also applies to a community or a network. The core activity often distinguishes one organization from another. It is not uncommon for it to be linked to the concept of core competencies—those which an organization (or group of people) are very good at.

Corporate Social Responsibility (CSR)

CSR means that companies (are willing to) bear responsibility for social issues such as air pollution, climate change or working conditions. They therefore take the social effects of their activities into account. This applies to all business processes, such as purchasing, production and marketing communication. CSR is not a project, but an integral vision of the core activities of a company (MVO Nederland, n.d.).

Dream

A very concrete proposition often starts with a big and idealistic dream, represented by a Big, Hairy, Audacious Goal (see BHAG). Imagine that everything would really work out, everyone would cooperate and nothing and nobody would throw a spanner in the works … the world would be plastic-free in 30 years, no one would ever go hungry again, there would be clean water and sanitation available for everyone … a dream is, therefore, a positive long-term goal.

Eco-efficiency and Eco-effectiveness

These concepts reflect the aim to reduce the use of raw materials and additives linked to the reduction of waste and pollution in the process of producing goods and related services. The result should be a cheaper as well as a more environmentally friendly product. This implies a more effective use of raw materials and products. *Eco*, therefore, does not only mean *ecological* but also *economical*.

External Check

This is the final step of the Design Phase, which tests the viability of the new company, business activity or intervention. Relevant questions are: Are you on the right track? Is it already there? Is it allowed? Is it possible? You can do this external check yourself or have it done by third parties. It is important to check the business model against people or information not yet included in its development up to the time of checking.

Externalizing

In the context of this publication, externalization means the (strategic) process in which the costs and/or effects of doing business are not passed on but indirectly recovered from customers, citizens or the environment (paraphrased from Ten Bos, 2010). They are costs made by the company but deliberately passed on to society (consciously or unconsciously—see also Buchanan & Stubblebine, 1962).

Future-Proof

A business model with a future-proof design allows a business model to have a long-term validity because it contributes to solving ecological and social issues, without compromising a sound economic basis.

Hybrid

The meaning of hybrid can be mixing dissimilar *matters*. To ensure that transactions (see Transaction) run smoothly, we usually express them in one particular unit, to make things easier. With financial transactions we emphasize the monetization of values: express everything in money. But transactions can also take place with *dissimilar* values, which we call hybrid values.

Hybrid Transactions

Hybrid transactions allow for using different types of value units simultaneously and interchangeably, such as money, time, energy, mobility and waste.

Impact

This is the often powerful and sometimes lasting effect that an event, action or choice has on people, their environment (natural, institutional, and/or social) and thus on the course of things that arise from that effect in the long term (Maas, 2011). Impact can be measured by the nature of the change that occurs as a result of an event, action or choice made (see also Transition).

Inclusion (1)

This is a broad concept that focuses, among other things, on involvement, integration, and participation. It is widely used in the discourse on immigrants, disadvantaged people and people with disabilities, but its scope is much wider. The inclusive society is a society in which everyone counts and in which everyone can participate in social, cultural and economic activities.

Inclusion (2)

This means recognizing and including disadvantaged groups in society based on equal rights and obligations. Inclusion is opposed to ableism (see Ableism). The concepts of inclusion and integration complement each other in contemporary society (Cambridge Dictionary, n.d.).

Inclusion (3)

Inclusion also means 'enabling every citizen, notably the most disadvantaged, to fully participate in society, including having a job, access to quality services, helping people participate actively in society, and getting back to work' (European Commission, n.d.).

Indicators

Indicators provide a way to measure a particular phenomenon from one or more perspectives. They are *objectively measurable constructions*, notions or entities based on a measurement which may lead to the conclusion that, for example, (strategic) objectives are being achieved or not. A combined set of indicators can serve as the basis for a monitoring system.

Life Cycle Analysis

Life Cycle Analysis or Assessment is a method of measuring the impact of a product and its associated services during and following the life cycle of that particular product, from cradle to grave. Initially, only the total environmental impact was considered. Nowadays, it is common to include other kinds of impacts (see Impact).

Loops (1)

These are (closed) processes in which a certain complex of raw materials in different compositions and/or functionalities follow one another, but finally come back again to the starting point. A loop can, therefore, be drawn schematically as a circle or a circular movement. It is common to distinguish between natural (biological, living matter) and technical (lifeless matter) loops (Ellen MacArthur Foundation, 2012).

Loops (2)

The circular economy focuses on material loops to reduce the use of raw materials and the generation of waste, and maximize the lifespan of products and (raw) materials. In this publication, a distinction is made between different types of loops. Moreover, the biological loop is included in various elaborations.

Model

A model is an abstract, coherent set of assumptions, suppositions and their interrelations that can constitute the foundation for the development of theories relating to a specific part of reality. It is also possible that a model is developed based on a particular theory.

Network

Based on information and communication technology, it is possible to set up networks in addition to the conventional centrally managed organization. These networks contain competencies that can be addressed when necessary. However, the actual network does not belong to anybody. This is also called *distributive* organization.

Parties

Also called stakeholders, these are interest parties, which can be any individual or group that can affect or be affected by the achievement of organizational goals (Freeman & Reed, 1983). Different stakeholders can have common, independent or even opposite interests. Perhaps even more difficult is that in this publication we often do not talk about an organization that has a certain business model, but about a platform with all kinds of parties, or a community or a number of stakeholders who create a business model together.

Platform

A platform is built based on brokering supply and demand. This can be achieved both physically and digitally. Consider Ebay.com, for example, where second-hand goods are traded (see: www.ebay.com), or FatLlama (see:

FatLlama.com) or Vinted (see: www.vinted.co.uk) where efforts are made to make better use of tools, among other things. The arrival of cryptotechnologies such as blockchain gives rise to new payment options on these platforms.

Sticky Problems

See Wicked problems.

Strategy (1)

This is a short- or long-term action perspective, setting out the route to arrive at the agreed objectives. For the concepts of sustainability, circularity and inclusivity, directly related strategies emerge. Consider, for example, the RE-strategies (recycling, repair, refurbishment, etc.) for the circular economy.

Strategy (2)

A strategy is a targeted plan through which an organization or a configuration of parties involved intends to achieve their goals. Realizing these goals requires making choices about possible routes and available resources.

Substitution

Substitution refers to replacing one material with a material that has a lower environmentally harmful impact or has a biological origin instead of a synthetic one. For example, replacing toxic technical materials such as asbestos with materials that have similar functional properties, but that do not harm the environment. A biological material fits within a natural loop of growth, use, and composting. The idea is that substitution contributes to sustainability or circularity.

Sustainability (1)

The aim is to arrive at a *radical* reduction in the use of raw materials, the consumption of energy, the emission of harmful substances, the negative impact on natural ecosystems (biodiversity), health, social cohesion, etc. Eco-efficiency and eco-effectiveness are central concepts.

Sustainability (2)

This includes the conscious and balanced organization of entrepreneurial activities to create value in three dimensions: People, Planet, Profit (PPP). The approach is that these contribute to prosperity and wellbeing in the short and long run. The so-called Triple-P is a concept developed by John Elkington (1997).

Sustainability (3)

'Sustainable development is the organizing principle for meeting human development goals while simultaneously sustaining the ability of natural systems to provide the natural resources and ecosystem services upon which the economy and society depend' (WCED, 1987).

Sustainability (4)

'Sustainable development is a development that meets the needs of the present without compromising the ability of future generations to meet their own needs' (WCED, 1987).

Template

In this publication, we use a fixed template consisting of the building blocks of the business model. The Business Model Template (BMT) consists of the Definition, Design and Result Stages. You are advised to follow it through from top to bottom. Based on a certain selected logic, variable content can be developed coherently within predefined places of the BMT.

Transaction

The bilateral (between two parties) or multilateral (between several parties) exchange of values with the goal of creating value for those involved. The basis for a transaction is the exchange of a service and a compensation (whether or not in monetary terms).

Transition

A transition is defined as a fundamental change in the fulfilment of societal needs and is the result of interacting and mutually reinforcing developments in areas such as economy, culture, technology, institutions, nature and the environment (adopted from Alkemade et al., 2011).

Value Creation

This involves creating value between parties through transactions, which can be a combination of material (goods) and intangible (services). The parties involved decide what is of value and this is not intrinsically linked to goods, services or events.

Value(s) Creation

In the value creation process, multiple values are always created for and by the parties involved at the same time. These values are subjective and depend on context (place and time) and the individual. So, what is of value for one individual may be very different from what is of value for someone else, even though they are part of the same transaction.

Value Proposition

This is the proposition, offer, or solution of an organization or a number of collaborating parties, often formulated in terms of the (future) *value* that the proposition has for the (potential) customer(s) and users. A value proposition defines concrete, verifiable results.

Wicked Problems, a.k.a. Sticky Problems

Complex issues that are connected to each other and which simultaneously demand a variety of solutions from multiple collaborating parties (see also Weber & Khademian, 2008). Sustainable development and climate transition are wicked problems, but so are individual aspects of sustainability such as regional food supply or plastic soup.

Those who need a comprehensive Thesaurus focused on the above concepts are recommended to consult mvotermen.wordpress.com (in Dutch), and for an English equivalent www.thesaurus.net. The authors do not bear any responsibility for the design, content or accuracy of these recommended thesauri.

References

Alkemade, F., Hekkert, M. P., & Negro, S. O. (2011). Transition policy and innovation policy: Friends or foes? *Environmental Innovation and Societal Transitions, 1*(1), 125–129. https://doi.org/10.1016/j.eist.2011.04.009.

Bollier, D. (2016). *Commoning as a transformative social paradigm.* Retrieved on 23 June 2019. thenextsystem.org/commoning-as-a-transformative-social-paradigm.

Buchanan, J. M., & Stubblebine, W. C. (1962). Externality. *Economica*, 29(116), 371–384. https://doi.org/10.2307/2551386.

Cambridge Dictionary. (n.d.). Inclusion. In *Cambridge dictionary.* www.dictionary.cambridge.org/dictionary/english/inclusion.

Collins, J. (2021). BHAG. *Jim Collins.* https://www.jimcollins.com/concepts/bhag.html.

Elkington, J. (1997). *Cannibals with Forks: The triple bottom line of 21st century business.* Oxford: Capstone.

Ellen MacArthur Foundation. (2012). *Towards the circular economy Vol. 1: Economic and business rationale for an accelerated transition* (p. 98). Ellen Mac Arthur Foundation. https://www.ellenmacarthurfoundation.org/assets/downloads/publications/Ellen-MacArthur-Foundation-Towards-the-Circular-Economy-vol.1.pdf.

Encyclopædia Britannica. (2013). *Albeism.* In Encyclopædia Britannica. www.britannica.com/topic/ableism.

European Commission. (n.d.). *Active inclusion.* European Commission. Retrieved on 24 September 2020. ec.europa.eu/social/main.jsp?catId=1059&langId=en.

Freeman, R. E. (1984). *Stakeholder management: A strategic approach.* New York: Pitman.

Freeman, R. E., & Reed, D. L. (1983). Stockholders and stakeholders: A new perspective on corporate governance. *California Management Review, 25*(3), 88–106. https://doi.org/10.2307/41165018.

Maas, K. (2011). Maatschappelijke prestaties van organisaties: Van outputmeting naar impactmeting [Social performance of organizations: from measuring output to measuring impact]. *Maandblad voor Accounting en Bedrijfseconomie*, November 2011.

MVO Nederland. (n.d.). *About CSR – Corporate sustainability and responsibility. MVO Nederland.* Retrieved on 24 September 2020. www.mvonederland.nl/en/about-mvo-nederland/about-csr-corporate-sustainability-and-responsibility.

Restakis, J. (2017). *Cooperative commonwealth & the partner state.* Retrieved on 23 June 2019. thenextsystem.org/cooperative-commonwealth-partner-state.

WCED. (1987). *Our common future*. Oxford University Press.
Weber, E. P., & Khademian, A. M. (2008). Wicked problems, knowledge challenges, and collaborative capacity builders in network settings. *Public Administration Review, 68*(2), 334–349. doi.org/10.1111/j.1540-6210.2007.00866.x.

Appendix C: Educational Assignments

The following assignments broadly follow the structure of the Business Model Template (BMT). Almost all of them can be used individually, in pairs, and in teams. They have been put in such a way that changing several words often results in a slightly different approach. This means that in class, different teams and groups of students can work side by side on more or less the same assignment and present the different outcomes to each other. We do not pretend that these assignments are exhaustive, but we do want you to work with the BMT.

Suggested Assignments for Building Block #1—Motive and Context

> **Assignment**
>
> Title: Mind Map Circular Economy
>
> Type: Individual and team
>
> Time: +/−1 hour
>
> *Assignment description:*
>
> Search for images, articles, and reports on the internet about the circular economy. Together, draw up a mind map of what you think is essential in that respect. It may be helpful to do this individually first and then compare the results and discuss them. If you want to, it could be useful to repeat this assignment with, for example, a word such as sustainability or inclusivity (see also Appendix B: Glossary).

J. Jonker and N. Faber, *Organizing for Sustainability*,
https://doi.org/10.1007/978-3-030-78157-6

The purpose of this assignment is to clarify the meaning of certain notions. You can do so during or before studying the theory.

Assignment

Title: Impact of humanity on the environment or the planet

Type: Individual, pairs, and class

Time: +/−30 minutes to 1 hour

Assignment description:

Individually or in pairs, search newspapers or the internet for a good example of an event or news item that clearly shows the impact of humanity on the planet. Look for facts from reliable sources to elaborate on this. Based on these materials, make a 60-second elevator pitch with one illustration in which you briefly explain this impact.

This assignment aims to discover ways in which humans negatively influence their environment or the planet. These forms of impact can be used positively later on during the BMT Result Stage.

Assignment

Title: The relationship between professional practice and the government's plans for a Circular Economy in the Netherlands by 2050

Type: Individual as a student or for a company

Time: +/−1 h 30 minutes

Assignment description:

Read the government-wide programme for a circular economy *A Circular Economy in the Netherlands by 2050* (Government, 2016; www.government.nl/documents/policy-notes/2016/09/14/a-circular-economy-in-the-netherlands-by-2050). From the five priorities, choose the priority that best suits your studies/future work or industry, and prepare a short text (200–300 words) about the impact (threats and opportunities) of those plans on your future profession, industry or sector. If you want to do this more extensively and systematically, you can also do this in the form of a SWOT or DESTEP analysis.

The purpose of this assignment is to think about what the cabinet plans actually mean for the future of the professional field for which you are studying or the sector in which a company that you would like to work for operates.

Assignment

Title: Create a one-liner for Building Block #1—Motive and Context

Type: Individual or pairs

Time: +/−15 minutes

Assignment description:

Read the quotes that belong to the Motive building block and come up with a catchy and original new one-liner that clearly indicates what problem in the world has had such an impact on you that you would like to solve this problem by making use of the BMT. If you want to go one step further, make a short video clip of your reason/pitch.

This assignment aims to formulate as clearly and concisely as possible what the core is of the challenge that you would like to take on.

Suggested Assignments for Building Block #2—Dream

Assignment

Title: Circular dream and core values

Type: Individual or group

Time: +/−1 hour

Assignment description:

Formulate a balanced sustainable and circular Dream for a company or case (if necessary as a mission and vision), and three associated core values. Be creative, think outside of the box: although it does not have to be feasible tomorrow, it should be imaginable. What you propose should fit into a transition towards a circular and sustainable society, five to ten years from now. Summarize the Dream in a catchy one-liner so that it becomes a value proposition (following the quotes as mentioned earlier). This assignment can be applied to both an existing organization and a business model that is to be developed.

The purpose of this assignment is to look further ahead at how a company/case could be part of a future circular and sustainable society and to formulate this in a Dream and a Proposition.

Assignment

Title: The internal organization: a reality check

Type: Individual or group

Time: +/−2 hours

Assignment description:

This assignment is meant for an existing business model and consists of two parts.

Part 1: Draw up a mind map of the current organization. You can use some of the elements below:

- Proposition
- Strategy (intentions versus practice?)
- Core activities, if possible described as business processes
- Competences (knowledge and skills)
- Culture (collective attitude of employees)
- Policy (for example purchasing policy, financing policy, or risk policy).

Based on these elements, indicate how sustainable, circular and inclusive this organization is. Concentrate on the core activities of the internal organization. Then describe the *ideal* sustainable organization. Use principles such as:

- In an ideal organization, the policy of the purchasing department is ...
- In an ideal organization, all employees can ...
- In an ideal organization, the corporate culture is ...
- In an ideal organization the strategy is set up ...

TIP: it can be useful to use the dream and core values that you formulated in a previous assignment as a guideline.

Part 2: Carry out a reality check with the results from Part 1 of this assignment.

Prepare a two-part overview:

a. Which parts do you think are feasible (and may already have been realized)?
b. What do you think is unfeasible? Carefully argue why it is not feasible now and what it will take to realize it in the future. What concrete steps need to be taken to get there?

The purpose of this assignment is to discover what criteria the internal organization should meet in order to participate as a company in a sustainable and circular economy.

Suggested Assignments for Building Block #3—Proposition

Assignment

Title: The worth(lessness) of things

Type: Individual in class

Time: +/−1 hour

Assignment description:

Find and bring a broken or discarded object. Think of an iron, a toaster, a mobile phone or similar. Have a look at it and describe why the thing is broken or discarded. Then think of and describe which different types of value are still contained in this object or can still be created with it. This assignment works especially well when it is used in class, and students discuss each other's objects.

The purpose of this assignment is to clarify how quickly or easily things are broken or discarded and to think about which value(s) they might have by circular standards.

Suggested Assignments for Building Block #4—Business Model Archetypes

Assignment

Title: Business Model Patterns

Type: Individual or group

Time: +/−2 hours

Assignment description:

Innovate the existing business model of a case/company using the business model pattern cards (businessmodellab.nl/en/tools—the instructions for using the cards are on the website).

This assignment aims to get inspiration from proven patterns in business models and use them to create your own business model.

Assignment

Title: Business Model Canvas (BMC) versus Business Model Template (BMT)

Type: Pairs or group

Time: +/−1 hour 30 minutes

Assignment description:

Choose a company from a list of sustainable companies given by the teacher and find out what their business model is. Elaborate their business model in the Osterwalder (2004) business model canvas (BMC). Use the internet to find all the information to do this. Which parts can be worked out well and which are more difficult? Can you include all created values in the model? What can you not put in this model, and why not? Then do this assignment again, but now elaborate on the business model using the BMT. Then make a comparison between the two elaborations and put the two elaborations and the equation into a PowerPoint presentation. Remember to draw some clear conclusions and make recommendations and, of course, mention your sources.

The purpose of this assignment is to work with the business model canvas to describe a sustainable company. The limitations of this model concern the thinking and acting of many companies and show how difficult it is to visualize all the values created.

Assignment

Title: Urban mining

Type: Group or class

Time: +/−3 hours

Assignment description:

This assignment works when done by a whole class. In preparation, it is useful to get familiar with the concept of urban mining, for example, by watching the Backlight documentary *Mobile Gold*:

www.vpro.nl/programmas/tegenlicht/backlight/mobilegold.html.

Part 1: Go outside (literally!) and come back with three examples of a product or waste stream that you think is suitable for urban mining. Take photos of the products or materials that you have in mind when the product and/or the residual flow has been processed.

Part 2: Develop your business case for a chosen residual flow. Answer, for example, the following questions:

- How are you going to do this? What is your value proposition?
- What materials are involved (volume, quality, stability, legal admissibility, etc.)?
- How did you get your materials?
- What logistics and sorting issues could come up here?
- How can you make money? What is a suitable revenue model?
- What is the impact of this business case expressed in several indicators (CO_2 reduction, heat consumption, fewer kilometres, etc.?)
- If it is not feasible now, what changes are needed (institutional, fiscal, legal, social, etc.) for this to be a good business case?

Part 3: Produce a PowerPoint presentation of your business model in which you explain these elements succinctly. Use this presentation as a pitch for your business model. If you have more time available, prepare a catchy video clip (see later in these teaching instructions).

Part 4: The teams present the previously formulated business models to each other. Each team has a number of points to give to other groups. Do this with large margins, for example, 1, 3, 5, and 10 points. The allocation of points is discussed within the teams. Use clear criteria for this: if you want to, you can explain this at the beginning of your assessment. The team that eventually receives the most points is the winner.

This assignment aims to introduce students to the concept of urban mining and show/discover value in everyday products and materials in their immediate environment.

You can also apply this assignment to existing waste streams such as mucky wastewater, flowers, other agricultural residues, professional clothing such as uniforms and so on.

Assignment

Title: Manufacturing industries vs. service sector

Type: Individual or group

Time: +/−1 hour 30 minutes

Assignment description:

Find existing examples of the three business model archetypes: platform, community-based and circular. For each archetype, look for an example focused on the manufacturing industry, and an example focused on the service sector. So you are looking for a total of six different examples. Compare these examples and discuss similarities and differences in the approach to the business model. The result can either be a paper or a presentation (or both).

This assignment aims to discover differences in the design of a business model for the manufacturing industry or the service sector. Doing this with the three different types will present the underlying principles for business models.

Suggested Assignments for Building Block #5—Parties

Assignment

Title: Loops and the Loop Ladder

Type: Individual or group

Time: +/−3 hours

Assignment description:

Both entrepreneurs and students can use this assignment.

For entrepreneurs: draw your current loop, for example by using one of the 31 cycles in the book *Organising for the Circular Economy* by Jonker et al. (2018). Improve the existing loop based on a number (three to five) of intended changes. Then place your own company on the loops ladder (see Fig. C.1). Where are you now and where do you want to be three, five or ten years from now? What is right for your company?

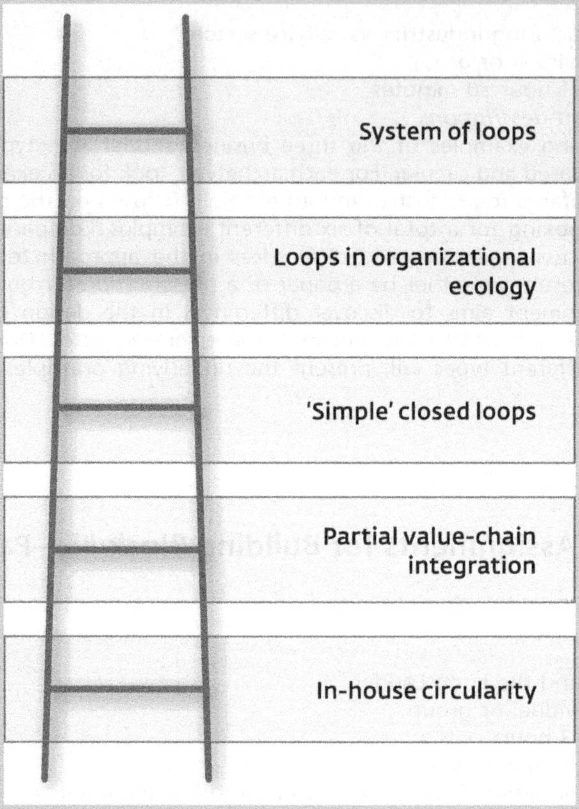

Fig. C.1 Loops ladder

For students: draw the loop of a given or practical case. Improve these based on intended changes. What does it take to realize these changes?

Now put the case on the loops ladder (see Fig. C.1). Where are they now, and where can the case be three, five or ten years from now?

This assignment aims to define the current loop and see opportunities by doing so to improve it for the future. These improvements can be inserted and tested against the loops ladder to outline a future perspective.

Assignment

Title: Network of external parties

Type: Individual or group

Time: +/−1 hour

Assignment description:

Draw a map of the external parties (based on Building Block #5—Parties). Start with the parties that are known now, for example customers, banks, and government. Indicate which roles these parties currently have and roughly what relationship your case or company has with them. You can use a list or a mind map structure for this.

Then outline the network of parties that are required in the desired future ideal-type loop situation (you could use the loop with intended changes from the previous assignment). Check and fill in which party could or should fulfil which role. Feel free to write down imaginary parts or typify roles to fill the loop. It is best to do some *wishful thinking* for this process. First of all, disregard all boundaries and limitations.

This assignment aims to visualize the external parties and their roles in a cycle and to supplement this with the necessary parties and roles without thinking in terms of limitations.

Assignment

Title: Stakeholder impact matrix

Type: Individual or group

Time: +/−2 hours

Assignment description:

Create a stakeholder impact matrix using the following steps (this assignment also relates to Building Block #9—Impact):

- Determine the main stakeholders for your company or case.
- Next, determine which value you can create for which stakeholders (see, for example, the *Value Creation* star in Chapter 5).
- Check what the relevance of this value is for each individual stakeholder.
- Check whether the impact you create is small, medium, or large. If necessary, use a limited set of indicators for this.
- Put your findings in a stakeholder impact matrix as follows:
  - x-axis: Impact of the created value (from small to very large)
  - y-axis: Relevance of the value to the stakeholder (from small to very large)

In the matrix, the upper right quadrant values create the highest impact and are the most relevant to the stakeholders.

The purpose of this assignment is to get an indication of the value a company can create and the impact this has on various stakeholders. This can be very useful for creating support and setting priorities.

Suggested Assignments for Building Block #6—Strategy

Assignment

Title: Advertise a circular mobile phone or laptop.

Type: Pairs or group

Time: +/−1 hour

Assignment description:

This assignment works best with multiple pairs or groups of students in a class. Create an advertisement for an imaginary circular mobile phone. The life cycle of the mobile phone must be closed with several parties. It is your decision how to approach this. Then choose a revenue model and elaborate it. Think of things like PAAS, deposit, lease take-back, rent, performance, or repairs. Include the proposition, prices, and terms that you have in mind in the advertisement. Also, write down the most important conditions. When this assignment is done with several groups, you can *sell* the ads to each other.

The advertisements can be presented to each other in different ways.

a. As a PowerPoint poster
b. In a detailed infographic. Put up printed infographics and walk past them together while teams take turns explaining them.
c. Cut and paste. Each team makes a poster on a flipchart. Put it up and present it to each other.

Then debate if and why it is really about a circular cell phone, or if there is, for example, a form of *greenwashing*. Discuss what you think is the most attractive proposition.

The purpose of this assignment is to get students to think about how a product can be made circular by focusing on a product that they use a lot every day (cell phones). It is not then about manufacturability or feasibility, but about the offer to the customer, the proposition.

Assignment

Title: Examples of corporate strategies

Type: Pairs or group

Time: +/−2 hours (depending on the number of companies you select)

Assignment description:

Identify and analyse the strategies of a number of companies using the different strategies provided in the book. You can do so by choosing three sustainable and three non-sustainable companies, but you could also take five circular companies. First make it clear what strategies you recognize and which aspects they are based on. In any case, this assignment requires you to find more (online) information about the companies involved. Do not look only at the information that the company provides (for example, on the website or in annual reports) but also look for critical articles or reports.

The purpose of this assignment is to gain more insight into different business strategies based on the available examples.

Assignment

Title: Obsolescence as a strategy

Type: Individual, pairs or teams

Time: +/−1 hour

Assignment description:

Part 1. Find three different concrete examples of planned obsolescence. Consider what has been done by the designers to ensure that the product ages and breaks down faster than necessary. Describe for each product what it would mean if this product was not designed with this strategy, but with a strategy of, for example, extending the lifespan. What would be the consequences of this change of strategy and for whom? Think beyond the obvious customers, but also think of the manufacturers themselves, the financiers, and other parties.

Part 2. Repeat this assignment, but now for perceived obsolescence. Then look not only at designers but also at marketers and advertisers. What would be the consequences if, for example, a PAAS strategy was adopted here?

This assignment aims to recognize practical examples of planned and perceived obsolescence, think about what impact this strategic choice will have, and consider how it can be done differently.

Assignment

Title: Your sustainable choices

Type: Individual

Time: +/−30 minutes to 1 hour

Assignment description:

Take a moment to see how you make sustainable choices in your own daily life. Take groups of activities such as dressing, living, travelling, hygiene, or eating. Find out for each example which choices you make. If possible, indicate the purpose of the strategic choice. Then try to form an opinion on the degree of sustainability of your own daily behaviour. After this, present the individual outcomes to each other in the classroom. This creates a beautiful and vibrant collection of examples of sustainable strategic choices that can be discussed.

This assignment aims to gain more insight into your own behaviour when it comes to sustainability.

Assignment

Title: Sustainable choices of companies

Type: Group

Time: +/−1 hour

Assignment description:

In the news or on the internet, find at least three examples of companies (or the government) that make strategic choices with a view to sustainability. For each example, determine what these choices are and why they were made. Give a clear indication of the purpose of a strategic choice. When was the choice made (so you can see how long a certain strategic choice has been operational), and what is the possible impact? This assignment works well in class, with several students or groups collecting examples and sharing their work results. This will result in a good collection of examples of sustainable strategic choices that you can discuss.

This assignment aims to gain more insight into the reasons why companies and governments make choices with regard to sustainability.

Assignment

Title: Strategic choice

Type: Individual or group

Time: +/−30 minutes

Assignment description:

For this assignment, you need a company or a case. Check which strategy from the BMT can serve as the primary strategy for the company or case concerned. If applicable, also indicate a secondary strategy. Also, see how these strategic choices have been translated into core activities. Give evidence as to why this strategy applies to this company or organization, but also provide counter-arguments. If possible, try to find out what the short- and long-term effects of these strategic choices are.

The purpose of this assignment is to apply the theory of strategic choices from the BMT to a company or case. Considering a secondary strategy will help you to think with a broader perspective.

Assignment

Title: Strategic poster

Type: Class divided into groups

Time: +/−1 hour 30 minutes + optional 30 minutes for the poster session

Assignment description:

You (the students) now work at a consultancy firm as sustainability managers for circularity. You support companies in their transition. To *sell* the six strategies for sustainability and circularity, your agency is looking for a good poster to promote to potential customers.

These posters must be easily understood and lead people to think.

Divide the class into six teams: one team for each strategy (Eco-efficiency, Product as a service, Use optimization, Lifespan extension, Cascading, and Community Building).

Now go outside and take pictures of an example of an object or situation that you are sure can be made more sustainable and circular with your assigned strategy. Create a poster that promotes this and makes people think. The poster should clearly show how you want to apply the strategy to achieve more sustainability and circularity. When people see the poster, they should want to get started with your strategy right away.

This assignment can be concluded with a classroom poster session in which all posters made are presented. Discuss each other's posters and the strategic elements that they highlight.

This assignment's aim is to playfully visualize the different strategies and discuss them on the basis of practical objects.

Suggested Assignments for Building Block #7—Core Activities

Assignment

Title: Material cycles

Type: Individual or group

Time: +/−2 hours

Assignment description:

For this assignment, you need a case or a company that makes a physical product. Make an overview of the materials used to produce the product in the case. Learn about the examples of cycles (infographics belonging to the *Organising for the Circular Economy* workbook [Jonker et al., 2018]). For your case, consider which cycle or cycles best match the materials in your overview. Then try to figure out how you can add, substitute, or otherwise change in a sustainable way to use these materials to close the cycle, using the examples and your own creativity. Show this in a cycle that applies particularly to your case.

The purpose of this assignment is to think about closing the cycle, starting from the materials. Because this is difficult, especially without specialist technical knowledge, we use many examples.

Assignment

Title: VAT (Value Added Tax) becomes SVAT (Sustainable Value Added TAX)

Type: Group

Time: +/−1h 30 minutes

Assignment description:

This assignment works best with several groups of students per class, each devising their own concept for SVAT. Think of a way to convert VAT (Value Added Tax) into SVAT (Sustainable Value Added Tax). In other words, think of a way to stimulate sustainability through taxes. Do not only think of tax but also the use of tax revenues. So also, what will you do with these tax revenues to promote sustainability? Think about three products (or categories) for which you would like to introduce the SVAT with a view of the circular economy. Consider how high the amount should be (approximately), how you want to implement it, and how it will be paid. And then, of course, there is the key question: who will pay? When this assignment is carried out in a classroom setting, discuss the concepts of each group together, and weigh them against each other. Who came up with the best implementation of SVAT?

The purpose of this assignment is to playfully consider the possibilities of stimulating sustainability (and circularity) through taxation.

Assignment

Title: From value creation to core activities

Type: Individual or group

Time: +/−2 hours

Assignment description:

For one specific case, make a concrete analysis of the 3Ps (People, Planet, Profit) in terms of value creation. Indicate which core activity or activities is/are required to create these values. Look at today's context, but also think about future possibilities. Draw up a timeline for each value: how long will it take for this value to emerge, or how long does it take for a specific value to be lost? Use estimates of time if necessary.

This assignment's purpose is to translate the intended value creation for the 3Ps into core activities and then translate this into a time frame. Hopefully, this will make the often somewhat abstract term *value creation* more concrete.

Suggested Assignments for Building Block #8—External Test

Assignment

Title: Learning from the competition

Type: Individual or group

Time: +/−1h 30 minutes

Assignment description:

Find three existing cases already active in your business model's field. Each case is briefly described in content and provided with at least one source (website). What are they doing? How do they do it? How long have they been doing that? And so on. Elaborate on this description of the cases systematically. What do you think they are doing very well in terms of sustainability, circularity, or inclusivity, and what could be improved? Complete the assignment with at least three clear-cut conclusions or recommendations to improve your case or business model.

This assignment aims to actively look at three comparable companies operating in the same field as the case that you are working on and to learn from the competition.

Suggested Assignments for Building Block #9—Impact

Assignment

Title: Your impact

Type: Group or class

Time: +/−30 minutes

Assignment description:

Have a group discussion fuelled by the question: What is the impact of your everyday decisions? Where do you buy things, what do you take into consideration, and where does your waste go? For example, use your three most recent purchases for this discussion.

The purpose of this assignment is to look in the mirror and to look critically at your impact. Discussing this with others creates new insights into the choices and considerations that consumers make every day.

Assignment

Title: Identifying impact in an annual report

Type: Pairs or group

Time: +/−1 hour

Assignment description:

Look up the most recent online annual report of a large (national) organization, for example a railway company, a domestic airline, or a bank. Identify several values in this report. Choose the three values with the greatest impact and find out how they are organized. Then try to find out what impact this will create.

This assignment aims to analyse how impact can be reported and how it is organized based on a concrete and recognizable example.

Assignment

Title: Impact indicators

Type: Group

Time: +/−2h 30 minutes

Assignment description:

Choose (for a case) the indicators with which you think you can measure the results of your business model. When necessary, draw inspiration from the annual reports of sustainably oriented companies. Then determine how you want to measure these indicators and the method to report on them. Write down what you expect from the output, outcome, and impact. If possible, use precise quantities. This is really the ambition for this assignment. So what is the CO_2 reduction, the residual value, what about fewer kilometres, can you show that people become less lonely, etc. Then write down what you expect in terms of yield. If that is difficult (often it is still difficult to determine), indicate whether you expect an increase or decrease in the indicators and quantities mentioned. The last step is to indicate how these forms of impact are interrelated.

This assignment's purpose is to materialize the impact of indicators and quantities, other than just financial indicators. The more concrete the quantities, the easier it is to set goals and report on them.

Suggested Assignments for Building Block #10—Value(s) Creation: Transaction Types

Assignment

Title: Revenue models and business model patterns

Type: Individual or group

Time: +/−2h 30 minutes

Assignment description:

Use the business model cards for this assignment. You can find them on businessmodellab.nl/en/tools/bedrijfsmodel-kaarten. We distinguish five dominant revenue models (sales, product as a service, cascade, reprise (take-back), and hybrid revenue model—Building Block #10). Divide the set of business model pattern cards between these business models. This is the dominant revenue model of the pattern: many cards have multiple revenue models. Now analyse the companies' per revenue models. What do they have in common? What are the differences? Are there patterns in the distribution of companies over the revenue models? Are there certain revenue models that always occur in the same combinations?

This assignment's purpose is to discover, based on the examples, similarities and differences in how the five dominant revenue models are expressed in practice. It also makes it possible to look at combinations of revenue models.

Assignment

Title: Data and information as a transaction

Type: Individual or group

Time: +/−45 minutes

Assignment description:

Find at least five devices that are now *smart*, but were not ten years ago. Write down for each device:

- What the *smartness* adds in terms of functionality
- What data is generated and how this is translated into information
- Who you think benefits from that.

Analyse what data goes to which parties and whether there are any financial transactions in return. Who earns from transactions with that data, does the relevant party know that, and are they rewarded accordingly?

This assignment aims to gain insight into the vast amounts of data that are currently generated by smart devices, and how and for whom this can be of value. This can serve as inspiration for using data-driven technology in your own case and translating it into transactions.

Assignment

Title: Elaborating the conventional revenue

Type: Individual or group

Time: +/−3 to 5 hours (depending on whether the complementary part is done as well)

Assignment description:

This assignment provides a concrete and simple step-by-step plan for developing a revenue model for a specific case. The steps are:

Step 1: The first step is the conventional link between value creation and a financial revenue model (money). The central question here is which revenues move between which parties? The underlying strategy is also important, such as product as a service or cascading.

Step 2: Determine the nature of this business model; how do the transactions take place? It is important to clearly describe between which parties transactions take place and at what frequency.

Step 3: Define additional factors that influence the earnings model, such as risk, interest (depreciation), maintenance, environmental impact (eco-tax), and other matters. Carefully select the factors that apply to you.

Step 4: Find out which costs are not included in the revenue model (the so-called *externalization*); think of pollution, loss of biodiversity, exhaustion, etc.

Step 5: A conventional revenue model is all about making financial profit. It is important here that sufficient revenues are offset against the costs. It is, of course, important whether there is a one-off or a recurring transaction and, for example, how much risk is taken (and by which party). Find out what this looks like, both with and without externalized costs.

This assignment aims to gain insight into financial revenue models and considerations that can be included.

Assignment

Title: Revenue model with hybrid values

Type: Group

Time: +/−1 hour

Assignment description:

Suppose that you are not only (or not at all) paying with money but that transactions are based on different values that can be used simultaneously. Discuss in a group how such a hybrid transaction model can contribute to transaction forms that can, among other things, promote sustainability and inclusivity. Discuss the advantages, disadvantages, and potential bottlenecks of such transaction models. If necessary, choose a case on which you focus this discussion. Discuss whether there are certain aspects of sustainability that lend themselves particularly to the use of hybrid transaction technology?

This assignment's aim is a broad discussion about the possibilities and limitations of hybrid transactions from the perspective of sustainability.

Assignment

Title: Revenue model with the help of blockchain.

Type: Group

Time: +/−1 hour

Assignment description:

For this assignment, it may be necessary to learn about blockchain technology and its possibilities and limitations. Discuss how blockchain technology can contribute to the development of alternative forms of transactions that can promote sustainability and circularity. Discuss the advantages, disadvantages, and possible bottlenecks of the use of blockchain technology. If it becomes too abstract, choose a case that you will focus on in this discussion. Discuss whether there are certain elements of circularity and sustainability that lend themselves particularly to the use of blockchain technology.

This assignment's aim is a broad discussion about the possibilities (or impossibilities) of blockchain technology from the perspective of sustainability.

General Assignments

Assignment

Title: Advice assignment based on the BMT

Type: Individual but preferably in (interdisciplinary) groups

Time: +/−40 to 400 hours (entirely dependent on the level of elaboration)

Assignment description:

This assignment involves the full elaboration of an advice assignment based on the BMT. Follow the steps, as described in the book. This can be done—after quite some preliminary work—in a two-day hackathon, it can be done in a 40-hour week of intensive education, or it can be spread over a period of seven or more weeks.

The value of this assignment increases when carried out by an interdisciplinary group of students.

Assignment

Title: Mini-hackathon

Type: Groups in class

Time: +/−3 hours

Assignment description:

This assignment is meant to be a mini-hackathon in the form of a seminar in which groups of students complete the BMT *live* in class in a very short time. This can, for example, be the completion of a teaching programme in which the BMT has been discussed. You are recommended to work with A2 prints of the empty BMT and a generous stock of Post-its®.

Choose a case or a value proposition in advance. Take 2 hours to complete the BMT. Use the Post-its® to move elements, text, and improvements. Pay attention to a precise, compact, complete, and consistent formulation. Move the Post-its® whenever necessary. Where possible, insert symbols or small drawings to make things clearer.

Now take 30 minutes to translate the Post-its® into a clear and neat text with, where applicable, illustrations (use a marker) on your template. Make sure that every section of the BMT is filled. Then check the relationship between the choices made in the various building blocks. Finish with a 30-minute poster session. Groups view each other's posters and give tips and suggestions to each other's posters using Post-its®.

This assignment aims to come to a fully completed BMT in a limited time. By filling it in completely, students get insight into the interrelation of the parts. The pressure of time stimulates creativity in finding solutions. Filling in the BMT in two steps forces you to formulate precisely and come to the essence of the issue at hand.

Assignment

Title: Video pitch Circular Business Model

Type: Group

Time: +/−4 hours

Assignment description:

Prepare a video pitch of 90–120 seconds in which you present your circular business model. Seven tips for making a good clip:

a. Keep it short (no longer than 2 minutes).
b. Make a script and storyboard before you start
c. Remember the 5 Ws:

   - Who are you (or who do you represent)?
   - What is the plan?
   - Where does it take place?
   - What results do you hope to achieve?
   - Why does this matter?

d. Show it! Telling something is good, showing something is better.
e. Do not hide your message. Make it a personal message to your audience.
f. Make sure people can hear you well.
g. Prepare a catchy opening. People quickly decide whether they find something interesting or not, so grab their attention immediately.

Some practical information. There is software available to make a clip with your smartphone or other recording devices. Windows offers Windows Live Movie Maker. This program is present on every Windows computer and, if not, can be downloaded for free. Apple has iMovie, which is present on every MacBook or iMac. Also, there are all kinds of helpful programs available online, such as Powtoon. However, do note that you often have to create an account for these types of programs and that the free version gives limited user rights, which limits re-editing a video. If you want to share the video publicly, pay attention to the image rights of others. Online you can find many free video clips such as Pexels and Pixabay as well as sound clips such as Zapsplat or Audiohub.

This assignment aims to quickly visualize the essence of a business model so that it can be shown to others (external parties). By making it visual, a concept or idea can be conveyed clearly in a short time.

References

Jonker, J., Stegeman, H., Faber, N., & Kothman, T. H. (2018). *Eén zwaluw belooft veel goeds – resultaten van het landelijke onderzoek 2016–2017 naar business modellen voor de circulaire economie*. Doetinchem: Stichting OCF 2.0.

Jonker, J, Kothman, I., Faber, N., & Montenegro Navarro, N. (2018). *Organising for the circular economy | a workbook for developing circular business models*. www.newbusinessmodels.info/ebook/organising-for-the-circular-economy-a-workbook-for-developing-circular-business-models.

Osterwalder, A. (2004). *The business model ontology: A proposition in a design science approach*. www.academia.edu/download/30373644/thebusiness-model-ontology.pdf.

Appendix D: Sustainable Development Goals

An end to extreme poverty, inequality, injustice, and climate change is the core of the UN Sustainable Development Goals (SDGs). The 193 member states of the United Nations have adopted this development agenda for 2015–2030. The agenda consists of 17 goals, which apply in all countries and for all people.

The goals are:

1. Elimination of all forms of (extreme) poverty
2. To end hunger, and ensure food security and sustainable agriculture
3. Healthcare for everyone
4. Inclusive, equal, and quality education for everyone
5. Equal rights for men and women and empowerment of women and girls
6. Clean water and sanitation for everyone
7. Access to affordable and sustainable energy for everyone
8. Inclusive and economic growth and employment, and decent work for all
9. Infrastructure for sustainable industrialization
10. To reduce inequality within and between countries
11. To make cities safe, resilient and sustainable
12. Sustainable consumption and production
13. To address climate change
14. Protection and sustainable use of the oceans and seas
15. Protection of ecosystems, forests, and biodiversity

J. Jonker and N. Faber, *Organizing for Sustainability*,
https://doi.org/10.1007/978-3-030-78157-6

16. To promote safety, public services, and justice for all
17. To reinforce the global partnership to achieve these goals.

Implementation of SDGs

Countries implement the SDGs at the national and international level. In 2016, the European Union and the UN, among others, committed themselves to the implementation of the goals. In July 2016, the UN made agreements about how progress can be monitored and measured (indicators). Based on this, reports will be published in the coming years.

Cooperation between ministries and with key-players in society is at the core of working on the SDGs from and by the Netherlands. The national government is monitoring what the Netherlands is doing with regard to the SDGs and what still needs to be done. The government is also looking at social initiatives that are already running on the themes of the various SDGs. An overview of these initiatives can be found on the SDG Nederland website. Like other countries, the Netherlands reports to the UN on progress.

Sources

https://sdgcompass.org/business-tools.
www.un.org/sustainabledevelopment/sustainable-development-goals.
ec.europa.eu/eurostat/web/sdi/indicators.

Appendix E: Sustainability Tools

Measuring Impact (Impact Wizard)

Website: impactwizard.eu.

Impact Wizard is a method used to create a clear picture of the social impact of your project. This method clearly shows the impact and allows for easy communication to the target group. It also allows you to increase your social impact.

CO_2 Calculator

Website: www.CO2logic.com/nl/services/CO2-calculator.

On the CO_2Logic site you will find a CO_2 calculator. With this calculator is it easy to calculate how much CO_2 emission there is for houses, cars, aeroplanes and companies. After the calculation, this CO_2 emission can be compensated for by investing in CO_2Logic climate projects.

Futureproof Community

Website: futureproof.community.

The matchmaking platform for sustainable entrepreneurs with over 800 solutions. The community provides insight into who is working on which challenge and which networks offer sustainable solutions, and helps with the realization of these solutions. Here you can find climate-neutral, circular, and inclusive business models and sustainable trade chains.

J. Jonker and N. Faber, *Organizing for Sustainability*,
https://doi.org/10.1007/978-3-030-78157-6

Appendix F: Templates

Extra copies of the BMT (Figs. F.1 and F.2).

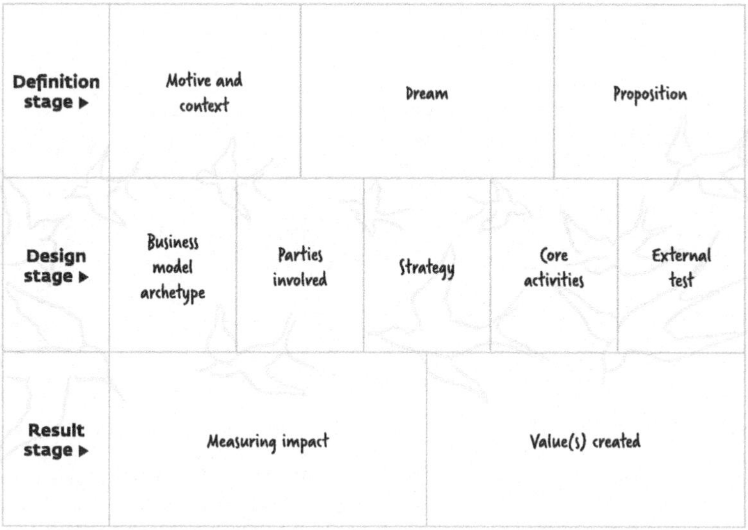

Fig. F.1 Business model template

J. Jonker and N. Faber, *Organizing for Sustainability*,
https://doi.org/10.1007/978-3-030-78157-6

Fig. F.2 Business model template (circular)

Index

J. Jonker and N. Faber, *Organizing for Sustainability*,
https://doi.org/10.1007/978-3-030-78157-6

The manufacturer's authorised representative in the EU is Springer Nature Customer Service Centre GmbH, Europaplatz 3, 69115 Heidelberg, Germany. If you have any concerns regarding our products, please contact ProductSafety@springernature.com

Printed and bound by CPI Group (UK) Ltd, Croydon, CR0 4YY
30/09/2026
02225450-0018